THE REAL HOOSIERS

Also by Jack McCallum

THE REAL
HOOSIERS

Crispus Attucks High School,
Oscar Robertson, and the
Hidden History of Hoops

JACK McCALLUM

NEW YORK

Hachette Books
Hachette Book Group
1290 Avenue of the Americas
New York, NY 10104
HachetteBooks.com
Twitter.com/HachetteBooks
Instagram.com/HachetteBooks

First Edition: March 2024

Published by Hachette Books, an imprint of Hachette Book Group, Inc. The Hachette Books name and logo is a trademark of the Hachette Book Group.

The Hachette Speakers Bureau provides a wide range of authors for speaking events. To find out more, go to hachettespeakersbureau.com or email HachetteSpeakers@hbgusa.com.

Books by Hachette Books may be purchased in bulk for business, educational, or promotional use. For information, please contact your local bookseller or Hachette Book Group Special Markets Department at special.markets@hbgusa.com.

The publisher is not responsible for websites (or their content) that are not owned by the publisher.

Print book interior design by Sheryl Kober.

Library of Congress Cataloging-in-Publication Data

Names: McCallum, Jack, 1949– author.
Title: The real Hoosiers: Crispus Attucks High School, Oscar Robertson, and the hidden history of hoops / Jack McCallum.
Description: New York, NY: Hachette Books, [2024] | Includes bibliographical references and index.
Identifiers: LCCN 2023042358 | ISBN 9780306830754 (hardcover) | ISBN 9780306830778 (ebook)
Subjects: LCSH: Crispus Attucks Tigers (Basketball team)—History—20th century. | Robertson, Oscar, 1938– | Crispus Attucks High School (Indianapolis, Ind.)—History—20th century. | Basketball—Indiana—History—20th century. | Racism in sports—United States—History—20th century. | Indiana—History—20th century.
Classification: LCC GV885.42.I4 M33 2024 | DDC 796.323/620977252—dc23/eng/20231023
LC record available at https://lccn.loc.gov/2023042358

ISBNs: 978-0-306-83075-4 (hardcover), 978-0-306-83077-8 (ebook)

Printed in the United States of America

LSC-C

Printing 1, 2023

To all those who never got the chance to play

A new vision began gradually to replace the dream of political power—a powerful movement, the rise of another ideal to guide the unguided, another pillar of fire by night after a clouded day. It was the ideal of "book learning"; the curiosity, born of compulsory ignorance, to know and test the power of the cabbalistic letters of the white man, the longing to know. Here at last seemed to have been discovered the mountain path to Canaan, longer than the highway of Emancipation and law, steep and rugged, but straight, leading to heights high enough to overlook life.

—W. E. B. Du Bois,
The Souls of Black Folk, 1903

Jordan River, chilly and cold,
it chills the body, but not the soul.
There ain't but one train that's on this track,
it runs to heaven and runs right back.

—"Every Time I Feel the Spirit," traditional
Negro spiritual sung at the first Crispus
Attucks High School commencement,1928

"Render your body to them," his father had taught, "but know your soul belongs to God."

—Edward P. Jones, *The Known World*, 2003

CONTENTS

CONTENTS

THE REAL HOOSIERS

Prologue

The eyes have you. They follow as you walk the halls of Crispus Attucks High School, a ninety-five-year-old fixture in the northwest section of Indianapolis, built near a confluence of three fetid waterways, built to keep Blacks in their place, built by haters, built to fail. The eyes are in every hallway, for each August an image of the most recent graduating class is affixed to a wall before the school year begins, a march of time from the front offices to the gymnasium, each photograph a message that history matters at Crispus Attucks High School.

Lauren Franklin, the Attucks principal, should walk the halls with a vat of potato salad, for each journey is a family reunion. She did not graduate from Attucks, but thirty-one members of her family stare down at her, and she *feels* them in her bones every school day. "My mother and father met at Attucks," she says, lost in reverie. "My grandmother, Marian Perkins, who's on the wall [Class of 1942], was alive when I got this job, and her message was, 'Don't you mess up my school now.'"

Eugene Strader, her maternal grandfather, is in the 1929 graduation photo. Her paternal grandfather, Warren Franklin, was a junior and a top student at Arsenal Technical High School in Indianapolis when he was told, in the summer of 1927, *Sorry, all Blacks in Indianapolis must go to Attucks.* They probably didn't say *sorry.* That order came from the powerful Indianapolis School Board. It would be too strong to say that the board was run by the Ku Klux Klan, but it would *not* be too strong to say that the Klan had its hand on the wheel of most board decisions back then. Warren Franklin did not graduate because he had to get a job, a familiar story; his was one of many lives disrupted by the segregation order.

But other lives were saved. Look, there in the 1932 class photo is the face of Willard B. Ransom. After his graduation from Attucks, he experienced years of racial prejudice in the US Army and in his law practice, so he organized the Indiana branch of the National Association for the Advancement of Colored People (NAACP) and spent the rest of his life in the civil rights movement, organizing protests and sit-ins in and around Indianapolis, everywhere from White Castle hamburger stands to downtown department stores.

Nearby is the Class of 1930 photo, which includes the remarkable Flonoi Adams, who went on to Purdue University and then into the army, where he received the Bronze Star for "meritorious achievement," as well as a dozen other military honors. He was the first of a parade of Attucks graduates to make their mark in the military. There, in the 1936 photo of Attucks's ninth graduating class is Charles Henry DeBow, a Tuskegee Airman who flew fifty-two World War II missions in the European theater. There in the 1937 photo is DeBow's classmate Graham Martin, who began what seemed destined to be a dismal life at the Dickensian-sounding Home for Friendless Colored Children before entering Attucks with an overpowering will to succeed. He became one of the "Golden Thirteen," the US Navy's first group of commissioned

Black officers. He returned to teach and coach at Attucks for almost forty years; the school's football field bears his name.

Another wall, another photo, this one from 1941, shows John Wesley Lee, who became the first African American commissioned, as an ensign, in the navy in 1947. Five years after Lee—look, there in the Class of 1946 photo—is Brigadier General Norris Overton, who once said, "Everything I achieved is because of Attucks." One year after Overton graduated—there, in the Class of 1947 photo—along came Harry Brooks Jr., who advanced to major general in the army, where his subordinate officers included Colin Powell, who later called Brooks "the conscience of the Army."

It wasn't just the Attucks males who were drawn to Uncle Sam. Alberta Stanley White, another graduate from that Class of 1937, joined the Women's Army Corps during World War II. While keeping up her grades, she, like many others at Attucks, also earned fifty cents a week as a domestic worker to help with the family expenses.

This inclination of early Attucks graduates to serve—a trend that continued; witness the ascension of Fred Davidson III (Class of 1959) to deputy assistant secretary of the navy in 1981—was no accident. From the time the school opened in 1927, Attucks had an aggressive ROTC program, as well as a kind of ineffable stay-in-line, almost militaristic philosophy. It was as if the Attucks brass had sought to make a mockery of an official Army War College study that concluded, "The black man could not control himself in the fear of danger to the extent the white man can. He is mentally inferior to the white man." That was written in 1925, sixteen years before DeBow climbed into a cockpit at the Tuskegee Army Flying School.

The return of so many Attucks products from World War II inspired a push against the institutional racism that prevailed in Indianapolis, which practiced a paternalistic not-now-but-soon philosophy of race relations. The veterans had served their country yet still could not get served at many lunch counters in the capital city, and their children were still being directed to a segregated school. A headline from the January 11, 1947, *Indianapolis Recorder*, the African American newspaper of record that still publishes today, tells of the fight, one that, as we shall see, lasted decades: "Vets Plan New Campaign Against Jimcrowism in Schools of City."

The soundtrack to Crispus Attucks High School, though, was more complex than "The Army Goes Rolling Along" or "Anchors Aweigh." Dozens of future jazz musicians[1] learned their craft at Attucks, which hired outstanding music teachers. It was a short walk from the high school to Indiana Avenue—the *Ave-noo*, as it came to be called—where nationally known acts like Cab Calloway and Louis Armstrong jammed with Attucks grads. Then along came David Baker—there he is, in the Class of 1949 photo—who as a teenager riding the streetcar to and from school would pull out his tuba and blow a few bass notes, much to the irritation of fellow passengers. Baker, who would be nominated for a Pulitzer Prize, kept on playing and would later direct an influential jazz department for the Jacobs School of Music at Indiana University (IU), an institution to which he may not have been admitted a decade or two earlier because of his skin color.

Something less improvisational? There's Rodney Stepp on the wall with the Class of 1969. He composed, keyboarded, and gamboled with the Spinners, a Rock and Roll Hall of Fame group with tight harmonies and tighter choreography, and can be seen in the background of *When We Were Kings*, the documentary about the 1974 Muhammad

---

1. A partial list of the great musicians who came out of Attucks must include Jimmy Coe, Slide Hampton, J. J. Johnson (who played with Miles Davis), Jimmy Spaulding, Virgil Jones, and the most famous of them all, John Leslie "Wes" Montgomery (who did not graduate). The most influential figure, however, might have been Russell W. Brown, a teacher and band director at Attucks for thirty years. Jazz critic David Johnson called Brown "one of the unsung heroes of 20th-Century American jazz."

Ali–George Foreman Rumble in the Jungle in Zaire, where the Spinners were invited to play.

Something more buttoned-down? Move to the Class of 1982 for the photo of Angela Brown, who played Adelaide in the Attucks production of *Guys and Dolls* and went on to become a celebrated dramatic soprano who specialized in portraying Verdi heroines.

You can stop anywhere, really, on your journey through the hallways and find some Attucks grad who made a difference, someone who overcame overwhelming odds and achieved amazing things after leaving a school that by its very existence demonstrated Indianapolis's corrosive hypocrisy. As historian Aram Goudsouzian put it in a piece for the *Indiana Magazine of History*, "Crispus Attucks High School established itself as the central institution in black Indianapolis, a source of pride, a base for community organization, and a training ground for future success."

On we go. There, in the Class of 1937 photo, is Harriette Bailey Conn, who became Indiana's deputy attorney general and a state representative, and who, like Ransom, never wavered in her fight for civil rights before her death in 1981. Conn graduated from Attucks when she was fourteen. David Leander Williams, a 1964 Attucks grad who wrote the comprehensive *African Americans in Indianapolis*, called her "a warrior." Three years after Conn, along came A'Leila Josephine Kirk, one of the first Black women accepted into Indiana University's School of Medicine. She went on to become chief of psychology at Danvers State Insane Asylum, at the time a groundbreaking institution.

S. Henry Bundles, there in the Class of 1943 photo, was the first African American to graduate from the Indiana University School of Journalism but found it impossible to land an editorial position because of his skin color. So he switched to the business side and became the circulation manager of the *Indianapolis News*. Bundles branched out and eventually became chairman of the Indianapolis Business Development

Foundation and, as an Indy 500 Festival director, a sometime driver of a pace car, never forgetting that in the early days of the Brickyard, he would not have been allowed to enter.

Firsts are all over the walls. There's Joseph D. Kimbrew ('46), Indianapolis's first Black fire chief. There's Taylor L. Baker Jr. ('53), the city's first Black prosecutor. There's Julia Carson ('55), the first African American woman to represent Indianapolis in the US Congress, who on a June day in 1999 presented Rosa Parks with the Congressional Gold Medal, the result of a bill that she had cosponsored. There's James Toler ('58), the city's first Black police chief. There's Janet Langhart ('59), who became Chicago's first Black "weathergirl" and later, among many other things (model, TV host, author), the "First Lady of the Pentagon" after marrying William Cohen, the secretary of defense under Bill Clinton.

While much of the white citizenry of Indianapolis regarded the school as one homogenous Black sea, all kinds moved through the halls of Attucks. Study the Class of 1965 photo and find the face of Bernard Parham, who early in life discovered that he had a head for chess. Parham helped organize a club at Attucks that played as a team in a kind of underground circuit that met at Douglass Park in the Black section of Indianapolis. "We couldn't go to places like Broad Ripple Park," said Parham in a 2022 interview, "or they'd kick us out. So, I'd get together with the white captains of the other Indianapolis schools, and we'd play informal matches." He became a grandmaster, has a move named after him (the Parham Attack), and, oh, yes, in 1964, the year before he graduated from Attucks, beat someone named Bobby Fischer in an exhibition. It's not folklore; you can look it up on chessgames.com.

There were, of course, more prominent sportsmen at Attucks than chessman Parham, who continues to play games at his home in Lafayette, Indiana. Go back to the hallway where the 1950s photos hang, back to 1953, and find Willie Gardner, one of the star-crossed souls of Attucks. Gardner, who was often referred to by his unusual middle name of Dill or his ironically bestowed nickname of "Wee Willie" (he stood 6'7"), was a brilliantly gifted basketball player valued by both the Harlem Globetrotters and the New York Knicks. But a heart condition ended his basketball career in 1957 and, combined with the effects of diabetes that took the lower part of both legs, ended his life in 2000.

Near Willie's photo is his onetime teammate and friend Hallie Bryant, the first African American to make a big splash in Indianapolis scholastic basketball. The photo was taken right after he was named the state's Mr. Basketball and months before he left for Indiana University, where he played three years and found that the Bloomington campus was not the best place to find success as a Black player in the 1950s. But Bryant moved on and carved out a career as both a Harlem Globetrotter and a one-man 'Trotter offshoot.

Move up to the Class of 1957. There is Albert Maxey, another basketball star who went west to play at the University of Nebraska. While he found the Cornhusker State not always accommodating to Blacks, he nevertheless stayed and became a policeman and husband to the late JoAnn Maxey, the first African American woman to serve as a state senator in Nebraska. When Dr. Martin Luther King Jr. passed through Lincoln one day in 1964, Maxey was on his detail.

Take a few steps back. Near Bryant and Gardner is their close friend, a kid by the name of Robertson. The photo identifies him as Bailey Robertson, but he usually went by "Flap," the prevailing theory on the derivation of his nickname being the way he flapped his wrist after he shot his deadly jumper. Yet there are those who subscribe to the theory that Flap earned the sobriquet by flapping his gums, and his coach, Ray Province Crowe, had more than one word with Flap about his chattiness. Crowe and Flap are immortalized together in the movie *Hoosiers*, portraying the coaches who watch in frustration as their team loses to Hickory High in the state championship game. Much more to come about *Hoosiers*, and much more to come about Flap, who died in 1994 at age fifty-eight.

Take a few more steps down the hall, and there he is, in the Class of 1956 photo, Oscar Palmer Robertson. Three years younger than his brother, Oscar resembles Flap but there's something more *guarded* about him. He's smiling, but tentatively. He is holding something back. In the years that follow, Oscar will hold many things back.

Stare at the photo and know that in that young face are multitudes. The story of the Great Migration that brought millions of Blacks from the South to the North, where they didn't always find what they were looking for. The story of a city, a state, and a country struggling to come to terms with race; the story of the oppressive prohibitions and the more insidious indignities that African Americans endured even—perhaps *especially*—in places that promoted their own enlightenment, their own chimera of equality, which accurately describes Indiana. The story of a school that was built because of a fear that Blacks were *taking over* the educational system, a precursive nod to the replacement theory now widely articulated on right-wing airwaves. The story of an underdog institution that, ultimately, united a city through sport, if only for a short while.

The story of a man who's known by one name—one *letter* for God's sake—yet is often overlooked, both as a pioneer of the game and as a pioneer of players' rights. Oscar, who turned eighty-five in November 2023, is not a Muhammad Ali either by temperament or inclination; yet he did so much to change the political climate of his sport as president of the players' union. It was his name on a lawsuit that stopped franchises from treating their players like so much chattel, and it was his forceful testimony in a heated congressional hearing that helped sway public opinion in the players' favor. Yet much of this is forgotten in the wake of his triple-double standard of excellence, which has made him more number than man.

There is, too, the story of a game that wasn't born in Indiana but grew up there and, pumped through with small-town energy, spread like a virus, its ancient rituals so binding that Robertson, clearly the most artful practitioner of the Hoosier Game, seems in some way an anomaly, his Attucks teams of the mid-1950s a 180-degree detour— stylistically and pigmentally—from the rural highways that defined the de facto state religion of Indiana. So dominant was the small-town ethos of Hoosier hoops that in the half century before Oscar's Attucks Tigers, no Indianapolis team had won the state championship in a sport generally considered to be *urban*.

In fact, the story of Crispus Attucks, as stirring and as organically connected to one of the game's singular figures as it is, has become swallowed up, like a mom-and-pop grocery in a corporate takeover, by the big-screen fiction of *Hoosiers*. A pity because the real story of the connections between Attucks and the real-life inspiration for *Hoosiers*, Milan High, is fascinating—and will be told here.

There is, finally, the story of both a sport and a country in flux. Oscar's Attucks teams came along when the game itself was moving ever so tentatively from its slowball/stallball roots, and Attucks helped move it. The NBA's twenty-four-second clock was put into practice in April 1954, a month after Oscar finished his sophomore season, the awkward statue-like set shots giving way to a more freewheeling, higher-octane game with shots taken on the move. You can *see* the game evolve through the Attucks teams of the 1950s.

As for changes in the country, consider these facts:

- When Oscar was a sophomore, Thurgood Marshall, a sometime participant in Indianapolis's racial skirmishes, was successfully arguing *Brown v. Board of Education of Topeka* before the Supreme Court.
- As Robertson and his family returned to Indianapolis from their annual summer visit to their Tennessee homeland in August 1955, a fourteen-year-old Black boy from Chicago

named Emmett Till was beaten, shot in the head, and thrown into the Tallahatchie River in Money, Mississippi.

- Three months later, in December 1955, as Attucks began its scorched-earth run to a second straight Indiana state championship, a woman named Rosa Parks refused to give up her seat on a bus in Montgomery, Alabama.

Oscar and his mates did not immerse themselves in the specifics of those events. They were kids with other priorities and other dreams. But more than most, certainly more than most of their white opponents, they had a sense of the bigger picture. Their lives in Indianapolis were defined by limits. There were places they couldn't go, things they couldn't say, emotions they couldn't act on. Transplants all, they lived in their own version of the Known World, most comfortable and content in the playgrounds and the gyms where they learned the game that captivated the state.

CHAPTER ONE

The Robertsons Move North . . . and Find a "Quiet" Racism

"Once in a while I think about how we came from all over the place. By chance we end up here. In this place. In Indianapolis. . . . It really is kind of amazing."

In the days before television turned our sports heroes into flesh and blood, we saw them as more myth than man, like the 1927 Notre Dame backfield—transformed into the Four Horsemen of the Apocalypse by a classics-loving sportswriter named Grantland Rice. Our heroes—Ruth, Grange, Dempsey—ran wild in our imaginations. As for Black stars, well, we knew little and cared less. Their collective histories tended to amalgamate into a single narrative. They migrated from the South. They had little money. Their fathers were absent. They had superhuman athletic abilities but didn't know how to cultivate them.

That was not entirely wrong—just the last part.

Yet there is a richness in the journeys of our older Black stars, also layered in myth, sustained by oral history. The story of the Robertson family's move from Tennessee to Indianapolis is archetypal yet distinct. There are millions like it, but each is a singular tale, baked through with strife and toil but also with love and fortitude, the themes of the families who took part in the Great Migration.

There is also, in the words of Bryan Stevenson, author of *Just Mercy*, "something that people don't talk about much in this exodus story." It's too sinister, too monstrous. "A lot of the leaving the South had to do with lynching and violence," said Stevenson in a 2022 interview at the Equal Justice Initiative (EJI) in Montgomery, Alabama, where he is executive director. "That reinforced the idea that it wasn't safe to play in white spaces." It didn't matter that the overwhelming majority of Blacks in the South didn't confront overt violence firsthand. They heard about it; they knew about it—particularly the African Americans born in the 1920s and 1930s, as Oscar Robertson was. "You can't understand the evolution of sports in the second half of the twentieth century," says Stevenson, "without understanding this massive relocation of African Americans that took place during the first half. And it is rooted in the trauma and terror that lynchings created."

Stevenson's EJI has documented 4,075 "racial terror lynchings" of African Americans between 1877 and 1950, a number that will probably grow as research continues. They happened primarily in Alabama, Arkansas, Florida, Georgia, Kentucky, Louisiana, Mississippi, North Carolina, South Carolina, Tennessee, Texas, and Virginia. But racial terror was not exclusive to the Deep South. As we shall see, it crept close to the Hoosier capital of Indianapolis, whose citizens prided themselves on their racial equanimity.

Oscar writes in his autobiography, *The Big O: My Life, My Times, My Game*, that his great-grandfather, Marshall Collier, was raised in slavery in Tennessee and lived to be 116. Marshall was what slaveowners called a "runner," not content to be someone's property, a battle his great-grandson would later fight in courtrooms and Washington, DC, hearing rooms. Indeed, the memory of his great-grandfather flows through Oscar, who was born on a snowy Thanksgiving Day in 1938, one hundred years to the day after Marshall's birth.

As family lore has it, Marshall never made it to freedom until after the Civil War. But despite getting apprehended time after time, he somehow avoided beatings. Perhaps, then, he also presaged the oldest Robertson brother, Bailey, known as "Flap," an avid conversationalist who could talk the shell off an egg. Oscar remembers Marshall as long and lanky but can't confirm family accounts of another startling tidbit about the man: that he stood seven feet, two inches tall. Oscar's father, Bailey Sr., was only 5'11", so Oscar, who finished his growing at 6'5", split that difference.

As Oscar writes of Marshall, "He lived through Reconstruction, the infestation of carpetbaggers, and, later still, the Klan nights. . . . When he passed from the earth, he was the oldest man in the United States, and he had never traveled above the Mason-Dixon Line." No way to prove if he was the oldest man, but the limited geographical journey that Marshall Collier took fits a pattern, and his heirs would live a variation of that in Indianapolis.

Robertson, a slave name, comes from his mother's side. (Slaves customarily took either the name of their "master" or the maternal surname.) The family's Tennessee history involves sharecropping and endless toil and home births. Bailey, Henry, and Oscar Palmer, in that order, were ushered into the world in a farmhouse on Tennessee State Highway 29 in Dickson County. They went to church, socialized on Sundays, attended a one-room schoolhouse (Oscar writes lovingly of a teacher with the wonderfully melodic name of Lizzie Gleaves, "who had to be god-sent"), and did everything they could to coexist with the white man. His grandmother even breastfed the children of the folks for whom she worked. Folklore holds that children take on the characteristics of those from whom they draw milk so—who knows?—perhaps a few white Tennessee folks are part Robertson. Oscar's reveries of Tennessee come across as elegiac, including his being born with a deformed foot that his mother and grandmother endlessly massaged to make it normal. Well, maybe.

The hard truths of Black life in the South, however, landed heavily upon his parents, Bailey and Mazell: no matter how hard they worked, no matter how hard they prayed, no matter how firmly they believed in whatever the American Dream was for a Black family in the South, they would get nowhere. A bleak economic future for their children, all three of them bright and curious boys, seemed preordained. "My father just felt there was no future, no education," Oscar said to Indianapolis writer Mark Montieth in an interview years ago. Millions of other Black families from the South came to the same conclusion. Between 1910 and 1970, about six million of them left the South, chronicled most eloquently in Isabel Wilkerson's wonderful 2010 book *The Warmth of Other Suns.*

Oscar, Flap, and Henry would find much commonality as they grew into teenagers and swapped family stories at Crispus Attucks High School. In a 2014 piece in *Indianapolis Monthly,* two of Oscar's teammates on the 1955–1956 Attucks team talked about their migration from the South: "Things were real bad for us—a lot of poverty, no hope," said Stanford Patton, a forward on the 1955 and 1956 Attucks teams. "We knew we were segregated. We knew where we could and couldn't live. We knew where we were wanted and weren't wanted. We were living in a caste system." (Wilkerson's riveting follow-up book, not incidentally, is titled *Caste.*)

Sam Milton, a guard who played with Oscar and Patton, put it this way: "In the South, my parents had worked on farms, and during the winter when there was no crop, you still stayed on the boss man's farm. So, in the summer, even after you'd done the crop, you wouldn't have no money because you still owed him for staying all winter. Indianapolis was a lot different. Here you could at least make your own living. But you still kind of knew where you couldn't go."

Willie Merriweather, the coleader (with Oscar) of the historic 1955 Attucks team, has a story similar to the Robertsons'. He, too, came from Tennessee, in his case Jackson, a town about an hour's drive east of Memphis. "My father was pretty lucky, relatively speaking," said Merriweather in a 2022 interview at his home near San Antonio. "He worked at International Harvester, a pretty good job for a Black man back then. And my mother worked [as a domestic] for the same family until she was seventy-two years old. My dad died when I was fifteen. That happened to a lot of African American men from that generation. Heart attack, bleeding ulcers. Diet, pressures they worked under, pressures of the time. A lot of them went too early."

The family of John Gipson, a center on the 1955 and 1956 Attucks teams, came from Mississippi, and he, like the Robertson boys, took summer visits back to the South. "I remember riding in a cotton wagon with an uncle who was several years older than me," said Gipson during a 2022 interview at his Indianapolis home, "and I heard him say, 'Man, there's gotta be something better than this.' I never forgot that." Gipson's mother died in childbirth when he was ten, and he and his sister were raised mostly by his aunt and uncle because his father traveled around looking for work as a cement finisher. "Life wasn't easy up here," says Gipson, "but, hey, we were all in the same boat, so we didn't talk about it much."

The family of Bill Scott, a guard on the 1955 team, came from Alabama to stay with his grandmother. Shortly after his mother arrived in Indy, she was raped and murdered after being dragged from a streetcar, and Scott spent the rest of his childhood living in a converted garage with his grandmother and an uncle who liked his liquor. Scott died at age sixty-one in 1998.

"Once in a while I think about how we came from all over the place," said Bill Hampton, who had a three-mile walk to Attucks that he "gladly" made after his family arrived from Kentucky. "By chance we end up here. In this place. In Indianapolis. And what we all accomplished together." He shakes his head. "Man, it really is kind of amazing."

———

The Robertsons set off for the North in 1942 from the small Dickson County town of Charlotte, picking a landing spot, as did most other migrating Black families, because a relative, sometimes even a distant-*distant* one, lived there. (Decades later a sign would be erected out on Highway 48 within the Charlotte limits, reading, "Oscar Robertson, Dickson County Native.") In the case of the Robertsons, Bailey had an aunt and cousins in Indy, and he had briefly worked in the town during World War I. Think of how the basketball world could be different except for a touch of fate. Had there been a Robertson aunt in Chicago, perhaps Oscar would have ended up on the South Side at DuSable High, whose products include musician Nat King Cole, singer Dinah Washington, comedian Redd Foxx, and NBA player Maurice Cheeks, not to mention a spectacular high school basketball team you'll hear about later. Had there been an uncle on the West Coast, the Robertsons might have followed the path that a family from Monroe, Louisiana, took to Oakland about the same time, and Oscar, a seminal guard, might have been a hoops legatee of Bill Russell, the seminal center four years his senior. Or it could have been Detroit or New York or Pittsburgh, other prominent destinations for those who packed hope and dreams, along with their clothes and fried chicken wrapped in wax paper, during the Great Migration.

But it was Indianapolis because Aunt Inez lived there. Their arrival came a decade and a half after the Indianapolis city council had adopted a resolution that made it unlawful for whites to establish residence "in a portion of the municipality inhabited principally by negroes" or for

Negroes to establish residence in a "white community" except with the written consent of a majority of persons of the opposite race inhabiting the neighborhood. To a degree, they took an eight-hour journey north to end up back in the South.

The boys sustained themselves along the way with food Mazell had packed, eating on the bus because at most of the stops along Highway 31W in Tennessee and Kentucky, Blacks were not allowed in restaurants. But the same would have been true in many parts of Indiana, though they didn't know that yet. It was no doubt with a sense of relief that mother and children arrived in Indy. But the ordeal was not over. Writes Oscar in *The Big O*,

> My aunt's house didn't have a phone; that luxury was simply out of the question, so my mom had no way of communicating with my father in Indianapolis. When we arrived at the bus station, nobody was there to greet us, and we had no way of getting in touch with my dad. So my mom, my brothers, and I gathered up our belongings and walked 24 long blocks from the station near the old Claypool hotel, all the way to Aunt Inez's house on the city's west side. Dad answered the door surprised. He'd had no idea we were coming. I was four years old.

Oscar and his brothers were part of a wave. Between 1940 and 1950 Indianapolis's Black population increased twice as fast as the overall population. It seems axiomatic that the journey to the North had to be made—the sacrifices of leaving behind a family and a "safe" life in the South notwithstanding—simply because so many millions made it. But renowned Hoosier-born historian Emma Lou Thornbrough, who taught for decades at Butler University, wrote in *The Indianapolis Story: School Segregation and Desegregation in a Northern City* that there were two minds about the advisability of the African American journey.

While one paper, the *Indianapolis Recorder*, welcomed them and insisted that their arrival was causing "neither residential or labor animosities," the *Freeman* urged blacks to stay in the South, saying that while they might find greater political freedom and better schools in the North, their economic opportunities would be limited. Most alarming, in the opinion of this ordinarily accommodationist paper, was the prospect of growing residential restrictions. "We have learned to forego some rights that are common, because we know the price," it asserted. "But we cannot give up our right to live where we choose. . . . Enforced grottoes [*sic*] will never sound good to the ears or appear well in history."

That turned out to be prophetic.

At that tender age of four, new Indianapolis resident Oscar Palmer Robertson knew what he was leaving behind—acres of Tennessee paradise and grandparent love—but nothing of what lay ahead. A smart and sensitive boy, he found out quickly. "To be a poor man is hard," wrote W. E. B. Du Bois in *The Souls of Black Folk*, "but to be a poor race in a land of dollars is the very bottom of hardships."

———

If you want a Hoosier historian's eyes to glaze over, then start to recite this sentence: *Indiana is either the* . . . He or she will complete it for you. *Indiana is either the most northern state in the South or the most southern state in the North.* The fact that it has become a Hoosier chestnut doesn't mean it isn't true. Lanier Holt, an associate professor of communication at Ohio State University, has a colorful variation, describing Indiana as "the middle finger of the South thrust into the center of the Midwest."

Adds Holt, who earned his doctorate at Indiana University, "Indiana is a very strange state with a very strange history of race relations."

The state's first constitution in 1816 was, like many constitutions, swollen with high-mindedness at the same time that it kept Blacks from voting, as did a subsequent constitution ratified in 1856. During an 1843 lecture in Richmond, Indiana, a city that borders Ohio, abolitionist Frederick Douglass was egged and beaten; he was later attacked in Pendleton, another Indiana town. The Indiana Constitution of 1851 outright banned Negroes and mulattos from coming into the state and even discussed colonizing them in Africa, a "solution" recommended by the governor. One delegate opined the following about Blacks: "I would say, and I say it in all sincerity and without any hard feelings toward them, that it would be better to kill them off at once. If there is no other way to get rid of them. We have not yet come to that point with the blacks, but we know how the Puritans did with the Indians who were infinitely more magnanimous and less important than this colored race."

Those who avidly defend Indiana's checkered racial history as relatively benign cling to one indisputable fact: it was not a slave state and fought bravely for the Union in the Civil War. That 1816 constitution was uncompromising in its explicitness that there should be no slavery. An inscription on Monument Circle, a striking fixture of downtown Indianapolis that will later figure prominently in the Oscar Robertson–Crispus Attucks story, notes that 210,497 "Indiana volunteers" died in the war for the Union.

No one has written more eloquently about Indiana's nuanced relationship with race than James H. Madison, a widely respected emeritus professor of history at Indiana University, and this is what he wrote about the mainstream Hoosier view of slavery in his 2014 book, *Hoosiers: A New History of Indiana*:

Few Hoosiers defended slavery. Many regarded it as a violation of the laws of God and man. A Fourth of July orator in Fort Wayne in 1835 pointed to "the gross inconsistency of styling ourselves the Friends of the rights of man, while we hold within our own borders millions of human beings in absolute and degrading servitude." At the same time, few whites in pioneer Indiana proposed to interfere in the South's peculiar institution. Even fewer proposed to alter the racial inequalities within Indiana.

Richard Pierce, a professor of history at Notre Dame, notes in his excellent book *Polite Protest: The Political Economy of Race in Indianapolis, 1920–1970* that many Indiana whites were sanguine about the arrival of Blacks from the South. That's because those African Americans tended not to upset norms at job sites in contrast to militant white Europeans, many of whom were union firebrands or even anarchists along the lines of Nicola Sacco and Bartolomeo Vanzetti, whose trial and eventual electrocution in 1927 roughly followed the construction and opening of Crispus Attucks High School.

There was a pragmatic side to the Hoosier rejection of slavery. "Yes, there was some sentiment about the morality of slavery, but it's not like white pioneers in Indiana were all that eager to have African Americans as neighbors," said Madison in a 2022 interview at his home in Bloomington. "Plus, most of the white pioneers were upland southerners who were not wealthy enough to own slaves. They referred to 'slave labor' as 'free labor.' That was competition for them."

As far as Indiana's history of educating (or not educating) African Americans, *tortuous* doesn't begin to describe it. Though an article in the first state constitution provided that a system of public education should be open to all, Blacks found perpetual roadblocks through the twentieth century. In the 1850s the Indiana Supreme Court ruled that attendance in public schools should be limited to white students even if Blacks wanted to pay their own tuition (as was sometimes the custom back then), explaining that Blacks were barred not because they "did not need education, nor because their wealth was such as to render aid undesirable, but because black children were deemed unfit associates of whites, as school companions."

In what should be looked at as a kind of political mantra, custom, not law, prevailed in Indiana, a kind of *quieter* racism. Hoosiers[1] considered themselves rural and didn't flinch when their capital was referred to as "Indy-No-Place." Its leaders rarely spoke out publicly in the manner of, say, James K. Vardaman, the governor of Mississippi from 1904 to 1908, who famously pronounced, "If it is necessary every Negro in the state will be lynched; it will be done to maintain white supremacy." Vardaman also fought resolutely against public schooling for Blacks. "The only effect of negro education," he wrote, "is to spoil a good field hand and make an insolent cook." Pity he's not around to weigh in on critical race theory. (Despite repeated calls for its renaming, Vardaman Hall, an administrative building, still stands on the Ole Miss campus.)

Indiana was a place where the desire of the white population for racial separateness was in large part uttered quietly, the Hoosier love affair with the Ku Klux Klan notwithstanding (see Chapter 8, and, granted, that is a major *notwithstanding*). Pro-white institutions did their work quietly, too, through real estate redlining, decades of all-Caucasian school board slates, and patronizing "Colored Folk" sections of newspapers.

This racial blindness can be capsulized in the person of Thomas Riley Marshall, Indiana's governor from 1909 to 1913 and later vice

---

1. One wades into the etymological quagmire of *Hoosier* with much trepidation. It is a maze with no exit. An entire wall at the Indiana Historical Society in Indianapolis is devoted to the name, which shows up as early as 1855 as a term to describe Indianans. Do the research, but Madison says he's always liked James Whitcomb Riley's story that early settlers often had vicious brawls, after which a passerby would spot a dislodged organ on the floor and ask, "Whose ear?"

president under Woodrow Wilson. Marshall, labeled a progressive for his time, did issue a moratorium on the sterilizations being conducted throughout Indiana under the faux science of eugenics. That undid a 1907 law signed by the previous governor, Frank Hanly, that "provided for the involuntary sterilization of confirmed criminals, idiots, imbeciles, and rapists." (Eugenics, which varied from state to state, did not explicitly mention the sterilization of Blacks but, not surprisingly, was carried out disproportionately on poor and minority populations.) Marshall was a man given to righteous proclamations about race but was congenitally opposed to confrontation and therefore disinclined to make real change. Madison refers to Marshall as "a liberal with the brakes on."

The Robertson family found a lot of that when it came to Indiana in the early 1940s. And to a large extent, the brakes stayed on.

CHAPTER TWO

Attucks Has a Zebra Problem

"Those hoods didn't mean anything to us."

O scar Robertson's sophomore season at Crispus Attucks did not begin in 1953 with a herald of trumpets, for these were not the days of LeBron James and Amateur Athletic Union (AAU) ball and national rankings for high school teams. Now, it is undeniable that coach Ray Crowe thought more of Oscar as a player than Oscar *thought* Crowe thought of him. Oscar writes in his autobiography that he was surprised and elated when he found out that he survived the final cut of "Ray the Razor," who had earned that sobriquet around the halls of Attucks because he had to cut so many players. "I walked home in a daze and about burst with pride when I told Bill Swatts, my friend," he wrote. But there is no evidence that Crowe even considered cutting him. Crowe had seen Oscar's talents with his own eyes and had gotten glowing reports from Oscar's junior high coach, Tom Sleet, a wholly reliable source revered by the Attucks players to whom he taught the game.

But perhaps Crowe was reticent to invest too much hope in the sophomore. Oscar's older brother Flap had eventually become one of Crowe's mainstays, but it had taken a while, and the coach was never pleased with big brother's gift of gab.

It's also possible that Oscar's all-around versatility worked against him at the outset of his relationship with Crowe. He was tall at 6'3", but not overwhelmingly so, therefore clearly not a center. Oscar could handle the ball but wasn't overtly flashy in the manner of Attucks's graduated star Hallie Bryant. Plus, it seemed as if the quiet kid liked rebounding. Was he a guard or a forward?

How wonderful it would be if we had the power to see people not as they are at the moment but as what they will *become*. Emily Dickinson passes away as a lonely spinster, mysterious to even her closest friends, considered not much more than an odd duck by the townspeople in Amherst, Massachusetts. But not long after she dies, her sister excavates a couple thousand of her poems, and next thing anyone knows, Emily Dickinson is the Belle of Amherst, a genius in the poetic pantheon beside Walt Whitman and Ralph Waldo Emerson—where she remains.

So, look again at Oscar, the sophomore, an unlikely agent of chaos. In just six months he would become the Kid with Potential to Be the Next Great Thing. By the following year Oscar was the It Kid of Indiana basketball; the year after that he was Maybe the Best Ever, the leader of a team known well beyond the state of Indiana, a team that broke barriers and went undefeated in his senior year. And a couple years after that, a photographer snapped Oscar in action for the University of Cincinnati against Kansas State, and he became something else again. The image caught him in midair, both feet far off the ground as if he had sprung from a trampoline, legs splayed in a get-the-hell-out-of-the-way posture, his hands holding the ball in a viselike grip, teammates and opponents standing around and ogling him, like they had just come upon the *David* on its perch in the Galleria dell'Accademia in Florence. Oscar was officially immortal.

But at the first practice in 1953, he was just Little Flap, another Attucks candidate who hopped to it when the Razor blew his whistle. It's impossible to know at this point whether Crowe planned to start Oscar right away because there were extenuating circumstances before his varsity debut. The sophomore had decided to take a crosstown bus to his first game, which was to be played at Arsenal Technical High School on the east side of Indianapolis. The opponent was Fort Wayne North Side. So, welcome to the world of Attucks basketball in the 1950s, where a home game was never at home.

The Attucks gym, see, was small—hardly a gym at all. Crowe had his teams run at the beginning of practice, and getting the work in required fifty laps around the gym. Attucks had last hosted a game in the late 1940s; in the early days of the school, when there was no gym at all, the Tigers had occasionally played games in the school auditorium, and, yes, you could fall off the stage, a most emphatic out of bounds. The Tigers were eternal vagabonds. Other Indiana high school teams played in virtual palaces—when Muncie Fieldhouse opened in 1928, it had a larger capacity than gyms at Indiana University and Purdue, and massive arenas were built in Vincennes, Michigan City, and Elkhart to fit the desires of the mad-for-high-school-basketball citizenry—but Attucks was constructed in second-class fashion. Used and out-of-date textbooks, hand-me-down uniforms, bargain-basement facilities—those were a way of life at Attucks. The hardest-working man in Indianapolis at that time was Alonzo Watford, the Attucks athletic director and scheduler charged with keeping the plates spinning.

Anyway, Oscar's bus to his first game got caught in traffic, as city buses tend to do, and then, near his stop, "some dude pulled a knife on me," he recounts in his autobiography. Why? "Just life on the streets." He arrived at the gym before tip-off, but still a little late, and began his high school career on the bench. For three minutes. Crowe then put him on the floor as a forward, and over the next three seasons he rarely came off unless Attucks was far ahead and Crowe was pushing the mercy button (or Oscar got into foul trouble, which happened way too frequently when he was an upperclassman). Attucks beat Fort Wayne North easily. Oscar scored fifteen points and committed four personal fouls, and the next day's *Indianapolis Star* reported that he demonstrated "poise unexpected of a sophomore." He always did.

The Attucks mainstay was expected to be guard William Mason, who had inherited the No. 34 jersey of Hallie Bryant, Indiana's 1953 Mr. Basketball. In fact, one of the few stories that Oscar kept in his scrapbook from the 1953–1954 season was a preseason piece about Attucks headlined "Tiger Teeth Sharp Even Without Stars." The only current player mentioned in the story was Mason.

Ray Crowe was beginning his fourth season as the Attucks head coach in Oscar's sophomore season. He and wife Betty were a powerful team at Attucks. In *The Ray Crowe Story*, a 1992 biography written by Kerry Marshall, Betty recalls many an afternoon when team members would be at the Crowe house taking a pregame nap. "I used to call them wall-to-wall carpet because they'd all stretch out on the living room," Betty told Marshall, "and I'd have to step between all of those long legs to get around the house." (Betty Ewing Crowe was Crowe's second wife, a charming Attucks Class of 1948 graduate, sixteen years his junior and not much older than his players.) Bill Hampton, a starting guard on the 1954–1955 team, remembered those days fondly in a 2022 interview. "We would go to Mr. Crowe's house," he said, "and Betty would feed us. It was like she was your family."

Ray never let the relationship between himself and his players get quite that cozy. He was very much their coach, very much in charge, more avuncular in manner than friendly. Attucks players were assigned to his homeroom, so every morning they saw Crowe's face and heard his lectures about staying on top of their academics. Crowe was also a respected math and physical education teacher, which meant something in those days. "Teachers occupied a unique position in the black community as symbols of its potential," writes Richard Pierce in *Polite Protest*, "and they were important members of the educated middle class." That was particularly true at Attucks, which through the years remained as proud of its faculty as of its athletic teams.

Crowe had gotten into education after realizing that his postcollege job at International Harvester, a major Indianapolis employer, wasn't taking him anywhere, a story familiar to Black Americans. He had started as a sweeper and moved to crane operator, but his mind had been trained for other things. So when a friend told him about a teaching opportunity at School 17—Black administrators in the Indianapolis system were always on the lookout for Black college grads to teach—he applied, got the job, and accepted it despite a pay cut. He did his student teaching at Attucks, and in a flipped-script scenario, Crowe at first had to feel his way among the Black population. Bob Collins, a columnist at the *Indianapolis Star* who became a Crowe confidante, remembered a surprising conversation with him later in life. Crowe "said the first day he walked into Attucks he was scared to death," Collins related in an oral history conducted by the Indiana Historical Society. "He said he never knew there were that many Black people in the world."

Crowe's background explains that. He grew up in the appropriately named Whiteland, Indiana, a farming community near the larger town of Franklin, twenty miles south of Indianapolis. He was the second of ten children born to Morten and Tommie Ann Crowe, who were tenant farmers. Ray always said that the Crowes were the only Black family in Whiteland, a ten-minute drive north from Greenwood where the United Klans of America was headquartered as late as the 1970s.[1]

---

1. Writing from Greenwood in 1977, the grand dragon of the Klan, William M. Chaney, petitioned the Indiana General Assembly to vote against the Equal Rights Amendment because it "would force women to share the same cells in jails and prisons with men and with black bucks."

In *The Ray Crowe Story*, Crowe tells Marshall that he knew most of the people in Whiteland and Franklin who "paraded around" in hoods. "We worked side by side with them in the fields during harvest and then had a big celebration meal with them when harvest was over," Crowe told Marshall. "Those hoods didn't mean anything to us. We were just another farm family trying to get by like everyone else."

Those sentiments largely summarize Crowe's feelings about race. Over the years and up until his death in 2003 at age eighty-eight, he never talked much about racial incidents that affected him personally. Surely there were many, but he mentioned only a few. He had to sit in the colored section of the Franklin movie theater. His family didn't even consider going to most of the town's restaurants. During his days at Indiana Central (now the University of Indianapolis), a player from Hanover College called him a racial epithet, but his teammates quickly came to his defense, and the Hanover president later called to apologize. On one other occasion the Indiana Central team was refused service at a restaurant in southern Indiana, so the coach, Harry Good, gathered up the team, and they ate somewhere else.

Throughout his seven years as Attucks's coach—through endless trips necessitated by an inadequate home gymnasium; through meals that had to be eaten on those buses because restaurants would not open their doors to Blacks; through horrendous, race-based officiating; through comments, veiled and otherwise, that Attucks was success-ful only because it had superior athletes—Ray Crowe mostly held his tongue. Mostly. We shall see those rare exceptions.

Ray had been a star athlete, but his younger brother, George, was in a different galaxy as one of the greatest athletes in Indiana history. George was named Indiana's first-ever Mr. Basketball as a senior in 1939, a title that had become hagiographic by the time Oscar won it in 1956. That an African American received it in 1939 speaks to Crowe's talent. George also starred in baseball and track at Indiana Central and after graduation would become a barnstorming basketball pro and, most famously, a major leaguer who played ten years with the Boston (then Milwaukee) Braves, the Cincinnati Reds, and the St. Louis Cardinals, mostly as a first baseman and pinch hitter. When Ray was hired as Attucks's head coach in 1950, the story warranted three paragraphs in the *Indianapolis Star* and noted early that he was the older brother of George Crowe.

In the long run, however, Ray was not swallowed up by the exploits of his younger brother. Ray was a strong and tough competitor who impressed his young charges at Attucks by running up a wall and dunking. He told Phillip Hoose, who wrote *Attucks! Oscar Robertson and the Basketball Team That Awakened a City*, that he learned to play the game in a barn and a hayloft, a very Caucasian-like path to Hoosier hoops glory. At Indiana Central, Ray was a tough and smart guard for the basketball team in the winter; in track, he ran the 100 and 220 and also competed in the low hurdles and shot put. He was a combination of speed and strength, a coiled force.

And while George was making a name in the big leagues, Ray was becoming one of the most famous basketball coaches in a state that reveres its coaches. Those three paragraphs in a local paper had turned into a certified national story when Crowe hung it up after the 1956–1957 season with 179 wins and two state championships. (That said, Crowe never really got his due as a coach—another story for later.) Crowe commanded respect with a tough-but-fair demeanor and a way of getting along with everyone, a man comfortable in both the boardroom—he would later serve as an Indiana state representative, an Indianapolis city councilman, and director of the Indianapolis Parks Department—and the locker room.

But the jury was still out on his coaching as he entered the 1953–1954 season. It's essential to remember that Indiana high school basketball coaches back then belonged to something like the philosopher class in ancient Greece. For a half century they had been revered as geniuses, molders of men, pillars of small communities. And they were all white.

Black head coaches were still a novelty in the 1950s, and certainly no Black coach would have been chosen to lead an integrated school.

Just as another Hoosier named John Wooden would later live by his "Pyramid of Success," Crowe had his guiding principles, which were nothing if not high-minded. Here they are as he laid them out:

Right will prevail.
Be right without fear. Unfair victory is bittersweet.
No team can beat you if you are right (you're at your best when you are right).
No team can beat you if it is wrong.
No team can beat you at your best; right is unbeatable.

Crowe wrote an article for a local newspaper about team building that demonstrated the classic "Attucks Attitude" about discipline and comportment, constant themes of lectures, both wanted and unwanted, by Russell Lane, the school's no-nonsense principal, who ruled from 1930 to 1957. Lane lived in fear of an incident involving his students or athletes that would provide oxygen to the argument that African Americans were by nature violent. As Lane stood in the Attucks doorway each morning waving a watch—"Two minutes! Two minutes!"—almost his every act as principal was designed to keep order. There were occasions when Lane drove Crowe to distraction, and there were other occasions when Crowe *sounded* like Lane.

At the same time, Crowe was beginning to get comfortable enough to speak out on an issue that had dogged him since he got the job in 1950: biased officiating. It was indeed a plague upon Indiana basketball. Granted, nothing is more predictable in sports than opponents evaluating officials' calls in different ways, but there is substantial evidence that white officials, as a class, were not to be trusted to rule fairly in games involving Black teams.

Biased officiating was a recurring theme for Collins of the *Star*, who over the years would become Attucks's biggest cheerleader. He attended several officiating meetings and came away with the opinion that "when Attucks started getting good some of these guys were absolute bigots." Added Collins in an oral history before his death in 1995, "One of them said, 'Let me tell you something. A minute to play, once that black hand comes around that white hand and slaps the ball away? You're gonna call a foul on the black player.'"

Race-biased officiating remained a problem at all levels of basketball for a long, long time, and who can say it's been eradicated? But in the 1950s, as the game was transitioning to a faster-paced, vertical one, white officials most assuredly could not help but make calls based upon their own basketball upbringing. That was true even in the NBA, which began to change for the better when it worked substantial numbers of Black officials into its ranks. (NBA refs are about equally divided by race these days.)

The answer back in the 1950s, of course, would have been to hire more Black officials. They were—excuse the phrase—in the minority, but they were out there. In Indiana and other places, however, there was a resistance to putting Blacks in power, another illustration of the sub rosa racism that prevailed at the time.

Bernard McPeak, a highly qualified Black referee who had officiated games in Pennsylvania for fifteen years and had even worked state championships, applied for membership in the Indiana Officials Association (IOA) in the early 1950s, around the time that officiating outrages were beginning to get talked about publicly. McPeak's application was denied by a 40–7 vote. The organization's president, Clayton Nichols, a McPeak supporter, was candid and bitter when asked why the vote went that way: "It was because of his color." In other words, Nichols screwed up and told the truth.

In reaction, the front-page headline in the *Indianapolis Recorder* screamed, "Referees' Prejudice Exposed by Official of Association!" In a sidebar story, the *Recorder* asked another official it considered to be fair about the vote, and he supported denying McPeak. His reasoning? Black officials would be ineffective because "the crowd would be against them." That crystallizes so many decisions, even today: *We can't do the right thing because it will cause too much upheaval, so let's keep doing the wrong thing.*

The McPeak vote happened three days before Attucks's final game of the 1952–1953 season, which was also the final game for Attucks immortals Hallie Bryant and Flap Robertson. That formidable twosome was two seasons removed from what had been dubbed the Miracle of 1950–1951, Crowe's first season, when Attucks made it all the way to the state's final four before losing. The key game along the way was its heart-pounding 80–79 victory over Anderson High, a storied Hoosier high school power, in the regional final on March 3, 1951. With little brother Oscar at home watching on TV, Flap had come off the bench to hit a jump shot from the corner with seconds to go for the victory, probably the second-most famous shot in Indiana high school history. (The first was soon to come, and Attucks would much rather talk about the Flap shot.)

Anyway, having won the sectional and the regional, Crowe's 1952–1953 Attucks squad was in the Sweet Sixteen, what Indiana called the "semi-states," against Shelbyville, which decided to use an age-old ploy: slow the game down. The score was tied 44–44 with less than a minute left and Attucks with possession. It was Bryant's game to win. He killed time with a dribble, then drove hard toward the basket, elevated, and shot what appeared to be a wide-open layup before he was knocked to the floor by two Shelbyville players converging from each side. The shot didn't go down, but the whistle blew.

Two free throws were coming, and Bryant was a deadly shooter.

But wait.

Referee Stan Dubis pointed toward Hallie. Instead of Hallie *being* fouled, Dubis had called a foul *on* Bryant for charging. Two shots for Shelbyville's Jim Plymate. Good on both. Shelbyville wins 46–44.

One account of the game said that the whistle came so late that Attucks's Winford O'Neal had tipped in Bryant's shot, and the Attucks fans had begun to celebrate *that* basket.

For the *Recorder* it was almost too much to endure, the officiating representing just one example of the racial climate that existed in Indianapolis. The outrage was best expressed by a *Recorder* writer named Charles S. Preston. A few days after the Shelbyville call, he wrote, "Many Negro young people and others who are trying to believe in the democratic America were asking this week: Is it always going to be true that officials will take the close games away from Attucks, the close fights away from Negro boxers? Has a person with a dark skin got a chance for fair play?"

The call sparked so much outrage that the IOA felt compelled to publicly back Dubis and state that it promoted fair-minded officiating "regardless of race, color or creed." The criticism, it should be noted, came not just from the Black newspaper in Indianapolis. "Such deplorable refereeing calls into question the very integrity of the tournament," wrote the reporter covering the game for the *Versailles Republican*.

Bryant was devastated by the call and said at the time, "This will be with me for the rest of my life." He knew that Black players were much more likely than others to get bad calls from white refs. Black athletes frequently just *looked* like they were doing something that demanded a whistle. During a game in the 1951–1952 season, Willie Gardner had already fouled out when he heard the referee call a foul on No. 13. "I'm right here," said Gardner, standing up from the bench and raising his hand.

Under pressure, the IOA rescinded its veto of McPeak a few months after the end of the 1952–1953 season. But Crowe, who himself refereed from time to time, was not necessarily happy when he saw McPeak at the scorers' table. "He was bending over backwards so it wouldn't look like he was giving us any breaks," Crowe said later. "He was killing us."

———

It was during these early Crowe years that the on-campus Butler University Fieldhouse (later named Hinkle Fieldhouse) became the de facto home court for Attucks. And what a home court it was. At the time it was built in 1928, it was the largest basketball arena in the country with a seating capacity of fifteen thousand—a couple thousand more if you squeezed. Attucks had become such crowd pleasers, and the hassle of constantly rearranged games was causing such confusion—where is *Attucks* playing tonight?—that the idea of a permanent home gym was logical. Hoose reports in *Attucks!* that athletic director Watford paid $300 to rent the fieldhouse, and no one knew if it would be a good move. But in Attucks's first game at Butler, the athletic marvel Gardner put on an aerial show, Hallie Bryant scored forty-two points, and the template was set: Butler would become Attucks's own little entertainment palace, much like the famous Harlem Rens had played in the Renaissance Ballroom and Casino on 138th Street back in the 1920s and 1930s.

The move to Butler also brought Attucks more into the mainstream for those who thought of the Tigers as a carnival act—or something worse. "We showed them we didn't have tails," Oscar said during a podcast with the Indianapolis Basketball Hall of Fame. "That was a myth for a long time, that Black people grew tails at midnight." Inevitably, though, Newton's laws of cultural physics kicked in: there was a reverse reaction. As Attucks grew more and more successful at Butler into and through the postseason—Butler was the principal arena for the state tournament—the reasons they played there started to get forgotten. The thinking became *Oh, Attucks is getting an unfair advantage because Butler is their home court.* That conveniently ignored the fact that Attucks had been, first, *forced* to play there by its inadequate gymnasium and, second, *asked* to play there because the Tigers were such a popular attraction that both teams made money on an Attucks game.

In the beginning the core audience for Attucks's games had been the Attucks community. And its belief in the basketball team came freighted with something else, something bigger. Just as Caucasian Hoosiers invested heavily in *our boys* to bring honor to the small town, so did African Americans in Indianapolis see something beyond basketball in their Tigers. As Aram Goudsouzian observes in his *Indiana Magazine of History* piece, a loss represented "not just a setback for a group of young basketball players; it was also a defeat for a people who daily experienced the reality of segregation and discrimination."

Ray Crowe carried that burden to the bench every night. And as he entered his fourth season, still without that ultimate state-championship goal so desperately desired by Attucks Nation, it would be fascinating to know whether he saw what he had in Flap's brother, a quiet but confident young man bound for glory.

CHAPTER THREE

Threats Mar the Outset of Oscar's Sophomore Season

"The worst Negro slum in America."

You had to grow up fast when you were a sophomore basketball player at Crispus Attucks in the 1953–1954 season, as Oscar Robertson was, and not just because you were trying to improve your skills and work your way into the good graces of Ray "The Razor" Crowe. Never playing in your home gym carried with it a high degree of unpredictability. Would you be able to get something good—or anything at all—to eat before or after the game? Would you be cheered for your sterling play or gawked at because white fans weren't used to seeing Black players? Would the rancor you felt in the air be subtle, or would you be called the N-word outright? "I heard it a few times during those trips," Oscar wrote in *The Big O*. "But being raised in the South I learned not to let that crap get to me; the taunts made me play harder."

Also, it's necessary to understand where the game was in the early 1950s. An Indianapolis newspaper photo shows an Attucks player in action; the caption reads, "Hallie Bryant goes *clear off the floor* [author emphasis] in completing this layup shot." Another caption to a photo from another game, describing a different kind of shot, reads, "Back in the 'good old days' a one-handed shot was enough to get you kicked off the team, but Attuck [*sic*] Tigers make deadly use of them."

But something else was going on here too. It had only been a few years since America absorbed the astonishing news in 1947 that a Black man was going to play baseball for the Brooklyn Dodgers. But even scarier than the sight of Jackie Robinson in a baseball uniform was the sight of oversized Black men in shorts and sneakers. Even with Robinson on the field, the game essentially *looked* the same. But an all-Black basketball team playing with high energy? That took on another dimension. In some corners of Indiana, that was apostasy.

It was apparently bothersome to the sports editor of the *Indianapolis Star*, a man with the colorful name of Jep Cadou Jr., who had somehow communicated with the dead inventor of the game to reach his opinion about the direction of the sport. Wrote Cadou early in the Attucks phenomenon, "[James] Naismith never intended players with 'jumping jack legs' would be able to rewrite basketball's traditional patterns."

Such opinions weren't just the province of the heartland. Later, as 7'1" Wilt Chamberlain began to dominate in the NBA, well-known sports columnist Shirley Povich wrote in *Sports Illustrated*, "Basketball is for the birds—the gooney birds. The game lost this particular patron years back when it went vertical and put the accent on carnival freaks who achieved upper space by growing into it. Who can applaud Wilt the Stilt or his ilk, when they outflank the basket from above and pelt it like an open city? These fellows are biological accidents who ought to be more usefully employed, like hiring out as rainmakers to sow a few clouds."

Careful men like Attucks principal Russell Lane understood these fears, and against this racial and cultural backdrop, he made clear that Attucks players were not to be too fancy, too showy, too Globetrotterish, too *Black*. Crowe was a math teacher as well as a coach, and his daily calculus involved figuring out how to harness his team's strength, power, and athleticism while also keeping it looking like a traditional Indiana high school basketball team at a time when reporters were taking note that a player was *clear off the floor*.

As if that weren't enough, early in Oscar's sophomore season Attucks became page-one news for something other than basketball. Nine days before its game against city rival Arsenal Tech, the largest high school in the state, sensational headlines splashed across the local papers. A Tech player named David Huff reported that on his way home from practice, three Black men had stepped out of a car and threatened him. He said one grabbed his collar, and the other two poked him with knives. Huff reported that the men said to him, "You're a good shot, but you better not play too good [against Attucks]. If you make one single point we'll come back and cut you wide open."

The story grew like a weed. Threats were reportedly received at the homes of Huff and Tech coach Charlie Maas, who was told to keep both Huff and another Tech player, Don Sexson, out of the game. Those threats were written, it was reported, on toilet paper (in *pencil*, it must be added).

Then the threats turned in Attucks's direction. Crowe received an unsigned note at his home instructing, "Do not play Winifred [his first name was Winford] O'Neal or William Mason if you value their lives." In an unusual bit of specificity for a desperate man, the writer added, "I have all my possessions bet on the game, including my car and house and I want to see Tech win."

Oscar too got a phone call, informing him that he would be shot if he played. Oscar told the caller to go to hell.

The story conjured up another sensational headline[1] from a year earlier against an Attucks player: "Hallie Bryant Threatened." Bryant

---

1. The headline about Bryant appeared directly under another that read "Rosenberg Spies Executed." Both were in the same large type. In Indianapolis, a threat to a star basketball player was most assuredly a news story as big as the execution of Julius and Ethel.

had been promised that $500 would be "mailed" to him on the following Monday if he stayed out of the Indiana-Kentucky All-Star Game. But if he played, he or a member of his family "could expect to be injured." Bryant, who was assigned a uniformed police guard, played anyway and led Indiana to victory with twenty-one points.

Oscar seemed to slough off TechGate in later years, even wondering aloud why gamblers would target Huff, who, in his view, was a "steady role player" and "that's about it." But it gave the authorities something to think about. Attucks principal Russell Lane must have been apoplectic at the thought that Attucks supporters were threatening violence. The *Indianapolis News* reported on a "parley" between school and police officials to discuss plans for a "heavy police guard" at the game and ran a photo that showed Lane and athletic director Watford with Tech reps and a couple of policemen. On the day before the game this headline appeared in the *News*, the story specifically naming Huff, Sexson, Mason, and Oscar as targets: "FBI May Probe Threats to Tech, Attucks Players."

Meanwhile, the *Indianapolis Recorder* was concerned about something else: reports that school officials were considering cancelling all future athletic contests between the two schools and scapegoating the Black community for not only the threats but also an outbreak of vandalism at Tech. The paper mentioned the earlier threat against Bryant and emphasized that no one had suggested ending the Indy-Kentucky summer competition.

Whether the FBI did investigate isn't clear, but no arrests were made, and the game, as we shall see, went off without trouble. But the incident was illustrative, laying bare some of the simmering racial tension that predominated in Indianapolis.

———

A certain genre of story tended to follow Attucks victories: coverage of postgame celebrations, which invariably took place on Indiana Avenue, the thoroughfare near Attucks and the beating heart of Black life in Indianapolis. What Beale Street was to Memphis, what Vine Street was to Kansas City, what Walnut Street was to Louisville, Indiana Avenue was to Indianapolis. White folks could celebrate all over the place—the city was *theirs*, most especially Monument Circle—but Black celebrations were largely centralized, one might even say *contained*. In his weekly *Voice from the Gallery* column for the *Indianapolis Recorder*, the estimable Andrew W. Ramsey, also an Attucks teacher, made this observation, and keep it in mind for what happens the following year: "They [those in charge, the authorities] know that out of the strong racial feelings sometimes develop incidents, which are blamed wholly on the Negro participants. And the police of the city, bowing to the philosophy of segregation, insist that all of the celebration of victories by Attucks's teams be held in the ghetto instead of the Circle where normally such celebrations are held."

Blacks lived together; Blacks celebrated together. "Indiana Avenue Whoops It Up" read one headline after Attucks's big win in the 1951 regionals, and another story contained the following passage: "Not since Joe Louis was crowned heavyweight boxing champion of the world had Indiana Ave. had such cause for jubilation."

Full-throated communions of like-minded souls did, indeed, often follow in the wake of African American triumphs. They were spawned by the exploits of Joe Louis,[2] a product of the radio age and one of America's first African American sports heroes, and kept alive by Jackie Robinson, the front-porch hero of the Black population of the 1940s.

---

2. A blues musician named William Arthur Gaither, who is buried in Crown Cemetery in Indianapolis, wrote an immensely popular tune in 1938 called "Champ Joe Louis," inspired by Louis's knockout of Max Schmeling in Yankee Stadium. Two lines went like this: "It was only two minutes and four seconds / 'Fore Schmeling was down on his knees."

Jackie get any hits last night? You hear about Jackie stealing home? Like a thief at night, baby! How did Jackie's Dodgers do?

That communion was the understandable product of a people frozen out of the larger American narrative, with Black news and Black achievement consigned to the back pages or, as was usually the case, not covered at all.

But African American celebrations had a side effect in places like Indianapolis. Thoughts about unruly, liquor-crazed Blacks going wild in the streets roiled the guts of a segment of the white population.

The fears of the white populace made their way into print from time to time but were most often just *out there*, part of the quiet racism that wafted through the Indy ether. After the 1951 victory over Anderson High, the Flap Robertson jump shot game, Corky Lamm, a columnist for the *Indianapolis News,* even gently derided this fear: "Attucks won the Sectional and the city's seams didn't come apart now, did they?"

That unreasonable fear of the Black celebration would haunt Oscar Robertson, infuriate him, with its pure inequitableness. Every fiber of Oscar's being—the way he lived, the way he played—was about *order.* He attended a school whose central dictum was decorum, whose students were counseled almost daily to *stay in line.* Yet they were sometimes prejudged as savages with uncontrollable urges. Oscar could never get past it.

In the wake of the threats to the Tech and Attucks players, the Indianapolis police responded not by searching for the callers and toilet-paper writers but by cracking down on establishments along Indiana Avenue, reasoning that African American gamblers were trying to fix the outcome. The police raided dozens of Black-owned businesses, prompting the *Recorder*'s Preston to respond, "No one can say whether the threateners are fans of Attucks or Walla Walla. And if the original threateners were Tiger supporters, what about the later bums who sent threats to Ray Crowe and his boys? We also see no call for the prosecutor to grab his trusty sledgehammer and start smashing up Indiana gambling joints in this connection."

It should be noted that the *Recorder* was quite naturally involved in any story about the *Ave-noo*. The paper was literally part of it, located at 518 Indiana Avenue. The publication gave the *Ave-noo* a degree of intellectual class, and in return the *Recorder* received cultural relevancy from being in the middle of the music, the night life, the movies, and the gambling. (When the newspaper moved from its location at 518 Indiana Avenue in the 1960s, many people believed something in its soul was lost.)

To be sure, there was gambling on Indiana Avenue. Archie Greathouse, a powerful and respected citizen who, as we shall see, was a major figure during the opening of Attucks in the 1920s, himself ran a gambling establishment. "In a society in which opportunity was systematically denied to African Americans," observes Paul Mullins, an anthropology professor at Indiana University–Purdue University Indianapolis (a mouthful that blessedly goes by IUPUI), in the *Indianapolis Encyclopedia*, "the entrepreneurship in vice industries at the margins of the law shaped the fortunes of many of the most prominent personalities who lived and worked along the Avenue." But Caucasians in Indianapolis were unduly worried about Black-patronized saloons because they were often places to meet, venues for potential organization, which was assuredly the case with Greathouse's place. That said, the big players on the *Ave-noo* were just as often white men, such as the notorious brothers Joe and Isaac "Tuffy" Mitchell, Archie "Joker" Young, and Harold "Goosie" Lee. (If you were a criminal in Indianapolis, you had damn better have a memorable nickname.)

It's important to understand that the outsized fear of gambling and gamblers was very real during this time, almost a greater concern than the promised violence. Basketball was only a couple years removed from a point-shaving scandal uncovered in the early 1950s, first at City College of

New York and eventually involving at least six schools, the biggest name among them being the University of Kentucky.[3] Ultimately, some thirty players admitted to taking bribes to fix eighty-six games.

Now, there was no proof that small-time gamblers who populated the clubs around the *Ave-noo* had any part, or even remotely the juice, to attempt to fix basketball games. But there was always a civic fear of just exactly what kind of mischief was happening down on the *Ave-noo*.

The mainstream Indianapolis papers tried to minimize, even diplomatize, the event. They took note that weeks after the game officials at Attucks and Tech announced plans for "exchange activities." The *Indianapolis Star* printed a story about it accompanied by a photo of the president of the Attucks student council (Julian Combs) shaking hands with the president of the Tech Student Affairs Organization (Jim O'Dell). *See? We got a black kid shaking hands with a white kid. No racial tension here.*

Indianapolis was like so much of America back then, a city that kept its secrets and hid the fact that there were two worlds: one seen by the public at large, the other hidden in the shadows, where Crispus Attucks was built. To fully grasp what Robertson and his friends and teammates ultimately accomplished, it's necessary to understand life as it was back then—that prejudice, strife, and hard times were baked into the culture.

———

In 1935, seven years before the Robertsons arrived in Indianapolis, Dean William Pickens of the national office of the NAACP made a speech that was both observational and a call to action. "Violation of

———
3. Kentucky coach Adolph Rupp, who asked reporters to put an asterisk next to the names of prospects who were Black so he would know not to recruit them, had once said about the emerging scandal, "They couldn't touch my boys with a ten-foot pole." But two of his best players, Alex Groza and Ralph Beard, were found guilty of shaving points. Both played for the Indianapolis Olympians, an NBA franchise, for four years in the early 1950s but were banished after the 1950–1951 season when the NBA barred for life any player connected to the scandal.

the unalienable rights of colored people to life, liberty, and the pursuit of happiness is more flagrant and vicious in Indianapolis and Indiana," said Pickens, "than in any other Northern or Western City and State." According to renowned historian Emma Lou Thornbrough, he then criticized the Black community's "lethargy and acquiescence" in accepting such discriminatory treatment (foreshadowing what Richard Pierce writes about in *Polite Protest*, though the Notre Dame professor always makes his points with compassion and understanding of the difficulty of fighting entrenched powers).

In 1939, Nathan Straus, the director of the US Housing Authority, toured a Black neighborhood near the Robertson home on the west side of Indianapolis. Make no mistake about it: neighborhoods were defined by skin color, not just by common practice or desire but also by statute, specifically the 1926 Indianapolis City Council ordinance that codified racial separation in housing. Writes Pierce,

> Council's bold attempt to maintain racially segregated neighborhoods was especially egregious because the ordinance was passed after the United States Supreme Court had ruled a similar Louisville law unconstitutional in 1917. Ordinance supporters on the council thought Indianapolis could avoid the court's censure because their ordinance did not expressly prohibit the sale of property or give any particular advantage to members of either race. It merely prohibited occupancy. The court failed to see the distinction and summarily struck down the Indianapolis ordinance, but its presence was not really needed because real estate agents refused to show African Americans property, outside of designated areas.

As Straus took his tour, accompanied by an uncomfortable Indianapolis mayor Reginald Sullivan, he concluded, "This isn't civilized," and told hizzoner that the area of west Indianapolis upon which he gazed was "the worst Negro slum in America."

The negative scrutiny came not just from outside. Around the same time, a survey by Flanner House, a social service organization in Indianapolis, called that area "one of the most unsightly, unsanitary, and deteriorated sectors of the city." It came with a seeming economic contradiction: Most of the adult men and many of the women were fully employed. They had left the South and achieved a big part of the dream of the Great Migration. Yet the squalid west side was the best they could do for housing. They were hemmed in.

The Robertsons lived near the confluence of three bodies of water, none of them pleasing: Fall Creek, White River, and the Central Canal. The area was variously called Frog Island, Bucktown, Naptown,[4] or Pat Ward's Bottoms. Though the identity of Pat Ward has been lost to history, everyone knew what the Bottoms were: a particularly blighted area of a particularly blighted area.

The area was seemingly cursed from the beginning. In 1821 a catastrophic flood sent water over the banks of the White River, killing livestock and washing away the shanties of the impoverished Irish and Germans who had settled there. A malaria outbreak followed, and the river acquired, according to Attucks grad David Leander Williams in *African Americans in Indianapolis*, the nickname "The River of Death." The remaining whites fled, and poor Blacks took over the low-lying area, which remained subject to flooding.

Those who lived in Frog Island paid a heavy price for their poverty. A 1917 study found that Indianapolis had the highest typhoid rate among the nation's twenty-nine largest cities, a condition that the study "laid

---

4. The origin of the name "Naptown" is no doubt musical. An influential but little-known singer/songwriter/pianist named Leroy Carr, who was raised in Indianapolis in the 1910s, released an album with a guitarist named Scrapper Blackwell titled *Naptown Blues: 1929–1934*. Carr died in 1935 at age thirty or thirty-one from an alcohol addiction, but his songs have been recorded by countless musicians, from Robert Johnson to Eric Clapton.

squarely at the feet of the city's lax sanitary codes." A particularly hideous structure located at 458–460 Agnes Street, not far from the Robertson house, could be seen as a disquieting symbol: a two-story outhouse that was at once a testament to urban ingenuity and a punch to the gut of common decency. The subject of an excavation led by Paul Mullins and his IUPUI students in 2011—"It was a bad city to be a pig," commented Mullins after analyzing the dietary remains of both the German and the African American residents—the outhouse was there until at least 1956. (Insurance records show it was gone by 1962.)

What's there now? IUPUI's Campus Center on a street known as University Boulevard. That must draw a joke or two from those students who are aware of the street's history.

Infant mortality rates were higher in Frog Island than in any other place in the city, and outbreaks of cholera were traced to the west side near the fetid water. Thus a pernicious racial aggression emerged: force a segment of the population into one poisonous area, then finger-point and blame that population for the inevitable health degradations that ensue.

In a fascinating bit of irony, Indianapolis had finished an ambitious public housing project in that part of town shortly before the Robertsons moved to the west side. Lockefield Gardens, erected between 1935 and 1938, was one of Franklin Delano Roosevelt's New Deal fever dreams come to fruition. Designated specifically for the Black population, it was Indianapolis's first public housing project. (Proposals for white housing had also been advanced but didn't go anywhere.) The 738 Lockefield units sat on a twenty-two-acre site near bustling Indiana Avenue, then at its zenith as the cultural heart of Black life in Indianapolis. (The units were fireproof, which is significant, given the grisly toll paid by many Black families who lived in flimsily constructed firetraps on the west side; see Chapter 16.)

IUPUI's Mullins writes in the *Encyclopedia of Indianapolis* that "local realtors and elected officials had aggressively fought the construction of

Lockefield." This was not surprising. Call it a do-nothing mentality or a genuine laissez-faire philosophy, but Hoosiers generally turned down federal assistance, a stance that endures today. Plus, the real estate lobby was never behind Lockefield because, as blogger Wildstyle Paschall put it in a post for *New American Indianapolis*, "Public housing for Blacks was considered a threat to the continuing prosperity of mostly white landlords' ability to extract profit from Black neighborhoods."

Nevertheless, Lockefield was by and large a splendid success. It was reliably reported that even white people wanted to live there, the ultimate encomium in post-Depression Indianapolis. "We were immensely proud of living in Lockefield," said David Williams, who was brought up there, in a 2022 interview. In *Polite Protest*, Pierce quotes an early Lockefield resident: "Living here gives a man a feeling that he's going somewhere." How rare that feeling was for Blacks back then.

In some way, though, Lockefield *accentuated* the economic hopelessness of thousands of Black families like the Robertsons. Over the years, Oscar has become associated with Lockefield because of the storied Dust Bowl where he and his brothers learned to hoop (Chapter 4). But though their first house in Indianapolis at 1005 Colton Street was *near* Lockefield, the Robertson family, like so many others, could not afford even public housing. (Colton Street, originally known as Rhode Island Street, once reached further east but was demolished for the construction of Lockefield, according to research done by Mullins.)

So, in practical terms, nearby Lockefield was as far away from the Robertsons' grasp as a Park Avenue mansion. In his post about Lockefield, Paschall contrasts the "massive, brand-new, state-of-the-art" public housing project with the "barbaric third-world conditions" that existed "right across the street."

Oscar invariably describes his house on Colton, which research by Mullins indicates was built in the 1890s, as "a standard shotgun shack," meaning a narrow rectangular house with the rooms extending one behind the other on each side of a narrow hallway. The roof was tar paper, and a big potbelly stove sat, according to Oscar, "smack-dab in the middle of the house." He writes in *The Big O*, "There was no heat in the wintertime. You would get under all the covers you could, but the wind would come right through the windows. You would hear people across the street arguing and fighting all the time. And gunshots at night."

There was running water indoors, but the privy was outside for much of the time Oscar lived there, which was the case for the entire Frog Island area. Municipal pickup of the accrued waste was at best sporadic. "The air was perpetually full of bad smells and festering diseases," Oscar writes.

There were gradations of poverty even within the Frog Island dwellings, and the Robertsons lived in what became known as Kinkaid's Hole, an imaginative lift from a Western titled *Bandits of the Badlands* that Oscar and his brothers saw at the Lido Theater at 786 Indiana Avenue. In that 1945 film, a violent fistfight takes place between an outlaw and a Texas Ranger in a pit known as Kinkaid's Hole.[5] Translation: Colton Street was a badass pit.

Still, Kinkaid's Hole was home, and home was what you knew and just about *all* you knew. Oscar and his brothers didn't go to the south side of Indianapolis because it was all white. They didn't go to the east side because it was, Oscar says, "too tough." There were some Black schoolmates on the north side of Indianapolis, but west siders didn't have the money or the means of transportation to get over there. And Blacks weren't wanted downtown among the white-owned businesses and didn't have money to spend there anyway. If they did go, there were

---

5. The *Bandits* screenwriter was Doris Schroeder, whose first screenplay was titled *Heart of a Jewess*. So we can safely call this a departure. *Bandits* starred Sunset Carson, a staple of 1940s B Westerns. David Williams knows the film and says that the entire venue for the fight, not just the pit, was known as Kinkaid's Hole. "But I like the pit story better anyway," he says.

unwritten rules. "Like we could buy a hot dog at Kresge's," says Willie Merriweather of a prominent five-and-dime store in Indianapolis, "but we couldn't eat it at the counter." (The downtown Kresge building was where the leader of the Indiana Klan made his headquarters in the 1920s.) Oscar says that he and his brothers didn't even do much "roaming around" their own neighborhood. They could go to three movie theaters in Indianapolis—the Indiana Theater, the Walker Theatre, and the Lido—but not the Loew's downtown. But even at that, Oscar and his crowd did not populate Indiana Avenue all that much. A few years later, when they were in college, they were more likely to go back to Indiana Avenue, probably to the Cotton Club; Merriweather remembers seeing a young Tina Turner perform there.

If you got sick in Frog Island you had a chance of getting into the best nearby hospital, which was General Hospital at 10th Street and Indiana Avenue. But it treated Black patients in only one ward, and if that was full, you were out of luck. Several attempts to build hospitals staffed with Black physicians for Black patients (Lincoln Hospital, Charity Hospital, Dr. Ward's Sanatorium, Provident Hospital) had all failed due to lack of funding. Black babies on the west side were pretty much born where the Robertson boys were born in Tennessee—at home with the help of midwives or Black doctors.

If you got in trouble in Indianapolis, well, it was a crapshoot as to whether you would find equal justice. In a case that held much interest in Black America in the late 1940s, a Black Indianapolis truck driver named Robert Austin Watts was granted a new murder trial by the US Supreme Court on the grounds that Blacks were excluded from his jury selection in Marion County and also that Watts was coerced into making a confession without counsel. That Supreme Court decision reversed a decision of the Indiana Supreme Court that had denied his petition for a new trial and set an execution date. The case was taken to the US Supreme Court by the NAACP and its lawyer, Thurgood Marshall.

Marshall was an occasional visitor to Indianapolis, where he appeared at the "Monster Meetings" held by the Senate Avenue YMCA.[6]

However, Watts was again found guilty, this time in a Bartholomew County court, of murdering Mary Lois Burney, and after appeals, Indiana governor Henry Schricker refused to commute Watts's sentence. He was executed on January 16, 1951. The case was remembered not so much for cries that Watts was innocent as for the casual way that the Hoosier state (and it was not alone) ignored minorities in jury selection.

What about recreational opportunities for a boy like Oscar in 1950s Indianapolis? As long as he was willing to make a two-and-a-half-mile walk, a Black kid from Naptown could enjoy the grassy expanses of Douglass Park on E. 25th Street, a forty-three-acre community park that opened in 1927 mainly to serve the Black community and named for abolitionist Frederick Douglass. Joe Louis was a frequent visitor to the park's golf course—it was built in 1926 after the Indianapolis Parks Department had ruled that Blacks were barred from the city's four municipal courses—as were African American pros like Charlie Sifford and Ted Rhodes, who were denied admission to the regular PGA Tour.

Kids like Oscar could also swim in the pool there. "But only in Douglass Park," says Merriweather. "Not Broad Ripple." Inevitably, Douglass became an overcrowded catastrophe, the only pool, it was estimated, for seventy thousand Blacks in Indianapolis. When it got hot, some Black kids had taken to swimming in the polluted Central Canal, Fall Creek, and White River, even though undercurrents, trash, broken bottles, and

---

6. A young African American physician named Dr. Henry L. Hummons was a key founder of the Senate Avenue Y. He was inspired to organize a place for Blacks when he was denied membership in the Indianapolis YMCA. Known locally as "the Colored Y," it was the largest institution of its kind by 1915 and kept growing in prominence, largely because of its support of athletics and its "Monster Meetings." The meetings were "public forums where men, and later women, could gather on Sunday afternoons between November and March to listen to lectures on a wide variety of topics," according to a piece in the *Indiana History Blog*. School desegregation in Indianapolis—or the lack thereof—became a monster Monster Meeting topic.

a high volume of *E. coli* made it dangerous. Oscar and his brothers didn't do that. They had another place to go, as we shall see.

What Black kids in Indianapolis could *not* enjoy were the rides at Riverside Park[7] at W. 30th Street between the White River and the Central Canal. It was in their neighborhood, but they were kept out by a whites-only policy established in 1919 by Lewis Coleman, the lawyer who owned the park. "I can still see that big sign up at Riverside," remembers Merriweather. "'Whites Only.' At least they were clear about it." Others from that era remembered another Riverside sign: "Dogs and Negroes Not Allowed." As late as 1954 the *Indianapolis Recorder* was editorializing against similar signs, which nevertheless remained in place for another decade.

Black kids could enter the park on something called "Colored Frolic Day" if they had collected a substantial number of bottle caps from Polk's Dairy, which was, says Williams, "a highly progressive company for its time." (Jazz great Wes Montgomery worked at Polk's for a while when he was making a name on Indiana Avenue.)

In the Indianapolis of their younger years, where did the Frog Island kids turn for their sports heroes? Oscar was born five months after Joe Louis's greatest triumph—the destruction of Max Schmeling at Yankee Stadium—so the heavyweight champ was pretty much done by 1951 when he got dropped by a Rocky Marciano left. Sugar Ray Robinson and Kid Gavilan took over for Louis, but they were never as important in galvanizing the Black community as Joe, a hero of the radio age.

From his home on Colton Street, Oscar could hear the thunderous roars of the engines from what was becoming a world-famous racetrack

---

7. Although some Blacks did patronize Riverside throughout the 1950s, the ban on Blacks was not officially overturned until 1963 after protests by the NAACP Youth Council. David Williams remembers walking through Riverside in 1964, finally unencumbered by thoughts that he could be grabbed by the shirt collar and tossed out. "I took my 8-millimeter camera along to film it," said Williams in a 2022 interview. "It's not like they wanted us; it was just economic. It was like the Montgomery bus boycott."

at 16th Street and Georgetown Road in the suburban enclave of Speed-way. But it didn't do much for him. "You're aware of it, of course, but it just seemed like you were totally on the outside looking in," Robertson told William Rhoden of the *New York Times* in 2015. "It was cultural. My dad never went [to the Indy 500]. I felt that they didn't want black people to come out there. I was just told blacks don't go there."

Jackie Robinson was by now a constant, but only a few other Blacks had managed to trickle into Major League Baseball, and the sport had not captured the soul of the African American community the way it would in the late 1950s with the ascendance of superstars like Willie Mays, Hank Aaron, Frank Robinson, and Ernie Banks. The baseball most familiar to Oscar and his friends was played by the Indianapolis Clowns, a well-established touring team that was part of the empire of Abe Saperstein, owner of the Harlem Globetrotters. The Indy team, which came to the city in 1944 as the Indianapolis-Cincinnati Clowns, was full of talented players (including Goose Tatum, also a Globetrotter), some of whom would have been big leaguers had they come along later. They also took the field in grass skirts and gave themselves names like Mofike, Wahoo, and Tarzan.

Basketball was not a haven for Black role models either. As late as 1947, about the time that young Oscar was making his way to the soon-to-be-famous playground to start playing hoops, the National Association of Intercollegiate Basketball (NAIB; later the National Association of Intercollegiate Athletes), whose tournament for small-college teams had been organized a decade earlier by none other than basketball creator James Naismith (Chapter 5), barred Black players from participating. That exclusion led a Hoosier hero to keep his team home from the event, which was played at the Municipal Auditorium in Kansas City, Missouri. That coach's name was John Wooden, then at Indiana State, which had a reserve African American player named Clarence Walker.

The following year the ban was lifted, and years later Wooden took credit for this.[8] However, the facts, as uncovered by Seth Davis in *Wooden: A Coach's Life*, aren't quite that simple. Davis says that Wooden had already informed Walker that he *wouldn't* be going with his teammates to the 1948 tournament in accordance with the NAIB dictates. However, after the prohibition was lifted, Walker was okayed to go, and Wooden later claimed that he had taken a principled stand. Walker still wasn't allowed to stay with the team in its downtown hotel and instead was housed with a local minister across the river in Kansas City, Kansas. This makes it fair to ask whether Wooden should have stayed home for that reason too.

"It should be noted," said Davis in a 2022 interview, "that Clarence Walker on other occasions praised John Wooden as a fair man, and that, on balance, Wooden took many principled stands on behalf of Black players."

At the risk of belaboring the point, the story is significant. The stakes were high for that 1948 tournament because the winner (which turned out to be Louisville by virtue of a win over a talented Wooden team in the final) was automatically invited to the Olympic trials. So it wasn't just a tournament. Many people are highly principled to a point, but how many don't have a bending point?

The NAIB execs, having been pressured into capitulating, promptly took credit for being the first tournament to welcome Black players. (The pivot play has always been important for organization leaders.) While the NAIB battle was going on, John McLendon, the first celebrated Black

---

8. Real credit for lifting the ban should go primarily to a man named Harry D. Henshel, who was a member of the US Olympic Basketball Committee, as well as the founder of the United States Committee Sports for Israel. That was in his spare time. In his real time he was an executive for the Bulova Watch Company. Henshel had heard that Manhattan College was not going to the tournament to protest the exclusion of Blacks, and then Siena College had refused Manhattan's spot. So Henshel went public with his opinion that the NAIB champion should perforce be eliminated from Olympic consideration. That got the attention of the NAIB honchos, who rescinded the ban in short order.

basketball coach and a man who would become known for a famous "secret game" he played against a white team (more on that later), was fuming. Historically Black schools, such as North Carolina Central University, where he coached, were not eligible to play in the NCAA tournament. "The NCAA may mean *NATIONAL COLLEGIATE ATHLETIC ASSOCIATION* to some people," he wrote in an uncharacteristically emotional statement, "but to us it means *NO COLORED ATHLETES ALLOWED.*"

So, though Blacks were allowed to compete in the National Invitational Tournament back then, college hoops offered up limited opportunities to young African Americans. Look to the pros? Not then. In the fall of 1950, as Oscar's big brother Flap and Hallie Bryant were preparing for their sophomore season at Attucks, Earl Lloyd of the Washington Capitols was taking the court as the first African American to play in the NBA. There were only a few—with the revolutionary Bill Russell still three seasons away—when Oscar took the court as a high school sophomore in 1953.

There was an Indianapolis entry in the NBA's nascent years, first the Indianapolis Jets and then the Olympians, but the Jets never caught on, and the Olympians, after an initial burst of popularity, were irreparably damaged by having point shavers Alex Groza and Ralph Beard on their roster. Oscar never did see much in them anyway. "I saw them play," he told Indianapolis writer Mark Montieth of the Olympians, "but I had no connection to the Olympians. They didn't have any black guys."

Not surprisingly, the sports role models who resonated with Oscar wore colorful red, white, and blue uniforms, traveled around the world, and performed warmup routines to the sounds of "Sweet Georgia Brown." The Globetrotters came to Indy every year, just like they came to every town every year, or so it seemed, and what was not to like? They seemed to be having fun, they were famous, they were skilled, and, more to the point, it was assumed that they made a lot of money.

As for the undertones of Uncle Tomism in their routines, few people talked about them back then, and that subject certainly wouldn't have been fodder for a kid in his preteens. (It's worth remembering that, aside from the clowning, the Trotters could really play. Of the many victories they achieved in legit games, the most famous was a 1948 win over the George Mikan–led Minneapolis Lakers, who were on their way to becoming an NBA powerhouse.) Oscar never remotely considered joining the Globies—that wasn't his style—but he admired them.

Later, Ray Crowe would come to hate the inevitable Globetrotter comparisons that were hung on his team because they were all Black, dunked in the layup line, ran the floor, and knew how to dribble and pass. But to the players, it was a compliment. Oscar vividly remembers meeting the Globetrotters in his senior year, by which time Willie Gardner was a Globie, and his interactions with the Trotters were among the highlights of Oscar's life to that point.

But here's where the story takes a twist. A kid from a foul-smelling ghetto, with no money and maybe no future, picks up a basketball. His role models are men who play to a carnival tune and treat each night like high-comedy vaudeville. His specific heroes are Marques Haynes, who did a propulsive fancy-dribbling act, and Goose Tatum, a talented player known as the Globetrotters' "clown prince." How did that combination produce a player like Oscar? How did it produce a kid who, from his earlier days, thought like a quarterback, a kid who seemed to bypass apprenticeship?

Oscar Robertson was an anomaly. He was Miles Davis, an artist who blew with the cats on 52nd Street but was also schooled in the rudiments at Juilliard. Oscar's Juilliard was a magical place called Crispus Attucks, his club an equally magic playground called the Dust Bowl.

CHAPTER FOUR

The Magic of the Dust Bowl

"They say all Attucks players aspire to be Harlem Globetrotters. With that grind, they already are."

Mostly because of the threats, but also because it was a city game and a natural rivalry—east side Arsenal Tech against west side Attucks—the 1953 mid-December showdown at Butler Fieldhouse was one of the most anticipated scholastic games in Indianapolis city history. About ten thousand spectators packed the arena, and there seemed to be almost as many police. According to some newspaper reports, FBI agents circulated among the crowd. The toilet-paper threatener was still at large (never to be apprehended). Of the five players targeted, only David Huff did not suit up, Tech coach Charlie Maas saying that he "cried like a baby" when his parents laid down the law that he was sitting out.

There was a lot of nervous looking around among the players in the pregame warmups, and, predictably, the game was not a classic. Oscar scored the first basket of the game—that will emerge as a trend—and

Attucks was never in trouble; a letdown in the fourth quarter was mainly responsible for Tech getting as close as it did in the 43–38 Attucks win. Best of all—certainly to Attucks principal Russell Lane—nothing had happened . . . including great basketball.

Now, the threats weren't completely forgotten by everyone. One Indy newspaper reported the game in the following manner: "Did last night's game in Butler Fieldhouse set a precedent which will plague Indianapolis high school basketball in future seasons? Will other parents be afraid to let their sons play, as were the parents of Tech's Dave Huff last night? Crispus Attucks' 43–38 defeat of Tech made history. It marked the first time in this state a youngster didn't play because of threats to his person."

But the response of the *Indianapolis News* was typical when it said that the game was "as polite and orderly as Emily Post," and school superintendent Herman L. Shibler immediately green-lit the game for next season. "There wouldn't be the tension there was in this one if they played a normally scheduled game every year," said Shibler.

Oscar played with a blank mask on his face except when directing his ire toward a teammate who made a bad play, something that would happen increasingly as time went on—which was not always to Ray Crowe's liking. For observers looking at Attucks from without, Oscar was not necessarily the team leader. By the end of the season, he would be mentioned as a first teamer on a couple of all-city teams and ignored on a couple others. Attucks also had center Winford O'Neal, dependable Harold Crenshaw, up-and-coming forward Willie Merriweather (who would end up high in the all-time Attucks greatness list), and senior leader William Mason. In the run-up to the city tournament in early January 1954, the *Indianapolis Star* wrote, "Attucks, beaten but once in eight starts, and that by the state's top ranking power Terre Haute Gerstmeyer, has no standout player as in previous years. But the Tigers have one of the better balanced clubs in the neighborhood."

Oscar wasn't just another sophomore, but neither was he a prodigy. Hallie Bryant had been a prodigy. But Crowe saw what Oscar could be and gradually started to move him to the backcourt where he could control the ball. (He was not called a *point guard* because that term did not exist.) He was heading toward 6'5", and so an "official" move to guard—that is, putting a *G* next to his name—would have been almost heretical. Oscar was still called a forward in most newspaper accounts, and the term *swingman* had not been invented. In those days, centers were big, forwards were medium sized, and guards were small, even in the pros. The pro models for guards at that time were players like Bobby Wanzer (6'0"), Slater Martin (5'10"), Celtic teammates Bob Cousy and Bill Sharman (both 6'1"), Andy Phillip (6'2"), and Bob Davies (6'1"). Carl Braun of the New York Knicks was a relative giant at 6'5".

By and large Crowe realized that Attucks was at its best when Oscar was initiating the action. It's a funny thing on a basketball team, even today: the moving of a superstar player onto the ball, in effect handing him the quarterback position, isn't necessarily declared. It's doubtful that Tyronn Lue made an official announcement during the 2015–2016 season that LeBron James would now be the de facto point guard for the Cleveland Cavaliers. LeBron just *took* the ball. Oscar Robertson, even at age fifteen, was the kind of player who just *took* the ball.

His confidence was unwavering, his basketball IQ off the charts. It was that way almost from the beginning. "He just had that *something*," says Hallie Bryant today. Genius takes many forms, and in Oscar Robertson it took the form of regularity, of consistency, of strength of purpose, of—dare we say—monotony, a ritualistic adherence to certain principles of that mystical and elusive art of *playing the right way*. He learned all of that on a sacrosanct piece of asphalt, where hundreds of Indianapolis players found their game, their identity, and their place of refuge—but only Oscar found immortality.

———

Oscar's earliest memory of playing basketball—the "emperor" of India-napolis street sports, as he put it—was in a vacant lot a few blocks from his home on Colton Street where somebody had put up a pole, a back-board, and a basketball hoop. "Soon all of the dribbling and running would send dirt, clay, and dust flying everywhere," he writes in *The Big O*. So somebody named it the Dust Bowl. When he couldn't find a ball, Oscar recalled, he used a "dingy rag ball [he'd] fashioned, held together by elastic" or "a pair of rolled-up socks tied together with string." That story fits comfortably into the Hoosier tradition.

He sometimes played indoors, specifically at the Senate Ave-nue YMCA after the Robertsons secured a family card. But Oscar's personal history, and the history of basketball, changed when he made his way to a court that was constructed in the southern end of the Lockefield housing project, now recognized as one of those *if-you-build-it-they-will-come* shrines. It originally had a dust surface and was described by Jim Cummings, a writer for the *Indianapolis Recorder*, as "cinders and gravel between two backboards and netless rims." But it had been paved by 1948, when Oscar was ten, so it wasn't dusty at all when he began playing there with regularity. Nevertheless, the Dust Bowl name was carried over because . . . why not? Legend through nomenclature.

The makeup of the game was almost entirely African American, owing to its location in the middle of Frog Island. Nicknames were born at the Dust Bowl, and those who are still alive remember players like Boo, Eddie Baby, Ox, Smooth Dan, and the clear winner, Chick Entrée, even if they don't remember their surnames. Just as African Ameri-cans didn't often go downtown, white kids didn't often come to the west side. Carl Short, who became a star at Indianapolis Manual—he was third-leading scorer in the city in the 1955–1956 season—used to ride his bike over to watch the games, but no one asked him to play until there was an injury and he was the only one available. When he had proved his mettle, Short would sometimes get into the games. "I'll take the white boy," they would say.

Short, a strong and athletic center, learned his basketball chops on a different kind of playground. "I lived about four blocks from Eli Lilly," he said, referencing the city's largest employer, then and now, "and they made us a playground. There was a great big box at the entrance and all you had to do was sign your name, and you could get basketballs, footballs, baseballs, whatever. It was a wonderful situation for a kid who wanted to play. But it wasn't the Dust Bowl."

Short wasn't rich or entitled, but his talent was hewn on a corporate court created by a corporate benefactor. Oscar learned on something magical born from dust.

By 1951, the year that Attucks basketball really came to life after the Flap shot against Anderson High, Cummings wrote, "This asphalt-covered court with its shabby backboards and worn-out nets is known all over town as the Lockefield Dust Bowl. . . . In the summer the bucketeers get going at the crack of dawn. . . . [T]hey shoot till long after dark."

Those "bucketeers" operated, for the most part, under order. As early as 1944, Anthony Watkins, an Indianapolis police officer, had established a Lockefield Police Athletic League club. By the time the Robertson boys were fixtures at the Dust Bowl, James "Bruiser" Gaines, another Indy policeman, was directing the club, and he organized the first Dust Bowl Tournament in 1948. (Both Watkins and Gaines, predictably, were Attucks graduates.)

Anthropology professor Paul Mullins has unearthed a trove of information about the tournament. "Thousands of people" rimmed the Dust Bowl court as spectators, Mullins writes, presaging the celebrated

Rucker Park tournaments in Harlem that began in 1950 and eventually drew players like Julius Erving and Connie Hawkins. The *Recorder* gave the tournament heavy coverage. The Stuart Mortuary team, led by Willie Gardner and Hallie Bryant, won the 1953 title. Joe Bertrand[1] made sure Stuart wasn't dead the next year when he led the morticians to their second straight championship.

And in 1956, five months after he had been named Indiana's Mr. Basketball, Oscar, suiting up for Dison Heating along with brother Flap and Attucks teammate Bill Brown, won the Dust Bowl championship. An action photo of Oscar in a Dison uniform appears in the Indiana Basketball Hall of Fame in New Castle.

To be sure, a high level of testosterone wafted through the Dust Bowl air, and sometimes the loudest voices, not the smartest ones, prevailed. But by and large, the Dust Bowl operated as a Darwinian democracy: If you can play, you can stay. Game to twenty, each basket counts two, win by one, no overtime. (Three-point shots? Didn't exist back then. Free throws? You're kidding, right?) Winners stay on. Call your own. Don't be a pussy. Don't be a clown. Talent talks; bullshit walks. There was just enough structure and organization that the Bowl was rarely a free-for-all. It holds a revered place in the history of Indiana basketball, and—who knows?—would Oscar Robertson have reached the realm of the immortal without this jewel in the heart of an Indianapolis housing project?

Oscar also supplemented his playground knowledge. "I used to read books by Clair Bee," he told Mark Montieth in an interview years ago, conjuring up a long-ago Long Island University coach considered an early genius of the game but now largely forgotten. Oscar also watched film of old players such as Joe Lapchick (a legend with the

---

1. Bertrand, who was born in Biloxi, Mississippi, and died at age fifty-nine, broke the basketball color barrier at Notre Dame, then became the first Black elected to a citywide office in Chicago, serving as city treasurer and an alderman under Mayor Richard Daley.

Original Celtics and later a famed coach at St. John's and with the New York Knicks). And Oscar wasn't too egotistical to borrow from his peers either. "There was a guy named Willie Posley [a teammate of Oscar's brother on the 1952–1953 Attucks team] and, boy, I copied his one great move," Oscar told Montieth. "You'd come to a defender with the ball in your right hand and you fake left hard with your left foot, boom, hit it, and go back to the right real hard off the dribble." Decades later, one of the greatest players ever was still remembering a move he had learned from an ordinary high school player.

Though the Dust Bowl carries with it a kind of into-the-mystic character, there was an honest, Calvinist ethic about the place. Players got better there because they worked their asses off and played hard. In his book *Attucks!*, Phillip Hoose puts it this way: "The court was rarely empty. There, even on snow-swept winter evenings and sweltering summer days, Frog Island warriors played a bruising form of basketball that bore little resemblance to the delicately patterned game whites learned in school programs elsewhere in Indiana."

Alas, shrines rust; dust blows in the wind. The final Dust Bowl tournament was contested in 1974. The site of the fabled court is now part of IUPUI, and a basketball court stands there, a clean, well-lighted place (credit to Hemingway), where the games are casual. The last word about the significance of the Dust Bowl comes from Mullins, the professor who has literally dug up memories about this important part of basketball life in the Hoosier state: "The Dust Bowl was a consequential Black public place, a space that incubated African-American politics without ever being seen as an especially politicized place."

———

The 1953–1954 season was an up-and-down one for Attucks. The arrhythmic schedule brought on by the constant scramble for a gymnasium—sometimes three games in four nights, sometimes no games for ten days—took a toll. (Attucks never did get a suitable gym until 1966.) Charles Preston[2] of the *Recorder* wrote, "They say all Attucks players aspire to be Harlem Globetrotters. With that grind, they already are."

Refereeing continued to be race based. Preston characterized the officiating in one game as "fantastically one-sided" against Attucks. More importantly, at various times injuries robbed Crowe of his entire frontcourt—O'Neal, Sheddrick Mitchell, and Merriweather—and it was mainly Oscar's inspired all-around play that kept the team afloat. Merriweather's injury was particularly damaging. A two-way player in football, he got clipped on his blind side in Attucks's final game of 1954–1955 and tore the cartilage in a knee. Merriweather played seven basketball games, but the knee finally gave out, and he was through for the season. "They kept me in the hospital for thirty days," he said in a 2022 interview. It's one of the oldest basketball stories in the books. Had his knee injury happened today, he would have received proper treatment and no doubt returned.

There were meaningful victories, including three straight wins heading into the sectionals, but also disappointing losses, such as one in a rematch with Tech, which played at full strength with Huff. After the game there was again much talk about questionable calls—Attucks believed it had gotten screwed, and Crowe spoke out about it. "This time we lost because of poor officiating," he said, an extremely un-Crowe-like statement. The *Indianapolis Recorder* gave a full-throated defense of Crowe's criticism, while the *Indianapolis News* took the opposing position, running a sidebar story characterizing the two referees, Cy Profitt

---

2. Preston was the only *Recorder* writer with white skin. An avowed communist, he was recognized as a crusader for equal rights. Preston wrote about his days with the *Recorder* and his career generally in a book titled *Nobody Called Me Charlie: The Story of a Radical White Journalist Writing for a Black Newspaper in the Civil Rights Era.*

and Erwin Thrasher, as "rated among the top 30 in the state" and opining that "it was not an easy game to officiate."

The closeness of the contest and the complaints about the refs only added to the budding Attucks-Tech rivalry, and both teams talked openly about desiring a rubber match, which could likely occur in the sectional finals.

That's what happened. Before the game Crowe emphasized the team mantra: *Build a big lead. Don't let the refs get involved. Make your statement out of the gate.* The Tigers listened, built a 12–0 lead behind Oscar and a now-healthy Mitchell, and never looked back in a 53–46 win that made them one of the favorites for the state championship. Robertson was not the star of this one. Wrote the *Indianapolis Star*, "A calm but sometimes sizzling Crispus Attucks team, led by the brilliant shooting and overall play of Sheddrick Mitchell, completed a successful defense of its Indianapolis sectional championship last night by upsetting a tired Tech quintet, 53 to 46."

By now Attucks had become more than a basketball team. It wasn't just the collective effect of all the atrocious referee calls and the racist catcalls at the games over the years. It wasn't just the fact that the school board wouldn't build Attucks a proper gym, even though the perpetual "homelessness" played havoc with young athletes' lives. It wasn't just that Attucks drew massive crowds to the Butler gym yet never used the warmup room, of which other teams availed themselves—Oscar said later that he didn't even know the room existed.

No, Attucks had morphed into something else. It had become the barometer by which to judge the racial climate in Indianapolis, serving, as sports often do, as an entrée to a conversation. While the sports story may have been Attucks beating Tech in that rubber match, Andrew W. Ramsey, the columnist for the *Indianapolis Recorder* and the writer most likely to invoke the bigger picture and rain on a parade, looked at the game and saw something else. He saw a climate of "poorly concealed racism." He wrote about watching a young white boy, maybe six or seven years old, call another young white boy an "N-lover" merely for applauding a good Attucks play. To view the game merely as two fine high school basketball teams going at it was not for Ramsey, who was also a Spanish teacher at Attucks: "That was why Negroes who take a beating from the white man in industry, in business, in religion, and in their living conditions were jubilant to see a symbol of white supremacy bite the dust."

Understand that the views of Ramsey were not always popular, even in the Black community, even with his editors at the *Recorder*. Indianapolis was, in the phrasing of Richard Pierce, a place of polite protest. But Ramsey would only grow more determined in his beliefs, to the point that he eventually would say that Attucks, for all its grandeur, should be "bulldozed to the ground," representing as it did the triumph of racial segregation. More on that later.

But the "Crowemen," as they were sometimes called in the press, soldiered on, getting closer and closer to the chance at a state championship that was always just out of their grasp. It nearly ended in the semifinals against Columbus High School, but along came Oscar, who hit a free throw with twenty-five seconds left for a 68–67 win.

That brought them to a showdown in what Indiana calls the "semi-state" against Milan High School, invariably described as "tiny" or "little" and most assuredly, as one newspaper put it, "the people's choice."

———

From a seat at Plump's Last Shot—the tavern he owns three miles north of Hinkle Fieldhouse in Indianapolis, the place where he became immortal—Bobby Plump, the éminence grise of Hoosier basketball, can tell you almost anything you want to know about 1950s hoops in Indiana. It is difficult to describe Plump, who is a numinous presence in Milan, way, way, *way* more famous than teammate William Jordan, who became an actor and has one of those I've-seen-him-somewhere faces. (He played the chairman of the Joint Chiefs in Jodie Foster's *Contact* among dozens of other roles.) Plump is not the best basketball player in Hoosier scholastic history, and his enduring fame comes largely from one made jump shot. As George McGinnis remembered, the late Bob "Slick" Leonard, one of the Hoosier state's best-known personalities, loved to chide Plump about being a one-shot wonder. "'Bobby,' he'd tell him," remembered McGinnis, who died in late 2023, "'if you didn't make that one damn shot, you'd be pumping gas somewhere.'"

Plump is not the most widely known Indiana schoolboy star; Oscar and somebody named Larry Bird hold that distinction. Further, Plump's 1954 state-championship-winning Milan team is not considered among the best in Indiana history, a distinction that by consensus goes to Oscar's Attucks teams; the Indianapolis Washington teams led by McGinnis and Steve Downing; the East Chicago Washington teams led by Pete Trgovich, Junior Bridgeman, and Tim Stoddard; the 1987 Marion team led by Jay Edwards and Lydon Jones; and the 2006 Lawrence North team led by Greg Oden and Mike Conley.

But Plump might be the most *organically perfect* Hoosier, the one who most closely models the mythical *ideal* of Indiana basketball, certainly old-school Indiana basketball. At the very least, he is in the company of Steve Alford and Damon Bailey in that respect. And he was clearly the straw that stirred the drink for the team that lives deeply in the soul of Indiana basketball.

"What I do know," says Plump now, "is that we were a helluva lot better than most people thought." Indeed, for eight decades Plump has been fighting against the idea that Milan was a scrappy, overachieving bunch that simply caught lightning in a bottle on one early spring evening in 1954. He is right to do so because the Indians, who came from a farming community much closer to Cincinnati (thirty-nine miles west) than Indianapolis (eighty-three miles southeast), were an outstanding team. "We had been playing together almost from first grade through twelfth grade," says Plump. Their secret weapon, he says, was the coach, a twenty-four-year-old man named Marvin Wood, who looked nothing like Gene Hackman and who had coached in what would become another hallowed spot in Hoosier basketball: French Lick, home of Bird.

"The key thing was that Marvin didn't have a big ego," says Plump. "He brought the eighth grade coach [Marc Combs, a 1933 graduate of Milan] over to show him a zone defense. And he put in a control offense that was years ahead of its time, sort of like Dean Smith's North Carolina four corners. We protected leads off it, sure, but we could also score."

Reasonable folks can disagree about that—there was a lot of *stall* in the *control* offense—but Milan was formidable. And with a male student population of only seventy-three, it was indeed small compared to other teams who had contested for the state championship over the years.

From the long view of history, Milan, in its racial makeup, demography, and style of play, represented the very essence of Indiana basketball.

A bit of necessary backtracking. Remember that a Black team like Attucks was still a novelty in the mid-1950s to many Hoosier fans. It wasn't until the 1942–1943 season that Arthur Trester, the tinhorn dictator who had ruled over the Indiana High School Athletic Association (IHSAA) since 1913—ironclad rule: there are no tinhorn dictators so tinhorn as the tinhorns who run amateur athletic associations—finally allowed Black and parochial schools, as well as the Indiana School for the Deaf, into a tournament that was promoted as the ne plus ultra of sports democracy. In a delicious bit of Catch-22 reasoning, Trester had long held that schools with so-called closed or private enrollments could not participate in the tournament, ignoring the fact that Attucks was closed because the white community had wanted it so and even mandated it as such by local statute. Had Trester applied his principle evenly, of course, all-*white* schools could not have competed because most of them were closed to Blacks, at least in Indianapolis, Gary, and Evansville.

Over the years Attucks officials entreated the IHSAA to change its rules, but Trester, who guarded his power like Midas guarded his gold, always said no until lawmakers forced his hand.

Much of the pressure that finally overwhelmed Trester came from Indianapolis's own Robert Brokenburr, the first African American elected to the state legislature. Brokenburr introduced legislation to empower the state government to take over the IHSAA, forcing Trester into a settlement that ended his absurd ban in late December 1941, two weeks after Pearl Harbor.

One final note: the award given annually to the Indiana scholastic player who best combines the qualities of "mental attitude, scholarship, leadership, and athletic ability in basketball" is *still* named for Arthur Trester.[3]

So, more than being the big, bad Black team that was beaten by the scrappy little guy, a tale as old as the two-handed set shot, Attucks was in fact the outlier in its 1954 contest against Milan. But the reality of that state tournament has been so hopelessly lost in myth, much of it cinematic, that it needs quite a lot of disentangling, a tale that will be coming in Chapter 6.

---

3. In 2021 the Crispus Attucks National Alumni Association petitioned the IHSAA to change the name of the Trester Award to the Ray Crowe Sportsmanship Award. The IHSAA didn't go for it and instead created the Ray Crowe Excellence in Leadership Award to be presented to a coach or administrator who makes significant and/or long-term contributions to interscholastic athletics. So Trester's name lives on.

CHAPTER FIVE

Hoops: The Hoosier State's Most Glorious Import

"There was a lot of racism and racial comments. It took me totally by surprise."

In the hours before their night game against Attucks at Butler Fieldhouse, the Milan High School players stayed at the Pennsylvania Hotel in downtown Indianapolis. They were well rested after an early afternoon game against Montezuma, which took no revenge. Though Milan was being played up as a kind of David in the tournament because of its small enrollment, its opponent was even smaller, with only thirty-six boys and a total enrollment of seventy-nine.

The Milan kids were confident, and why wouldn't they be? They had gotten all the way to the state's final four the year before, losing to a powerful South Bend Central team that eventually won the championship, and most of the team was back, a core that had been playing together for a decade. They knew by then that Attucks had had an extremely tough game in the late afternoon, at one point trailing by fourteen points and just squeezing by Columbus, with Oscar controlling the game in the final moments.

As Bobby Plump and his teammates enjoyed an early dinner before the evening showdown against Attucks, more than a few fans recognized the Milan farm boys. They had expected to be cast as villains against a hometown team; after all, Indianapolis fans had suffered years of frustration in trying to win a state championship. But that's not what this all-white team encountered.

"There was a lot of racism and racial comments," Plump said during a 2022 interview at his bar. "It took me totally by surprise." The subject of the lead-up to Milan's game against Attucks makes him sad, and Plump is by and large a happy man. He has talked openly over the years about the comments he heard, but in a post–George Floyd world, they're almost too cruel to repeat. The theme was singular: *Beat those N-words.* That's what the Milan players heard in downtown Indianapolis before their game against the home team. *Beat those N-words.*

The message was unambiguous. It wasn't about social class. Like Oscar and his Attucks teammates, Plump and the Milan guys weren't rich or part of the Indiana power elite. "I never had a telephone growing up," said Plump, who was raised in Pierceville, two miles west of and smaller than Milan. "We didn't have electricity until I was thirteen. When I graduated from high school, we still didn't have running water." It wasn't about fans rooting for the scrappy underdog against the favorite either—Milan was every bit as touted as Attucks, perhaps even more so, because of the extensive history of Indianapolis teams folding in the stretch and Milan's appearance in the 1953 Final Four.

No, the favored status conveyed upon Milan was strictly about pigmentation. It's impossible to know how seventeen- and eighteen-year-old kids processed that message seventy years ago, but they certainly understood it. There were no Blacks in Milan, and from the time Plump and his teammates had started playing ball together, they rarely if ever played against an African American. When the ball was thrown up that night in Butler Fieldhouse, the Milan boys might have intuited that Attucks represented something different, perhaps a vision of the future. But they also understood that they, not Attucks, represented the ruling class in Indiana basketball. Milan hoops, not Attucks hoops, was in the Hoosier DNA. Milan players, not Attucks players, were the princes of Indiana, which holds a revered place in the history of roundball.

———

There were 18 men in the class. I selected two captains and had them choose sides. When the teams were chosen I placed the men on the floor. There were three forwards, three centers and three backs on each team.

I chose two of the center men to jump, then threw the ball between them. It was the start of the first basketball game and the finish of the trouble with that class.

—James Naismith, *Basketball: Its Origin and Development*

Every fan of basketball knows at least part of the story.[1] In the winter of 1891, Dr. James Naismith, an intelligent, serious-minded, and deeply religious physical education instructor at the Young Men's Christian Association Training College in Springfield, Massachusetts, cobbled together a game that he hoped would satisfy the rambunctious urges of his class of "incorrigibles." "Basket Ball," as he christened it, was a

---

1. Unlike most sports, which have multistreamed creation stories, the Naismith-Springfield tale has enjoyed an uninterrupted cruise down a single waterway over the years. We all bought in. Well, with one exception. Herkimer, a town of seven thousand tucked away in central New York's Mohawk Valley, has made a claim that it is the real birthplace of basketball. I don't know if its claims hold any water, though a "Herkimer Hoops" shirt would be awesome. For further info, Google a *Washington Post* story about Herkimer.

success from the beginning, as witnessed by its lightning spread around the country and even overseas.

In no place was the rapidity of that growth so evident as in Indiana. That's the simple statement that prompts a difficult question: How did it get to the Hoosier state so quickly? For decades the story went that a Naismith disciple named Nicholas McCay (almost always spelled incorrectly as McKay), a proponent of Naismith's brand of "muscular Christianity" and a YMCA official at his first posting in Crawfordsville, Indiana, took the game there directly from Springfield, almost as if he were delivering a UPS package. "Indiana basketball's unlikely Johnny Appleseed," Tom Graham and Rachel Graham Cody labeled McCay in their 2006 book *Getting Open: The Unknown Story of Bill Garrett and the Integration of College Basketball*. A sign standing on W. Main Street in Crawfordsville reads, "The Cradle of Basketball." It refers to a game that was played on March 16, 1894, between YMCA players of Crawfordsville and Lafayette inside a second-floor gymnasium in the town's Terminal Building. The following day the *Crawfordsville Journal-Review* reported on the game: "Basket ball is a new game, but if the interest taken in the contest last night is any criterion, it is bound to be popular."

But any number of "basket ball" missionaries, YMCA and otherwise, could have circulated the game. Just a month after he hung the peach baskets, Naismith wrote an article about his brainchild for the *Triangle*, the YMCA's widely distributed newsletter. Those missionaries who read about the game may well have included McCay since research indicates that he graduated from Springfield a full academic year *before* Naismith arrived. Here is Naismith's introductory paragraph to that article:

We present to our readers, a new game of ball, which seems to have those elements in it which ought to make it popular among the associations. It fills the same place in the gymnasium that football does in the athletic field, and any number of men may play at it, and each one gets plenty of exercise. At the same time, it calls for physical judgment and coordination of every muscle and gives all around development. It can be played by teams from different Associations, and combined skill with courage and agility, so that the better team wins.

Yeoman's work done by the Indiana Historical Bureau indeed suggests that the Indiana creation story is much more nuanced than the simple McCay delivery tale. A report as early as July 1892, just seven months after Naismith's first "basket ball" skirmish, announced that "basketball" (modern spelling) would be played at a "field day" at North Manchester University, which is about two hours north of Indianapolis. Four months later the *Indianapolis Sun* had an interesting account of "basket ball" activities among some scrappy athletes at Evansville, "a sort of indoor foot ball that is almost as murderous as the original game." The reference to football being "murderous" is apt because concern about that sport had a huge impact on the development and rapid spread of basketball. A hybrid of soccer and rugby, American football came along in the 1870s, followed by broken bones, concussions, and even death. Oddly enough, one of the low points of the game, played largely without protective equipment, occurred in basketball country, in Naismith's Springfield, where in the fall of 1894 Harvard and Yale played a particularly violent game that resulted in the hospitalization of five players.[2]

Stories in the *Indianapolis News* in February and April 1893 report that students at Earlham College in Richmond, Indiana, were playing

---

2. Wrote the *New York Times* of that football game, "The record of French duels for the last dozen years fails to show such a list of casualties as this one game of football produced. Black eyes, sore shins, and strained backs cut no figure in this contest." The violence went on for at least another decade until President Teddy Roosevelt summoned a parley of college officials that helped pave the way for changes that made the game safer. Sort of. The safety of football is still on the debating table.

basketball and that there was even a "basketball league" at the Indianapolis YMCA. Other accounts predating the game in Crawfordsville mention games in Connersville, Columbus, Ridgeville, and even a YMCA game between host Evansville and Terre Haute.

No matter who gets the credit, though, the game was a snug fit for the Indiana ethos. "Basketball was the by-product of a very rational, very rigid, very white world of values and institutions during the first decades of the game's existence," writes Nelson George in his 1992 book *Elevating the Game: Black Men and Basketball*. In practical terms, basketball was perfect for Indiana's rural geography. You didn't need much—some kind of ball and an iron ring, items that could be easily found or fashioned by farm families. Folklore grew around the primitive means that future Hoosier stars used to get started in Naismith's game. Homer Stonebraker of Wingate, the first Indiana high school superstar, learned the game by putting a small ring on a woodshed in his barnyard and shooting with a rubber ball the size of a tennis ball. Indiana University coach Branch McCracken, writes Scott Ellsworth in *The Secret Game*, grew up shooting an inflated pig bladder at a fruit basket. DIY hoops, that's the way they did it in Indiana.

Though it would come to be played by giant men, early basketball was a game writ small, a game for towns and farms, a game that could be played in isolation or utilized as an instrument of town unity and pride, a game uniquely suited to Indiana, which took to it with a vengeance.

And with an eye to color—or the lack of it. By 1916, writes James H. Madison in *Hoosiers*, the Indiana High School Athletic Association (IHSAA) had 450 member schools—and not one Black participant.

———

Despite the apparent existence of that early YMCA league in Indianapolis, the Hoosier capital did not have a true basketball presence for decades into the twentieth century. And it didn't have a true schoolboy hero until Attucks's Hallie Bryant in the early 1950s. As basketball began its viral spread through the state, Indianapolis's best athlete was a Black man who got almost no publicity in the mainstream press. Marshall Walter Taylor, later to be called Major Taylor, was an early arrival in the Great Migration. In 1887 he moved with his parents and siblings from Louisville, Kentucky, to a small farm in what was then widely called Bucktown, not far from where the Robertson family would decades later make their home. Taylor's father had gotten work as a coachman for the wealthy Southard family. Albert Burley Southard was a superintendent of the Indianapolis Peru Chicago Railroad and lived in a mansion on N. Meridian Street. From the ages of eight to twelve, Taylor lived with the family and got private schooling, along with Southard's son, Daniel, who became a close friend. Taylor was a lucky boy. For a while. The Southard family moved to Chicago when Taylor was twelve, and he was largely on his own after that.

He got the nickname Major because he wore a military uniform when he performed tricks outside Harry T. Hearsey's downtown bicycle shop. Major began winning both sprints and long races in and around Indianapolis, at which point he was asked to leave the city because other riders didn't want to compete against him. *If you can't beat 'em, exile 'em.* He later gained worldwide fame as a racer but couldn't beat the racism he faced, and he died penniless at the age of fifty-three, first buried in an unmarked grave in the welfare section of a cemetery near Chicago. According to a post by Sharon Butsch Freeland in HistoricIndianapolis.com, a group of former racers had his body exhumed and moved to a more prominent spot in the cemetery, the bill footed by the Schwinn Bicycle Company.

Taylor does have a legacy in Indy: the Major Taylor Velodrome Park. One other thing about him: right before he was asked to leave the city in 1896, he joined the See-Saw Cycling Club, formed by Indianapolis's Black cyclists, who were not eligible for membership in the all-white

Zig-Zag Cycling Club. Oscar Robertson would have signed on to the See-Saw Club in a minute.

———

The secret sauce for the spread of basketball in Indiana was the state high school tournament, created by small-town enmity and propelled by small-town energy. Crawfordsville and Lebanon went back and forth through the early years of the twentieth century, each claiming supremacy as the best high school team in Indiana. Though the Indiana High School Athletic Association existed as early as 1899, it was the Indiana University Booster Club—being a booster club, the members probably smelled money—that stepped in to create an official competition in March 1911. The event had a small-town feel from the beginning with twelve teams competing: Anderson, Bluffton, Crawfordsville, Evansville, Lafayette, Lebanon, Morristown, New Albany, Oaktown, Rochester, Valparaiso, and Walton. No Shortridge, no Broad Ripple, no Emmerich Manual, all well-established high schools in Indianapolis. (Crispus Attucks didn't yet exist.) Fittingly—certainly Nicholas McCay would say so—Crawfordsville won that first championship.

The IHSAA got involved the following year, and that brought in the busy hands of Arthur Trester, who was named the organization's "permanent secretary" before getting the title of commissioner. He was the top man in the IHSAA for thirty-one years—he died in 1944, shortly after his Orwellian rule barring Black and parochial schools from tournament participation was rescinded—during which the tourney kept growing to the point that it was widely recognized as the nation's top amateur event. That Trester continually ignored pleas and legal challenges to open the tournament to Black and Catholic schools was rarely (if ever) mentioned in the press until African American legislators began to hammer away at the issue in the early 1940s.

Trester was like a lot of men in charge of amateur organizations in those days. And these days. Expand the organization but centralize power. Hire yes men as employees. Show up. Work hard—or look like you are. You don't have to always do the right thing, but do the *big* thing, the *profitable* thing. *Own* the event—and Trester certainly owned the Indiana tournament. More accurately, Trester owned the IHSAA, and the IHSAA owned the tournament. Many in the know give more credit to a sportswriter named Bill Fox Jr. of the *Indianapolis News* for growing the tournament itself. It was Fox who coined the phrase *Hoosier hysteria* in the 1930s when he told the *Saturday Evening Post*, "High school gymnasiums are our nightclubs."

But it was Trester who knew whom to court, whom to kowtow to, and whom to bully. "Trester wouldn't give his mother a complimentary ticket to the tournament," Bob Collins, the cut-to-the-chase *Indianapolis Star* columnist, once said. Whatever else the IHSAA did, the tournament was the signature event and Trester the signature figure. "Mr. Arthur Tressler [sic] was largely responsible for the splendid organization of the high schools in Indiana, one of the first states to conduct a series of tournaments," wrote Naismith in his book.

Ol' Mr. Peach Basket himself came to Indiana in 1925 to visit the tournament—at that point it was still being held at Indiana University—which by then had drawn attention from all over the country (though not from the Black population). If Naismith, who later would become a mentor to the first famous Black coach, John McLendon, noticed there were no African American faces on the court or in the audience, he didn't say anything about it. Always homespun, Professor Peach Basket spins this tale about his Hoosier visit:

> I was to speak at the final game of the tournament, and arrived at the Coliseum to find that the doors had been closed. At the door, I presented a reserved seat ticket and an officials badge,

only to be informed by the guard that he could allow no one to enter. I explained to him that I was to speak there that evening, but he only smiled and shook his head. As I stood there chuckling to myself, the captain of police stepped up to me and asked what the trouble was. He asked my name and when I told him he exploded, "Good Lord. Man. Why didn't you say so long ago?"

The all-white tournament bathed in an atmosphere of myth and the caressive graces of small-town America. Wingate, a tiny, tiny town northwest of Indianapolis, was full-on hoop crazed by the early 1900s. The high school team, selected from a male enrollment of sixteen, had no place to practice except a small corner of a basement, the wintry outdoors, and a gym seven miles away in New Richmond, a town that years later would serve as Hickory in *Hoosiers*. Wingate won back-to-back state championships in 1913 and 1914, a tale still commemorated by a sign on Indiana State Road 25 coming into town. (One of its victims along the way to its second title was Milan.) In a story for the *Indy Star*, Kyle Neddenriep uncovered the coverage from the Wingate newspaper as news of the first state championship made it back to town: "Each telegram containing good news was hailed with cheers, shooting of anvils, firecrackers, ringing of bells, and like demonstrations. At night, when word of the final victory came, a candle parade was formed and marched all over town ending at a huge bonfire at the school grounds, when men, women, and children marched around, blowing horns, beating drums, sacrificing hats, and doing a number of other jolly stunts to work off the exuberance of joy at the outcome."

Tiny in size (population 446 in 1910), Wingate was nonetheless titanic in personnel in the form of Stonebraker, a well-muscled, superbly athletic, 6'4", two-hundred-pound giant and Indiana's first mythic hoops hero, a center so dominant he once scored eighty points in a 108–8 victory, which we can safely classify as *pouring it on*. Could one come up with a better name for a giant from the mists of history than Homer Stonebraker, later a star at Wabash College and a twice-elected sheriff of Cass County?

In the mid-1920s Wingate's team finally got an indoor practice facility, specifically a livery stable (no shots higher than twenty feet, Steph Curry, because they'd hit the roof) it rented from the town. Three bucks for a practice, six for a game. The story goes that the stable did have six rows of reserved seats, and all were presold, making Wingate an early practitioner of the season-ticket plan. That is *so* Indiana.

Yes, legends were made in the Indiana tournament, which moved around from a few different Indiana University facilities to the Old Coliseum and the Exposition Building in Indianapolis before arriving at its Butler home in 1945, where it stayed through the Oscar years and beyond. Shelbyville did not win the 1917 championship (Lebanon High School did), but its captain, a set-shooting artist named Paul Cross, achieved greater immortality as the town's first World War I victim. Cross died in France on June 5, 1918, a year after his graduation. The school still gives out the Paul Cross Award for leadership, and townspeople still play in the Paul Cross Gymnasium in the civic center.

The next mythic hero of schoolboy Hoosier basketball was a regular-sized forward named Robert "Fuzzy" Vandivier, who led Franklin High School's Wonder Five to a threepeat in 1920, 1921, and 1922 and continued his stardom at Franklin College along with several of his high school teammates. Many of us tend to be seduced by the heroes we first meet as kids, and so it was that John Wooden long proclaimed Vandivier the best guard he ever saw. Wrote Dana Hunsinger Benbow in an *Indy Star* story in 2020, "During the Wonder Five era, Mean's Drug Store in Franklin was where the public went to buy basketball tickets. Long lines were common outside the store before a big game, often forming before the store opened. Located on Jefferson Street on the northeast corner of the public square, the store was a sort of unofficial Wonder Five headquarters."

Many still call Wooden "the best they ever saw," famously tenacious when he led Martinsville to the 1927 state championship. "Until Oscar Robertson came around, John Wooden was the all-time Indiana basketball hero," says Bob Collins. "He was the player that all other players were compared to. He left each game wearing part of the floor."

And, well, there were some legendary bad boys, too, such as James Dean, a bespectacled hoopster at Fairmount High near Marion, Indiana, where the star-crossed *Rebel Without a Cause* star was born.[3]

Traditions grew quickly in the rich small-town soil. The Indiana Basketball Hall of Fame in New Castle is packed with state championship iconography, all manner of bells, barrels, and even rolling pins. The 1929 state champion came from Frankfort, a small high school less than an hour's drive northwest of Indianapolis. Its mascot? Do you have to ask? A hot dog.

Inevitably, this philosopher class of white coaches emerged from schoolboy Hoosier hoops, gods of fundamentals and discipline, men, it seemed, who followed Naismith in robes and sandals the way Plato tailed Socrates. They were often the most powerful men in their communities, comparable to preachers, men like Marion Crawley at Lafayette Jefferson and Everett Case at Frankfort, whose camps a knowledge-hungry Ray Crowe would attend before he took the Attucks job. "There was no way to calculate what Crawley meant to those flat lands," Collins said. "He got teams from Klondike, Dayton all over. Same with Case up in Frankfort. They had kids from all over.

---

3. Dean, a certified movie idol when he died in a car crash in 1955 at age 24, was no Rebel Without a Game as an athlete. In a terrific story for the *Indy Star*, Benbow delves into Dean's extensive high school sports career, which included his being named the school's "Top Athlete of the Year" for his exploits in baseball (third baseman), track (pole vault, hurdles, relays), and most of all basketball (set-shooting guard).

Move the father in, give him a job at one of the factories there, and the kid would play basketball for the team."

Yes, as long as you were Caucasian, high school basketball was the state's primary diversion from November to March, and nothing else came close. It was Trester who established the inviolate rule of Tuesday and Friday games, which still stands in many states. College ball? Play on Monday and Saturday, for all we care, just not on Tuesday and Friday. It all reached a frenzied climax with the tournament, the destination craved by every high school player with a basket in his barn and hope in his heart. Only in Indiana would the pro arena (home of the NBA's Indiana Pacers) be modeled to look like a *high school gym*, as Gainbridge Fieldhouse (originally Conseco followed by Bankers Life) was.

As we shall see, an entirely different brand of basketball—the Black game—was spreading throughout the country on a different course, largely ignored by white fans and major media. But the Indiana model was the Platonic ideal of the game, and Hoosier high school grads were soon pollinating teams all over the country. Michigan State once fielded a starting team composed entirely of Hoosiers, even though Michigan was considered a good basketball state. Hoosiers headed south too: at one Vanderbilt–Ole Miss game, twelve of the twenty players came from southern Indiana. Graham and Cody write in *Getting Open* that Cal Berkeley's pep band once greeted the University of Southern California team by playing "Back Home Again in Indiana" because so many Hoosiers were on it.

In his book *Wish It Lasted Forever*, noted *Boston Globe* writer Dan Shaughnessy talks about a conversation he had with Larry Bird about Hoosier basketball. "It's something you don't understand," Bird said, "unless you live there."

———

Bobby Plump and his Milan High mates did live there, right smack in the sweet spot of Hoosier high school basketball, a small-town team (the smallest since Stonebraker's Wingate teams) that had played together forever, played fundamentally, played with the confidence that came from outsized community support. So when the time came to meet Attucks, the Black kids from the big city? No big deal. Gene White, a starting forward for Milan, claimed that his team had the game won before it started, that the Milan players saw fear in the eyes of the Tigers before the opening buzzer. As for Oscar Robertson, the Milan scouting report listed him last, with no special instructions on how to handle him. He was a sophomore whose brother had made a famous shot years before. Means nothing.

Over the years very little has been written about the Milan-Attucks game that took place at Butler Fieldhouse on March 13, 1954—alas, no film evidence seems to exist—and what has been written is usually inaccurate, a farrago of fact and fiction culled together from YouTube and the *Hoosiers* movie. In truth, there isn't much to say. Plump can go into chapter and verse about the championship final win over Muncie Central (when he became a folk hero), but of the Attucks game he says, "We had their number. We were playing with confidence. We played a great game that night. It was obvious how good Oscar was, but we didn't let him take over the game. I'm glad we got him when he was a sophomore because... after that year? No way."

Oscar, who can be ungenerous about his unpleasant memories, is quite complimentary (by Oscar standards) about Milan and Plump in this one, though he does take note of his team's injuries, a fair point. He writes in *The Big O*,

> I can't honestly tell you that exhaustion had anything to do with what happened next. Milan had a strong team. They started fast and shot 60% in the first half and captured a comfortable lead.

Bobby Plump shot the hell out of the ball and ended up leading all scoring with twenty-eight. I played okay with 22. We had another forward who would be critical to our winning our first championship. His name was Willie Merriweather. But he was out with an injury. We were outmanned. If we'd had Winford O'Neal and Merriweather, I would have liked our chances.

Ray Crowe was equally complimentary to Milan, as Kerry Marshall writes in *The Ray Crowe Story*: "They played like a machine. Even with our pressure defense we couldn't force them out of their offense and defensively they played a zone better than any team we would see. It was one of those cases where we flat out got beat. I hate to lose, but when it happens like it did against Milan, all you can do is take your hat off to them and say, 'Nice game.'"

In its write-up of the game, the *Indianapolis Recorder* targeted exhaustion from the Columbus game as the culprit. Willie Merriweather went in a different direction. "If I would've played," he said in a 2022 interview, "we would've won. I'm sorry, but that's the truth."

Plump describes the Attucks game strategically. "We had them by five points at halftime, and there was no question we were going to our four corners," he said. "See, we had it as an offensive weapon, not just a stalling maneuver. We were comfortable playing that way. Attucks wasn't." Some accounts of the game in Indianapolis newspapers don't even mention Oscar's name. (In the All-Sectional team named by the *Recorder*, Oscar gained only honorable mention, while Sheddrick Mitchell, Bill Mason, and Harold Crenshaw were first team.)

The final was 65–52, so any thought that Milan, called the "smooth small-towners" in the *Recorder*, had stalled its way to victory against Attucks is nonsense. (One Milan player, Bob Engel, remembers Crowe coming into the locker room after the game and shaking every Milan hand.) Now, classic Indiana stallball did happen the following week in

Milan's state championship game against Muncie Central. That was the night that Milan became mythopoeic, the night that all kinds of Hoosier basketball history got all kinds of confused, the night that hatched *Hoosiers*.

As for Oscar Robertson, he would lose exactly one game over the next twenty-four months—and even that rates an asterisk.

———

Muncie Central, Milan's opponent in the state final, was Indiana basketball royalty when it went up against Milan. A school of about two thousand in 1954, Muncie had won state championships in 1928, 1931, 1951, and 1952 and had finished runner-up in 1923, 1927, and 1930. And remember, this was a single-class tournament—big schools and small schools all lumped together, the Hoosier system until 1998. Against Muncie, Plump and crew played classic Indiana basketball. "We were tired by then," said Plump. "We kind of had to play that way. They were really the favorites."

Philip Raisor, a Muncie star who would later become a well-known poet and the author of a book partly about this era of Hoosier basketball—he would have a fateful meeting with Oscar and Attucks the following season—agrees with that. "I don't know of any team I ever played on that was overconfident," said Raisor, "but we expected to win. Certainly I expected us to win. On the other hand, you see *Hoosiers* and it looks like Milan comes in like these little old country boys. They knew how to play and we knew that. It wasn't just Plump. Ray Craft was a very, very good player."

Unlike the Milan-Attucks game, this complete game is available on YouTube. Bring along an energy drink because, as an exemplar of basketball, it's not enthralling. For long stretches of the game, Plump stands in one place, at the center of the court between the free throw circle and midcourt, and just holds the ball, even when Milan is trailing, which was much of the second half. "I stood for four minutes and seventeen seconds," said Plump, almost proudly, speaking of a point in the game when Milan was losing 28–26. (Most other accounts put it at four minutes, fourteen seconds; you're free to go to YouTube and count.) The main danger, it would seem, was that even Plump, who jab-stepped now and then, would get lulled to sleep, forget which was his pivot foot, and commit a travel. Then again, the referees would have had to be awake to call it. "A lot of people thought that it was an easy game to officiate because of the low score," said Cyril Birge, who officiated the game, in an interview reported in *Referee* magazine in 2018. "But it wasn't. There was mental pressure all the time that you were going to miss something, that your attention might get lax because of the slow game."

In keeping with the times, of course, Muncie stayed back and watched it all, like spectators at an afternoon matinee. "Well, why *would* the defense come out?" Plump says. "They were ahead." Well, okay. But sitting back and watching was what *every* defense did back then, it seemed, whether it was ahead or behind. Plump shrugged that off. "I guess the defense figured there were always enough good dribblers to keep it away from them," he said. In other words, that's the way they did it back then, so that's the way they did it.

Finally, Milan called a timeout (ACTION!). A little more than three minutes remained, and Muncie was still ahead 28–26. "We decided in the timeout that we're still not going to shoot," remembers Plump. "Think about it. Fourth quarter, we're behind, fifteen thousand fans in the stands, state final . . . and *we're still not going to shoot.*"

Eventually, Milan begins a weave, the aggressive part of the stall, and—surprise!—Plump puts up a one-hander. Front rim. No good. Muncie rebounds. But Milan forces a turnover with unusually aggressive defense, and Craft makes a tying jump shot, in retrospect as important a shot as there was in the game. It's 28–28. Muncie misses,

Milan rebounds, and Plump is fouled. Plump calmly swishes two, his old-fashioned one-handed push shot unerring. Milan leads 30–28. With forty-five seconds left, Muncie ties the score on an inside shot by Gene Flowers, who was later a star at Indiana University.

Plump eats away at the clock. Milan calls a timeout to plot a strategy that could have been written on the scoreboard. Plump is going to hold it, then shoot it. Craft is supposed to throw it in to Plump, but instead Plump, temporarily brain-locked, takes it out-of-bounds and throws it to Craft. Craft gives it back. "It worked out better that way," Craft would say later, "because Bobby could get in position." Plump dribbles away the time, guarded by Jimmy Barnes, one of three African American players on Muncie's team. "Jimmy would've been all over him," Raisor says today, "except the coach told him to stay back. Go figure."

Six seconds left. Plump's face, as Bob Collins wrote later, is "an inscrutable mask." Plump jab-steps left, dribbles back right, goes up for a classic-looking jump shot from just outside the foul line extended, the kind of shot that was just coming into vogue at that time, maybe a little more one-handed at the apex than a modern jumper's, the kind of shot that Oscar often took. Plump had missed eight of his ten shots to that point. But not this one. "We'd seen him make that shot thousands of times," another Milan player, Glen Butte, told the *South Bend Tribune* in 2014, "behind Schroder's barn in Pierceville."

Though no one grasped it at the time, the moment the ball went through the basket, Bobby Plump and his team became immortal . . . as did the entire phenomenon of homespun Hoosier hoops.

A postscript: After the game, Milan coach Marvin Wood, described as a "5–6 bundle of basketball brains" by Angelo Angelopoulos of the *Indianapolis News*, visited the losing locker room and basically apologized to the Muncie team. "I hated to stand out there and hold the ball, boys, but that's the only way we could do it." Yeah, that helped a lot.

CHAPTER SIX

Separating Fact from Fiction in *Hoosiers*

"'Watching the paint dry' was something my dad used to say to me."

O scar Robertson was never one for following sports news that didn't involve Attucks, and even then he never lost himself in it. The scrapbooks he kept as a high school kid are haphazard; there's as much about brother Flap as about Attucks's final two triumphant seasons. He has often said that the day after the loss to Milan, a Sunday, he was in the Senate Avenue YMCA gym by himself in the morning, working on his game, thinking ahead to the 1954–1955 season.

So, Milan's state championship and certainly the attendant mythologization of the event were of no concern to him or most anyone else on the west side of Indianapolis. And make no mistake about it—there was quite a lot of mythologizing going on.

Immediately after the win over Muncie, Bobby Plump and his teammates had been genially "kidnapped" (Plump's word) by an Indianapolis policeman named Pat Stark, who had been their escort for the tournament. Stark had served in the same capacity in the previous year and requested to be Milan's guy. "I guess he just liked us," says Plump today. "He had promised that he would give us a ride around the monument if we won it all." Stark arranged for a caravan of Cadillacs, packed with Milan players, to follow him, sirens blaring, from Butler Fieldhouse through the Indianapolis streets to Monument Circle in the center of town, a distance of about six miles. Then Stark led the parade the wrong way around the circle, several times. "Pat damn near got fired for it," said Plump, "and, tell the truth, he probably should've."

The following morning the team went to church together at Saints Peter and Paul Cathedral on 14th and Meridian Streets near the hotel. Plump and several others were Lutherans and, ignorant of the rituals, were told to follow the lead of assistant coach Clarence Kelly, a Catholic. "We did it for a while, and then Clarence decided to fake us out a couple times," says Plump, who did some standing when he should have been sitting and some sitting when he should have been standing.

Then it was time for the two-hour ride home. The players were looking forward to reminiscing about the game and maybe catching some sleep. But it turned into a ride they would never forget. Had I-74 been around back then, it would have been an entirely different trip, but the Milan caravan led by Stark traveled on byways like State Roads 46 and 10. They were surprised to find lots of well-wishers along the way, even a "Congratulations, Milan" sign painted on a cattle truck in the center square of Greensburg. "We couldn't believe it," said Plump.

The traffic kept building because cars kept joining the caravan, which grew to eighteen miles long. Plump knows of a man who jumped out of his car nine miles from Milan and arrived home before his wife. When the heroes were finally placed on a makeshift platform at the school, there were "people as far as you could see," remembered Bob Collins, who called it "Indiana's Woodstock."

Plump is still dumbfounded and can't find the words to explain it. "Back then we thought, 'Well, this is just how it goes when you win a state championship.' But *that* many people? There had to be fifteen to twenty thousand, and maybe as many as thirty. How do I explain that? I can't."

———

This is a necessary detour, though it may not be a popular one in all quarters. When Ted Green debuted his documentary *Attucks: The School That Opened a City* at the Madam Walker Theatre in 2016, he noticed a disapproving buzz when Bobby Plump, one of the invited guests, walked in. He understood. "It was like: 'Jeez, even at an Attucks event we get Bobby Plump?'" said Green, laughing at the memory.

It's nothing personal against Plump, who over the years has been an unabashed booster of Attucks and much more in touch with reality than many Milanites. It's just that the Attucks story—the real one—has become subsumed by the fictional story. Over the years so much confusion about *Hoosiers* has sprung up that it seems imperative to separate fact from fiction. The movie's popularity ($28.6 million at the box office, a permanent place among the best sports films ever, a one-word evocation of a time and place) has obscured historical truth, which—obvious point, perhaps, but still worth making—should matter. Oscar and many of those in the Attucks camp are furious either with the movie, the misguided interpretations of it, or both, and that is entirely understandable.

There is little doubt that *Hoosiers* is yoked, culturally and politically, to a conservative mind-set. After ESPN Classic showed the footage of Milan's actual state championship game, NPR's Bob Cook, a Hoosier by birth, as he announces on his broadcast, opined that the team ("the Paul Bunyan of schoolboy sports") represented the "triumph of the small-town way of life, the pull-up-your-bootstraps ideal, that no matter where you are from and what disadvantage you may have, if you work hard, you'll succeed." In fairness, Cook also believed that the story plugged into small-town America's fears about school consolidation, that small schools were being swallowed up by larger regional districts, an argument that continues today.

Hoosiers was released at the height of America's love affair with President Ronald Reagan, whom one can imagine holding court over coffee with the Hickory hicks, extolling the virtues of the chest pass right along with supply-side economics. The movie plugs into the Hoosier state's essential ruralness and is nothing if not a valentine to small-town life. It sends the message, even if unintentionally, that the values—nay, the entire value *system*—of small-town, rural America is unassailably the model paradigm, the true-blue *correct* American model.

To a certain extent, *Hoosiers* asks that we stop time. Indiana may not have a monopoly on small-town nostalgia, but the Hoosier state does seem to bathe in it more than most. In a memorable 2019 *New Yorker* essay, Robert Gottlieb took apart one of Indiana's icons, writer Booth Tarkington, for letting his look-backward conservatism turn him from one of America's great novelists (Pulitzer Prizes for *The Magnificent Ambersons* and *Alice Adams*) into a "hack" and a writer "relentlessly scornful of anything 'modern'" with "crotchety views." His fatal flaw, writes Gottlieb, was his "deeply rooted, unappeasable need to look longingly backward, an impulse that goes beyond nostalgia."[1]

You can actually stop time in Indiana by taking Exit 115 off Interstate 70 at Knightstown, the small town where stands the Hoosier Gym, preserved in all its dusty yet frequently varnished glory, the venue where all the home games in *Hoosiers* were shot. "Right here," said Rex, an older gentleman who was doing the tours on the day of this visitation,

---

1. It could also be that Tarkington got old. Kurt Vonnegut, the *best* writer that Indiana sent off into the world, said (during a 1996 PBS interview), "It's just a fact that American male writers have done their best work by the time they're fifty-five. It's pretty junky after that. It's just an actuarial matter." Tarkington was forty-nine when he wrote *The Magnificent Ambersons* and fifty-two when he wrote *Alice Adams* but was still cranking out books up until his death at age seventy-seven.

"is where Strap knelt down to deliver his prayer before the final." We were down in the small locker room that, yes, looked exactly like it does when Gene Hackman's Norman Dale says, "I love you guys," and Preacher tells the tale of David reaching for his stone and slaying the giant Philistine. For Rex, and for thousands of Hoosier pilgrims, it is a religious moment.

It is crucial to note that director David Anspaugh and screenwriter Angelo Pizzo, though both Hoosier-born (Pizzo has few equals in his devotion to Indiana University hoops), spent much of their lives in Los Angeles in the movie business. They didn't sit down with the intention of deifying small-town America. But that message is the default extraction from *Hoosiers*, serving to promote the idea that values, cohesion, loyalty, unselfishness—all those things we associate with the best in athletics—cannot possibly come from any other place than a Hickory, Indiana.

The wellspring of kinship for kids at Attucks, however, came from a wholly different place. They were united by the insults and the ignorance of others. "In those days," Oscar said in a podcast with the Indiana Basketball Hall of Fame, "no one said good things about Black people." Though the Attucks players rarely talked about it, their bonds were strengthened by common mistreatment, not the balm of small-town adoration. "We were born in the South and came here in the back of the bus," said Robertson on the podcast. "Couldn't go downtown, couldn't go here, couldn't go there. There were things we could do and couldn't do." Movies rarely have room for everything, and there was no room for the Attucks experience in *Hoosiers*.

Like so many things in our culture, the film has undergone a new reckoning in a post–George Floyd world. So let us take a meandering stroll through the movie and connect whatever dots should be connected between this particularly rich era of Indiana schoolboy basketball and what it all means to Attucks basketball.

Let's make this point clear: Pizzo and Anspaugh were entitled to make a movie about any subject they wanted. People have criticized them for not making the Attucks story. Well, they didn't choose to make the Attucks story. Don't tell a writer and a director what they *should have* made. The story about a fictional high school called Hickory in a fictional town called Hickory was the story closest to their hearts. And heart produces art.

Furthermore, *Hoosiers*[2] is not based upon or adapted from a book, magazine, or newspaper article or any other piece of nonfiction material, as was, say, the 2023 HBO series about the Los Angeles Lakers, titled *Winning Time*. That series was adapted from a book by Jeff Pearlman called *Showtime: Magic, Kareem, Riley, and the Los Angeles Lakers Dynasty of the 1980s*. When critics found so much deviation from Pearlman's historically reliable tome, there was outrage. That is understandable. The creators of the drama and Pearlman (mostly) defended the changes as necessary for dramatic tension, narrative arc, and so forth. That, too, is understandable. In choosing to largely invent a story, however, Pizzo and Anspaugh should not be held accountable in the same way as the *Winning Time* crew was for, say, turning a real-life Jerry West into a raving lunatic Jerry West. His name in the series, after all, is Jerry West, and Jerry West is still very much breathing.

Having said all that, was *Hoosiers* inspired by the Milan High story? Absolutely, positively. Pizzo and Anspaugh, both Indiana University grads and both athletes and sports fans, *absorbed* the Milan story as kids. It seeped through their pores, as it did through the pores of hundreds of thousands of Hoosier kids. Sure, in the movie Hickory High wins the state championship in 1952 (not 1954), the team is coached by an aging, cantankerous coot played by Gene Hackman (not an energetic

---

2. The movie almost had a different title. The studio hated *Hoosiers* because it was convinced it would limit international sales. What? They don't know about torn-off ears in Paris? The higher-ups wanted *The Last Shot*. But after the movie scored astronomically high at its first test screening, the head of Orion Studios told Anspaugh and Pizzo, "Okay, you can have your damn title." At subsequent cocktail parties, the exec no doubt took credit for the name.

twenty-four-year-old named Marvin Wood), and the winning shot is made by a reluctant introvert named Jimmy Chitwood (not a popular and voluble high school hero named Bobby Plump). But that doesn't mean that Hickory is not, to a large degree, Milan.

As a result, an inevitable racial tension crept into *Hoosiers*. Since Hickory = Milan in the minds of most, it must follow that South Bend Central = Attucks. It didn't matter that the Milan-Attucks game was in the "semi-states" and not the finals, and had there been a true stand-in for South Bend Central, it would have been Muncie Central, not Attucks. The fame of Oscar Robertson combined with the popularity of *Hoosiers* assured that, over time, at least in Indiana, it would be Oscar's team that lost to the white kids.

The South Bend Central of *Hoosiers* is, in fact, a racially mixed team, as was Muncie, which had three Black players on the roster. At the beginning of the game in the film, two white starters can be seen coming out for the fictional South Bend Central, and one white player even makes a basket during the game. But the action focuses mostly on South Bend's two stars, both of whom are Black, one a guard named Boyle, the other an unnamed center. Neither looks anything like Robertson. But in the minds of many, Oscar is out there, getting beat by the white boys. And over time the state final opponents in *Hoosiers* have transmogrified into mythic archetypes that not only suggest reality but positively define it.

Hickory/Milan—disciplined, fundamental, heroic, winners, Caucasian

South Bend Central—athletically talented but ultimately flawed, losers, Black

In a spectacularly tone-deaf move, albeit one easily explained by marketing, the NBA's Indiana Pacers wore replica Hickory High jerseys for ten games during the 2015–2016 season. It was only in the *following* year that they got around to honoring Robertson's Crispus Attucks teams, which were, you know, real.

———

A few other points about a movie that is deeply embedded in the heart of Indiana basketball and will likely remain there through the ages.

Oscar was not asked to be a part of the movie. "We knew we had no shot with Oscar and, anyway, we didn't want him because then he would've been *Oscar Robertson*," said Pizzo. "Not enough people knew Ray Crowe, so that was good, and Ray suggested Bailey [Flap Robertson]. They were great, wonderful people. Ray had absolutely no criticism of anything we did. You could tell he was a very special man." (Not surprisingly, Crowe received some criticism for appearing in the movie. Oscar was among those critics. But Oscar stayed away from criticizing his brother, at least publicly.)

Plump is not in the movie—"I don't know why," he says, "but they just didn't ask me"—but Milan teammate Ray Craft plays the tournament official who shows Hackman and his team into the building and then informs them that it's time for tip-off. In real life, the adult Craft was more an official part of Indiana schoolboy basketball than Plump—Craft coached at Milan and Clinton Central and was assistant commissioner of the Indiana High School Athletic Association for twenty-five years.

A memorable line from the movie, one that seems to define the countrified, 1950s flavor of Hickory High, is a complete accident. It's delivered by Shooter, the dipsomaniacal assistant coach played by Dennis Hopper. "And, boys," he says, breaking a huddle, "don't get caught watching the paint dry." Anspaugh cut right after Hopper delivered it, and everyone stood around like . . . they were watching the paint dry.

"I had written some banal coaching line that I don't remember, and Dennis, obviously, didn't remember it either," says Pizzo. "Dennis—bless his soul—had a lot of years of drug abuse and some of his brain cells were gone, and there were lots of times he couldn't remember dialogue, and what he would do was just make shit up and throw it out there. Sometimes it would be terrible, but some good things would come out of it." (Hopper's line about his suit, "a real humdinger," was another ad-lib.)

Hopper apologized to Anspaugh and Pizzo and told them, "'Watching the paint dry' was something my dad used to say to me all the time." They decided to keep it in the movie.[3] "The funny thing," says Pizzo, "is that's on T-shirts now. Just another example of how serendipitous this movie stuff can be."

In the original script, Pizzo had written that Hopper's Shooter escapes from the hospital and joins the team for the final game. "Dennis begged me to take that out of the script," says Pizzo. "He was a year and a half into his own sobriety, and he had failed many times before, and he did not want to signal that it was okay not to follow the rules. So, I listened to him and kept him in the hospital. And when we tested the film, the audience went crazy when they see Dennis jumping up and down in the hospital room celebrating." (Hopper died in 2010 at age seventy-four of prostate cancer; Pizzo says he had stayed sober for the rest of his life.)

Though Crispus Attucks High School has no role in *Hoosiers*, two of its Indy rivals do. The filmmakers needed an audience to partially fill Butler Fieldhouse and convinced Shortridge and Broad Ripple to move up a scheduled game by two weeks and play it at Butler. Fortunately for the filmmakers, Indiana fans know how to act at a basketball game.

The actor (Maris Valainis) who plays last-shot hero Jimmy Chitwood got cut from his Indiana high school team three years in a row.

---

3. Among the memorabilia in Plump's Last Shot bar is a large *Hoosiers* poster signed by Anspaugh and Pizzo that reads, "To Bobby Plump, a man who never got caught watchin' the paint dry."

And Anspaugh and Pizzo were ready to cut him when he repeatedly missed the last shot in rehearsals. Pizzo remembers,

> He was just throwing up brick after brick when the crowd was in there. We had ten dress rehearsals, and he didn't make one. You could tell the crowd was getting tense. Gene Hackman said, "You gotta move him up." Bobby Plump said later, "I was closer to the basket than the shot in the movie." But we didn't want the shot from the elbow. We wanted it farther out.
>
> When it was time to actually film it, Maris makes the first one. We had been so concerned about him making the shot that we hadn't even talked about what would happen afterward. So, everything that happens—the joy, the crowd racing the court, the cheerleaders crying, Ray Crowe consoling his players, the place went *insane*—is all spontaneous. It was as much relief as anything. But it was authentic.

They did another take, and Valainis again made the shot. "But the first one was so good," says Pizzo, "that we took everything from that."

One of the better players on either team was Wade Schenck, who plays Ollie, the student-manager pressed into service. Schenck had a proclivity for dribbling behind his back during the filming, and Anspaugh had to tell him to stop doing that.

The saddest epilogue to *Hoosiers* is well known: Kent Poole, who played Merle Webb, committed suicide in 2003. He had been suffering from depression. Merle was the character who said before the state final, "Let's win this one for all the small schools that never had a chance to get here." Later, a filmmaker named Landry Long made a short film about Poole that is available on YouTube. Since there are always connections in Indiana basketball, Long is the son of Brad Long, who played Buddy in *Hoosiers*.

And since there are always connections upon connections, Brad Long is the son of a man, Gary Long, for whom Pizzo used to shag balls at Indiana University. "He was one of my heroes growing up," says Pizzo. Long, a member of the Indiana Basketball Hall of Fame, was an honorable mention All-American in 1961. "I only found out the connection after we cast Brad," says Pizzo. "We picked him because he just looked like a Hoosier."

There's not much to say about *Hoosiers* co-star Barbara Hershey and her character of Myra Fleener. She disliked everything about the movie except for Gene Hackman. She correctly felt that her relationship with Hackman's Norman Dale character is not explored thoroughly; too much was left on the cutting room floor.

As for Hackman, well, he is the heart of *Hoosiers*, but nothing about dealing with him was easy for the filmmakers. "He constantly referred to us as amateurs," says Pizzo, "which compared to him we were." It was the first movie for both Anspaugh and Pizzo, who would go on to write and direct *Rudy* in 1993, and the thirty-sixth for Hackman, including *Bonnie and Clyde, The French Connection, The Conversation, Young Frankenstein*, and all three *Superman* movies. Pizzo remembers,[4]

Gene took it out mostly on David. I don't think he liked me particularly either, but he came from the theater where there was a tradition of not changing a word of dialogue unless you asked. He held to that.

But I learned a lot from him. Gene would often say, "See this line right here? I don't need to *say* it. The camera will be on my face, and my *face* will say it." I pulled ten lines of dialogue out because of that.

---

4. I have never met Anspaugh but am friendly with Pizzo. The interview with Pizzo for this section took place at his home in Bloomington, Indiana.

I really don't enjoy watching *Hoosiers*. I hear some bad dialogue. I see mistakes. My perspective is too warped. But one thing I recognize is that if we had cast a subpar actor in that role of Norman Dale, I would've been exposed as a mediocre writer. He took dialogue that was sometimes not good or average and made it seem real. Gene was never easy—he was a black cloud. But having my first film be acted by people like Gene Hackman and Dennis Hopper? There are no words for how lucky I was.

In the end, Hackman gave a very Hackman-esque seal of approval. "I don't know how you pulled it off," he told the movie's director and writer when he saw them, "but you pulled it off."

———

In talking to commentator Bill Simmons about sports movies, Spike Lee had this to say about *Hoosiers*:

In some ways *Hoosiers* is similar to *Rocky*, although better made, containing much better performances. At the time, the NBA was becoming rife with black players, while Georgetown had been establishing a dominating presence in the fabric of the college game, so what do you do? You fill a nostalgic need with a fantasy, turn back the clock to a much simpler time, a time . . . when "nigras" knew their place. They are usually warmly embraced, these pictures about how wonderful and fine it was when, basically, n—s weren't around. [Word elision was in the original piece.]

Spike made *Do the Right Thing* and *He Got Game*, invented Mars Blackmon, directed Michael Jordan, and attended seventeen thousand

New York Knicks games, many of them awful. He deserves his say, and that's what he thinks about *Hoosiers*.

Here's what Oscar has to say:

> I ask you this: When the fictional version of Milan . . . reaches the championship game in *Hoosiers*, what does it mean that the filmmakers twisted the truth? Instead of having Milan defeat Muncie Central and an integrated team with two black guys on it, which is what happened in real life, Hickory defeated a fictional team of black players, coached exclusively by black men, whose rooting section consists of black men, women, boys, and girls. Is the proverbial race card being played?

Here is how Pizzo answers both Lee and Robertson: "*Hoosiers* is not a documentary. It's not a docudrama. We never mention that it's based on a true story. Whenever I would do interviews, I would say it's *inspired* by something that happened. But it's not one hundred percent Milan. These are completely new characters made out of whole cloth by me."

Absolutely true. But can we blame Oscar for his anger? Can we say he's wrong? Is it not understandable? For all that he and his teammates went through, and for all that they would accomplish over the next two seasons, the personification of Indiana basketball remains a fictional white team from a small town, not the Black team from Indianapolis whose *actual* accomplishments dwarf all others.

Through the years there have been hundreds and hundreds of complaints from Milan citizens about the movie. The town's consensus: You didn't tell the *Hoosiers* story correctly. You changed things. We didn't wear that many pairs of overalls. Our coach was young, not old. We all got along. On and on.

The proper answer to that is . . . be thankful. Pizzo and Anspaugh gave you an outsized place in history. They didn't set out to make a documentary about your basketball team because that's not the way film works. There have been books and articles about Milan, and for that be grateful. Bobby Plump has always taken that approach—"Hell, I'm just glad we're remembered!"—and shut up about the historical inaccuracies. A team that would achieve far more than Milan would get ignored for years because it was located on the poor west side of Indianapolis, where the faces were Black and no one wanted to go, a place that no one wanted to celebrate.

CHAPTER SEVEN

The Secret Spread of Black Basketball

"I don't think he could make my team."

Within Crispus Attucks High School, there was a heightened anticipation about the 1954–1955 season, Oscar Robertson's junior year. Seventy-six players tried out for the team, meaning that Ray the Razor really had to sharpen his blade. Still, there was the lingering suspicion in some quarters that Black teams would fold in the clutch. Preseason stories about Attucks were a trifle subdued and roughly followed this model in the *Indianapolis Star* before the 1954–1955 season opener:

> Loss by graduation of stalwart starters like Harold Crenshaw, Winford O'Neal, and William Mason ought to be enough to make anybody say his prayers. But judging from the looks of the Crispus Attucks leftovers, they may be forgotten much sooner than one would suppose. [Coach Ray] Crowe has three returning regulars and three other lettermen for a nucleus, and 11 of the 12 boys suiting up Friday night at Fort Wayne North Side will stretch six feet or better. Sheddrick Mitchell

and Willie Merriweather, a couple of six-four seniors, and six-three junior Oscar Robertson are holdover regulars.

So Oscar (who probably was taller than 6'3") was one of the "leftovers." He didn't feel like a leftover. He felt strong and confident, hardened by a summer working both on his grandparents' Tennessee farm and at an asphalt paving company in Indianapolis, as well as by a couple rounds of domestic turmoil.

First, Oscar's parents divorced. That his mom and dad weren't getting along wasn't a revelation to Oscar and his brothers, but divorce was still a shock, particularly when his father took another wife, Ivora Helms. "We were black people from the country, raised with a deep religious background," Oscar wrote in *The Big O*, "and we never heard of divorce, let alone knew about it happening to people like us."

Second, the family was uprooted from its Colton Street home, and not because of the split. The Indianapolis branch of Indiana University (later Indiana University–Purdue University Indianapolis), seeking to expand its Medical Center property around City Hospital, had asked the city to declare a fifteen-acre tract on Frog Island as a "blighted area," which meant it would be razed. It didn't have to ask very hard; Indiana's white establishment was all behind it. The Robertson house at 1005 Colton was in the middle of that tract. The Indianapolis Redevelopment Commission, which had been established in 1944 "as one of scores of local agencies across the country that directed transformations in post-war cities" (according to IUPUI anthropology professor Paul Mullins), gave its approval, and for weeks Indy's newspapers reported on a summer "slum tour" sponsored by the Indianapolis Junior Chamber of Commerce. That group was recognized, as Emma Lou Thornbrough put it, as "the most influential institution in the city," led by an imposing man named William Henry Book, who all but ran the city for three decades beginning in the 1930s.

Judged from the distance of history, those stories (the *Indianapolis News* and the *Indianapolis Star* were firmly in line with the politics and societal views of Book) had a look-how-badly-the-other-half-lives tone, presented as they were under the assumption that civic improvement would ensue if only unsightly Black housing would magically disappear. Oscar describes the relocation simply in his autobiography: "The summer before my junior year, the city took the land on Colton Street to build a hospital, and we had to move."

It's worth noting, remembering Richard Pierce's idea of the "polite protest" that prevailed in Indianapolis, that the Attucks yearbook covered these civic developments with unwavering optimism. Since we wouldn't expect students of the 1950s to proffer criticisms of civic leaders in the pages of a yearbook, it's safe to assume that this cheerleading commentary from the 1956 yearbook came from the Attucks higher-ups: "The roaring of the bulldozers, the 'put-put' of concrete mixers, and other sounds are reminders that Crispus Attucks is in the center of a redevelopment program. Old houses are rapidly being replaced by new modern dwellings."

The slum clearance, which displaced about ten thousand people, the overwhelming majority of them African American, coincided with the divorce of the Robertson parents. Now, Oscar had no great love for the shotgun shack on Colton, but the family probably would have stayed on if it hadn't been uprooted. Mother and sons first moved nearby to 3945 Boulevard Place, but Mazell, who was working two jobs (as a beautician and as a cook for an Indianapolis family), couldn't make the payments, even with Flap on scholarship at Indiana Central, so they moved down the street to another property on Boulevard. That made his walk to Attucks 24 blocks, but Oscar didn't care: he would have walked 124 blocks on his hands to go to Attucks.

That all-too-familiar scenario of dislocation represents the flip side of the Great Migration. Minority families, locked into the Deep South world of economic deprivation, limited or nonexistent educational opportunities, and unconcealed racism, were lured northward by the promise of a better life. To be fair, many found it. But they also found, as Oscar and his brothers did, moldering housing in sulfurous sections of cities, segregated schools (fortunately, the Robertsons landed at an exceedingly good one), limited job opportunities, and a kind of community branding that enforced the idea of inferiority, of "otherness."

The slum clearance/displacement had a profound effect, obviously, on Attucks's students and specifically on its basketball players, the majority of whom came from the west side. IUPUI's Mullins took note of this in any number of academic articles. He uncovered a 1952 story in the *Indianapolis Recorder* that listed that year's twelve Attucks basketball players and found that, several years hence, nearly all of their homes were gone, and, as he writes, "many of the very streets have been erased." The former homes of Hallie Bryant, Willie Posley, and the Robertsons are now under the Indiana University Medical Center, for example, and Willie Gardner's home on N. Missouri sits under state office complexes.

"The land was taken legally under urban renewal funding, identified for 'slum clearance,'" said Mullins in a 2022 interview. "So, everyone was compensated, but how much is not known. In these situations, generally, compensation is not substantial enough." Then, too, many of the residents on the west side didn't own their homes, so any compensation didn't go to them anyway. After their displacement, they had nothing, not even a roof over their heads.

"Does the university have mixed feelings about all this?" says Mullins. "Of course. The university has a measure of uneasiness now a half-century later. Many of our students are the grandchildren and great-grandchildren of the people we displaced. The number is something like five thousand households from the 1950s through the early 1980s. My office today is a short walk from where the Robertsons were brought up. I think a lot about that."

The divorce did result in a change to Oscar's practice habits. He still balled at the Dust Bowl from time to time and never forgot his roots there. But more and more he worked on his solitary moves at his father's new home a few blocks from Oscar's new digs. The *Indianapolis Recorder*'s Charles S. Preston made note of it in a preseason story, writing, "Willie Merriweather has grown an inch and a half, Oscar Robertson is shooting goals all day long in an alley behind Cornelius Avenue—and away we go."

Merriweather's importance to this 1954–1955 Attucks team can't be overstated. It's probably too strong to say that Oscar *revered* two teammates during his time at Attucks, but two stand out for how much he respected them: Merriweather from this 1955 team and Al Maxey from the 1956 state championship team. Both had enormous ability (Merriweather starred at Purdue, Maxey at Nebraska), and they were also tough guys, down-in-the-trenches types. One of Merriweather's specialties was grabbing a rebound with one hand and giving his opponent a subtle elbow with the other arm. "I wouldn't call myself a hatchet man," Merriweather says today, "but let's say I was strong-armed." Oscar wasn't soft, but there was some Gretzky to his game. His magic worked best when he had a couple of persuaders around him.

Then, too, Merriweather had a background similar to Oscar's. The Merriweathers had also come from Tennessee in search of a better life; his dad landed that job at International Harvester, and his mother worked as a domestic, including for the Simon family, which has owned the Indiana Pacers for forty years. And like the Robertson boys, Merriweather went back each summer to toil on his grandparents' farm. "Pigs, cattle, a couple mules, plowing, a hundred and twenty-five acres," remembers Merriweather. "Oh, there was a lot to do, that's for sure."

Whatever personal turmoil Oscar felt, he rarely showed anything. Hundreds of fans accompanied the Tigers to their opening game, which meant a 230-mile round-trip to Fort Wayne. It was part of a doubleheader—Fort Wayne Central against Marion, Attucks–Fort Wayne North in the nightcap. Keep in mind that the city of Fort Wayne was basketball royalty back then, the locale of a solid NBA franchise (the Pistons, owned by a staunchly antiunion industrialist named Fred Zollner) led by a bald California-bred, Stanford-educated, offensive-minded forward named George Yardley. This was going to be a big night for Fort Wayne hoops.

Except it wasn't. Any doubt that the "leftovers" were ready to pick up the Attucks baton was quickly removed. Wrote the *Indianapolis News* of Attucks's 1954–1955 debut,

> Who's going to hold that Tiger this year?
> That's the leading question in state basketball circles today after Crispus Attucks's amazingly smooth and easy 75–64 triumph over a good North Side of Ft. Wayne team.
> Attucks' high-scoring front line—Oscar Robertson, Willie Merriweather and Sheddrick Mitchell—poured 49 points through the hoops. Oscar got 19, the others 15 each.

The press reports on Attucks were starting to steer away from mentions of race. Attucks was no longer described as a "colored" team or a "Negro team" as was so often the case in the early 1950s when the "Crowemen" first started to make noise. But it's still imperative to understand how manifestly *different* Attucks appeared when the team took the floor and how relatively recently Blacks had been invited to join the Hoosier basketball party. Right up until Crowe's Bryant-Gardner-Flap teams, there wasn't any kind of Black *game* in Indiana; there were more like Black *sightings*, reported as if the players were fossils excavated on archaeological digs. *Look, a colored boy is playing!* That's not surprising considering how the game of basketball spread on two mostly parallel tracks—one white, one Black—that intersected at certain points but, for the most part, kept their distance from each other, wary rivals trying to master a new game.

———

Baseball was the sport through which we once gauged our nation's racial separation. It was the most popular sport in America—in some ways the *only* sport, from at least the 1870s through the 1950s—and Jackie Robinson's breaking the color barrier in 1947 was a worldwide story. (The role of National League president Ford Frick in the acceptance of Robinson has been overlooked. Frick, who became baseball's commissioner in 1951, was a fair-minded Hoosier, born in Wawaka, a town in northern Indiana.) We can hardly call baseball in its formative years exactly "democratic," unless we're comparing it to basketball. Writes Alex Painter in *Blackball in the Hoosier Heartland*,

> Contrary to what may be considered popular belief, it was not impossible for blacks to break into organized baseball ("historically regarded as the white dominated major and minor leagues") during the latter half of the 19th century. However, it has been firmly established that about half of the participation from black ballplayers prior to 1900 was through all black teams in otherwise all white leagues. As one historian writes, "This apparently was considered more palatable. You may not want the group of players on your team, but you would be willing to play against them."

Basketball in its formative years was almost exclusively a Black *or* white attraction. Its appeal to African Americans was obvious, says Bryan Stevenson, founder and executive director of the Equal Justice Initiative.

It was a very accessible sport, as compared to baseball or football, and, most obviously, the more elite sports, sports that required money like tennis, golf, etc. Recreation is one of the main things that came out of segregation, because it was created and resonated within the community. If you wanted to develop skills that people could appreciate and recognize and applaud, you had to do that in that sport space, or perhaps in the church music space. It wasn't possible to do it in the mainstream. So, basketball became a really important way for a lot of people to distinguish themselves and create identities.

Many substantial histories of Negro League Baseball have been written, and so we know a lot about Josh Gibson, Buck Leonard, and Oscar Charleston, the antecedents of immortals such as Willie Mays and Hank Aaron, who started in segregated ball and finally made it to The Show. (For a while in the 1940s and 1950s, Charleston's brother, Bennie, ran the athletic program at the Senate Avenue YMCA.) But Black basketball before 1950? The average mind pretty much goes to the Harlem Globetrotters and that's it.

But there was so much more. While James Naismith is known to virtually every hoops fan, the name of Edwin Bancroft Henderson has been all but lost. Henderson did as much as anyone to spread the game to the Black populace in the early years. Though hoops eventually evolved into a playground game, some structure was needed just to learn the rudiments. What were the rules? What could and couldn't you do with the ball? What was this new game supposed to look like? Indoor football? Lacrosse without sticks?

Young people who wanted to learn the game needed facilities, which the Black masses generally lacked, and a unified voice to teach and disseminate the game. White America had YMCAs and physical education teachers, and even white immigrant populations had the AAU, which quite early on spoke up on behalf of teaching basketball as a tool for Americanization, particularly on New York City's Lower East Side, where the game grew rapidly. At the same time, as Claude Johnson points out in his excellent *The Black Fives: The Epic Story of Basketball's Forgotten Era*, "The AAU, despite its stated ideals, would prohibit African American membership until 1914." This meant that any AAU member team that competed against a Black club risked disqualification from further amateur competition.

In 1902 things started to change for Black players, at least in the Washington, DC, area, with the opening of True Reformer's Hall, the first post-Reconstruction building to be financed, designed, and built entirely by African Americans. That building became, as Johnson writes on his Black Fives Foundation website (an indispensable source about early Black basketball), "the center of the region's Black basketball scene." Along came E. B. Henderson. A native of Washington, DC, Henderson earned a bachelor's from Howard University and a master's from Columbia, but it was during three summers of physical education training at Harvard in the early 1900s that he learned basketball, the game having spread naturally from Naismith's lair in Springfield to other parts of the Northeast. Henderson began teaching in the segregated DC public school system, where he introduced the sport to Black students and eventually organized a team at the 12th Street Colored YMCA. So, while Naismith's army was using midwestern Y's as birthing centers for the game, Henderson was doing the same at one Y in our deeply segregated nation's capital. Going forward, Black YMCAs would become extremely important in spreading the game, including the powerful Senate Avenue Y in Indianapolis.

Henderson's teaching, writes Johnson, represented the first time that African Americans played basketball on a wide-scale basis, "earning Henderson distinction as the 'Father of Black Basketball and the District of Columbia as the Birthplace of Black Basketball.'"

As was the case in Indiana, the game moved quickly when there were rivalries. Strike a match with fundamentals; light it on fire through competition. Eventually Henderson became a physical education instructor at Howard, then and now one of the nation's most successful historically Black colleges, and his first varsity team in 1911 was formed largely from the best of his 12th Street Y guys.

By then Black basketball had started to flourish elsewhere, particularly in Philadelphia, Pittsburgh, and New York. The latter was home to the Smart Set Athletic Club, formed in 1904 in the Stuyvesant Heights section of Brooklyn, "a powerful uniting force in the overall African American community of greater New York City," as Johnson writes. Also, the club could ball. In 1908, the Smart Set was declared "the Colored Basketball World Champions," a largely ceremonial title conjured up by Lester Walton, a writer from the *New York Age*, then the nation's leading Black newspaper. The Smart Set—widely known as the "Grave Diggers" because they just killed everybody—won again in 1909 but ceded the title in 1910 to Henderson's 12th Street Y powerhouse, which had managed to snag the Smart Set's best player, Hudson "Huddy" Oliver, one of the game's first stars and one of the first examples of cross-pollination among exclusive teams.

The Globetrotters came along in the 1920s, originating not in Harlem, by the way, but on the South Side of Chicago. Originally called the Savoy Big Five, the peripatetic Globies stormed basketball, rampaging jesters in red, white, and blue. Whether the Globies were "good" for basketball is a freighted question not easily answered. Whatever you say about their "Sweet Georgia Brown" hijinks, Abe Saperstein's traveling circus entertained millions of people over the years, provided employment for hundreds of Black players—Attucks products Bryant, Gardner, and Cleveland Harp among them—and brought fun and ball-handling skill to the game. But the Globies came to be too often the *only* manifestation of Black basketball, reinforcing the idea that Black players were foremost entertainers, fundamentally unsound, clownish. Black players were already fighting that stereotype in a game that large segments of the public could not understand. Even most of Walton's missives about Black basketball for a Black newspaper were put in the "Music and Stage" section of the *New York Age*.

Johnson's book and website notwithstanding, so much of early Black basketball is lost to history, such as the stories of the assorted Black students who found their way onto rosters at white colleges. Those athletes were usually of a type: good students and multisport stars who could help colleges and universities in multiple ways by manning various sports teams—more bang for the scholarship buck—while enabling those institutions to publicize their beneficence in *giving Black athletes a chance*. Samuel Ransom is believed to have been the first African American in college basketball; he played at Beloit College in Wisconsin in 1906 and was also an outstanding performer in football, baseball, and track. Fenwick Watkins fit the same pattern—he was a multisport star when he played basketball at the University of Vermont one year after Ransom. Cleveland Abbott was another of this type: he starred in basketball at South Dakota State and also played football, baseball, and tennis, and ran track.

A few years later, along came one of the true greats of Black basketball's early days. Cumberland Posey was born into wealth (his father was an engineer and eventually a partner of industrialist Henry Clay Frick) in suburban Pittsburgh. Posey starred in basketball at Penn State for two years, then formed the Monticello Athletic Association team (which won the 1912 Colored World Basketball Championship), after which he played basketball at Duquesne for three years under the name Charles Cumbert. (The NCAA was officially around in 1910, but we can agree that its enforcement division wasn't so assiduous about investigations back then.) Posey also had an even more outsized career in baseball with the Negro Baseball League's Homestead Grays, as a player, manager, and owner.

The real victims (that might be a strong word, but only by a little) of the Globetrotter hegemony were the legit Black powerhouse teams of the early days, who played superb all-around basketball and rarely clowned. They were teams like the New York Rens (who began as the New York Renaissance Big Five), named for the Renaissance Ballroom and Casino in Harlem, and the Loendi Big Five of Pittsburgh, named after an all-Black social club and organized by—who else?—Cumberland Posey. While Loendi won four straight Colored World Championships between 1920 and 1923, the Rens are without a doubt the greatest team with the least-known résumé. From 1927 through 1948—granted, record keeping was not exactly perfect—the Rens won 2,318 games and lost 381, for a percentage of .859. And they did it all while playing as a perennial road show. "It seems like I spent my whole life on the road," Tarzan Cooper, a great Rens center during the 1930s, told *Sports Illustrated* back in 1979. "When I look back on my playing days, all I see is that old bus. It was a rough ride in those days. Blacks couldn't stay in most hotels, and sometimes we had to drive 400 miles to find a hotel."

Most of these names go unmentioned, and most of these stories go untold, as Black basketball, from the early 1900s through the 1950s, consisted of an almost secret society that featured superb players who never made it into the mainstream public consciousness. How many Black athletes suffered that same fate? And how many never got the chance to play at all?

———

A remarkable man named John McLendon is that rare figure who fits snugly into both white and Black narratives about the spread of basketball in the first half of the last century. A Kansas native born in 1915, McLendon fell in love with hoops early and wanted to attend Springfield College because that's where Naismith hung up his first peach baskets. The good doctor was long gone by that time, having accepted a professor's job at the University of Kansas, and McLendon's father suggested that his son knock on Naismith's door and ask him to become his advisor. The family couldn't afford to send young John to Springfield anyway and wanted him to stay in the home state. As the story goes, Naismith heard McLendon out and replied, "Fathers are always right. I will be your advisor."

Yet, despite having the game's inventor on his side, McLendon was still prohibited from playing on the Kansas team because of the color of his skin. Could Naismith, by all accounts a fair and just man, have done more for racial equality, at least as far as basketball went? If research on that question has been done, this chronicler was unable to find it. During the nine years he coached Kansas beginning with the 1898–1899 season, Naismith never coached a Black player and seems to have never said much (or anything) about African Americans being excluded from the game.

To deepen the McLendon story, another Naismith mentee, Forrest Clare Allen, called Phog for his foghorn voice, was the powerful, well-respected Kansas coach when McLendon showed up at the first season practice in 1933. "I was sitting there with the other guys, and Phog Allen is calling some of the guys out to do some of the drills that he's doing," McLendon says in Scott Ellsworth's *The Secret Game*. "But he never did call me. And so I said to myself, 'Well, this is a hopeless situation.'" McLendon never did get on the court.[1]

What is clear is McLendon's enduring respect for Naismith, who never stopped being a guide and a sounding board until Naismith's death at age seventy-eight in 1939, just before McLendon began his long and

---

1. Though it's been written that Phog Allen, a dominant figure on the Kansas campus, also drained the school pool rather than have McLendon (an excellent swimmer) use it, that is not the case. Phog tangled with McLendon about it, and once called him a "smart aleck," but McLendon won a battle of wills to open the pool to African Americans. Custodians were apparently the only people to have drained the pool. The best source for all the McLendon-at-Kansas information is Milton S. Katz's excellent biography *Breaking Through: John B. McLendon, Basketball Legend and Civil Rights Pioneer*, along with the Ellsworth book.

illustrious career as a coach and fast-break pioneer. McLendon deserves a place in history if only for his participation in the famed secret game skillfully told by Ellsworth. It was a legit contest, with referees, between McLendon's North Carolina College team and a team from the Duke University medical school (the would-be docs had a local reputation as a strong ballclub), considered the first collegiate basketball game in which Blacks and whites competed on the same court—the humble gym on the campus of North Carolina College. The date was March 12, 1944, a Sunday. The Duke team arrived quietly. The gym doors were locked. "If the Durham cops, or the Klan, caught wind of what was going down, there was no telling what the consequences might be," wrote Ellsworth, who detailed McLendon's nervousness before the game.

McLendon's Eagles, tentative at first, doubled up their opponents 88–44. That wasn't surprising. "Black college basketball in the 30s, 40s, and 50s," wrote Billy Packer and Roland Lazenby in their 1991 book *The Golden Game*, "was among the best in the country." Then players from the two teams talked and ate together for hours.

To repeat, a basketball *game* had to be played in secret, in America, at a time when Tuskegee Airmen were flying bombing missions and dying in the European theater.

One postscript: The following day, a Black soldier from New York named Edward Green, a private stationed with a field artillery unit at Camp Livingston in Louisiana, failed to move quickly enough to the back of the bus after being ordered to do so by the driver, Odell Lachney. According to Stevenson's Equal Justice Initiative, which researches such incidents, Lachney stopped the bus and pulled out a gun. Heeding the wishes of a white passenger not to fire shots on the bus, he forced the soldier outside. Green begged for his life, but Lachney shot him in the heart. No charges were filed.

A second postscript: In 1960, the US national basketball team, so loaded with talent that it has been referred to as "the first Dream Team," met the Cleveland Pipers of the National Basketball Industrial League. McLendon was the Pipers coach, which made him the first African American to lead a professional team, though that accolade is usually given to Bill Russell, who became the first Black head coach in the NBA when he took over the Boston Celtics in 1966. McLendon's Pipers won that game 101–96, making him the first coach to beat an Olympic team, which was led by, oh yes, cocaptains Oscar Robertson and Jerry West.

———

It is not accurate to say that Black players were ignored in Indiana in the decades before Attucks's rise to prominence. In fact, they were almost always identified as curiosity pieces. *The tall Negro. The high-jumping black. The tan talent. The sepia sensation.* Even the *Indianapolis Recorder* searched the Crayola box for adjectives. There weren't many African American players, so it was a story—and sometimes trouble—when some made it onto a team.

In 1946, Frank Barnes, the coach at Shelbyville High School, put three Blacks in his starting lineup—Emerson Johnson, Marshall Murray, and Bill Garrett, a Hoosier immortal with a story to be detailed later. Barnes knew what he was in for since he had received hate mail for playing two African Americans, Tom Sadler and Jelly Brown, way back in 1940. But *three* Black players? That was violating the unspoken quota, a fungible number over the years. Back in the 1940s it was probably something like *You can start two Blacks on the road but only one at home, and it would be safer to start none.* Write Tom Graham and Rachel Graham Cody in *Getting Open*, the book about Garrett, "After Shelbyville's first game of the 1946–47 season—a win at home—a few adult fans started a whispering campaign against Barnes's use of three black starters, with one local trying to drum up support to run Barnes out of town."

Predictably, the Shelbyville Bears were often referred to as the Black Bears, and Barnes got more than his share of hate mail, which was no doubt replaced by missives of praise when his charges won the state tournament behind the talented Garrett. Parents of Black players usually did not travel to the most racist towns, and the three Black players were not allowed to stay with the team at their chosen hotel in Indianapolis for the state tournament; they boarded at a nearby rooming house. It's no surprise, then, that Bobby Plump heard *Beat those N-words* seven years later.

The Shelbyville racial mix was an anomaly. Beyond the racism (subtle or overt) that kept Black players away from the game, a high percentage of African Americans simply didn't complete their educations. They weren't encouraged by their teachers and were enrolled in nonacademic tracks that emphasized work over study. Economic realities at home forced them to quit school and take jobs; witness Willie Gardner in the 1950s, who quit Attucks a couple times to set pins at a bowling alley, only to be coaxed back by Ray Crowe. (The coach also bought clothing for Gardner.) The Hoosier tradition had no paradigm—or a very hazy one—for a Black player to attend college. College was for white boys. That's why the Black Hoosiers who made a name in the 1930s and 1940s deserve so much credit and more acclaim. Here are a few who preceded Garrett.

The first two can be introduced as a matched set—Dave DeJernett and Jack Mann, who battled each other in two memorable state playoff games back when Black players were very unusual. DeJernett's Washington team beat Mann's Muncie Central team for the 1930 state championship, and a season later Mann beat DeJernett in the round of eight en route to the 1931 state title. Remember that had these Black stars been playing for Attucks, they would not have been allowed in the tournament. Stanley Warren, a 1951 Attucks graduate who became a distinguished historian and educator, wryly notes in an essay for the Indiana Historical Society that the anomaly of individual Black stars pacing their predominantly white teams to wins in a tournament in which Black schools were barred "seemed to slip by unnoticed by the media and IHSAA officials."

DeJernett[2] might have been distracted in that game; during the tournament a letter arrived at Washington High, saying that he would be killed if he played in the tournament. He played anyway. Both Mann and DeJernett are in the Indiana Basketball Hall of Fame.

George Crowe, the aforementioned younger brother of Ray, was the star of a Franklin High team (coached by the estimable Fuzzy Vandivier) that made it to the finals of the 1939 state championship before losing to Frankfort. (Frankly, it was a great tournament.) But against all odds considering the racial climate of the time, George was named Indiana's first-ever Mr. Basketball. Crowe made the usual Black star trek: stints with the Rens and two other Black touring teams (the Los Angeles Red Devils and the Harlem Yankees) before really making his mark in baseball with the Cincinnati Reds.

Seven years after Crowe, another Black player, Johnny Wilson, known (almost inevitably) as "Jumpin' Johnny" because of his leaping ability, was Mr. Basketball after he set scoring records at Anderson High, which he led to the state championship when he scored thirty of his team's sixty-seven points in the climactic victory over Fort Wayne Central. Yet it's a safe bet that, throughout Indiana, Bobby Plump is

---

2. DeJernett lived a life that was both extraordinary and tragic, a not atypical reality for a Black star who couldn't find his place once the games were over. DeJernett played at Indiana Central and also starred in football and track, checking the usual boxes for Black players. After college he had stints with the Globetrotters and the Rens, the obvious landing spots for talented Black players back then. He fought in World War II but had a hard time finding a good job when he returned. He worked for a moving company and a janitorial supply company in Indianapolis. He began drinking. His hometown forgot about him. He got a DUI, then hit a six-year-old boy with his car when he was drunk. (The boy lived and was not injured seriously.) DeJernett died of a heart attack at age fifty-two; once known as Big Dave, he was known in death as Drunk Dave. In 2020, Gregg Doyel, an *Indianapolis Star* writer who has crafted several memorable stories about forgotten Indiana heroes, wrote about a visit to DeJernett's gravesite, discovering that the granite slab doesn't mention his World War II service or anything about basketball.

twice as well known as Jumpin' Johnny, who went on to set scoring records at Anderson College, now known as Anderson University in South Carolina.

Wilson was part of that long line of Hoosier folk heroes who DIY-ed themselves to basketball excellence. He learned the game by putting rags and a rock in an old sock and shooting it into a bushel basket, something like Naismith's charges in the Springfield Y. Among Wilson's high school teammates was an athlete who became better known than either of them: Carl Erskine, the great Brooklyn Dodgers pitcher—as of late July 2023 the only surviving Boy of Summer. (Erskine's relationship with Jumpin' Johnny is beautifully detailed in Ted Green's 2022 documentary about Erskine, *The Best We've Got: The Carl Erskine Story*.) In a 2019 story by Dana Hunsinger Benbow of the *Indy Star*, Erskine talks about being approached by Jackie Robinson one day early in Robinson's career with the Dodgers.

> "Hey, Erskine," Robinson asked, "how come you don't have a problem with this black and white thing?"
> "Well, I grew up with Johnny Wilson," Erskine told Robinson. "He was my buddy. And so, I don't have a problem."

Wilson had problems though. He was clearly the outstanding player of a 1946 All-Star Game between Indiana and Kentucky (a game that Oscar would dominate ten years later; see Chapter 17) in which he was the first Black ever to compete against a Kentucky team. Indiana won, and Wilson scored twenty-seven points, but the wristwatch—Wilson always remembered that it was worth $100—went to a white player from Kentucky named John Edward "Sonny" Allen, who scored fewer points and played for the losing team. (Allen was an outstanding player, and later a coach, at Morehead State College, where the baseball field was named in his honor.) Benbow reports that after complaints about the snubbing from a local sportswriter, readers sent in enough donations to buy Wilson a watch, making Jumpin' Johnny's cause a progenitor of today's GoFundMe campaigns.

A few weeks before the All-Star Game, Wilson's story began to intersect with the story of Garrett, the boyhood star from Shelbyville. Indiana coach Branch McCracken was invited to speak at the Anderson YMCA at a banquet celebrating Anderson's state championship. This was 1946, and there still had not been a Black player in the Big Ten, in keeping with the so-called gentlemen's agreement among the administrators and coaches in that conference. (In general, there is nothing so ungentlemanly as a gentlemen's agreement.)

It's important to look at the context of the time. Black servicemen were coming home from serving in World War II, yet couldn't get good jobs or equal access to education. African American newspapers had editorialized about the inequities, and even the Hoosier white sporting press had begun to cast its eye on the blatant discrimination in the Big Ten.

There were catalysts for that questioning. There was already talk about a rising Black star in the Brooklyn Dodgers organization who was on his way to breaking the color barrier in Major League Baseball. A countrified Hoosier named Ford Frick was president of the National League, and he was behind the ascension. Two years earlier that baseball player had been a US Army lieutenant court-martialed for refusing to give up a seat on a shuttle bus in Fort Hood, Texas. The officer had written a letter explaining the situation to Truman K. Gibson, the assistant secretary of war, in which he not only outlined the incident but hinted—ever so subtly—that the army was not going to come out looking too good should he be convicted. Here is a portion of that letter:

> You can see I need your advice. I don't care what the outcome of the trial is because I know I am being framed and the charges aren't too bad. I would like to get your advice about

the publicity. I have a lot of good publicity out and I feel I have numerous friends on the press but I first want to hear from you before I do anything I will be sorry for later on. Sir, as I said I don't mind trouble but I do believe in fair play and justice. I feel that I'm being taken in this case and I will tell people about it unless the trial is fair. Let me hear from you so I will know what steps to take.

Lt. Jack Robinson was subsequently cleared.

So, McCracken must have been of two minds when someone in the Anderson crowd asked the question about Jumpin' Johnny that was on everyone's mind. As reported by Graham and Cody in *Getting Open*, it was framed this way: "If Wilson comes to IU, would he play basketball?"

McCracken pondered it. He must have weighed the tenor of the times (more and more calls for equality) as well as the painful experience with racial prejudice of a close friend, a Jewish referee who was unable to get a whistle-blowing job in the Big Ten. McCracken probably even knew something about the early Black players in the East such as Fenwick Watkins and Cumberland Posey, and he had likely heard of George Gregory Jr., who had cocaptained an outstanding Columbia University team in 1931, joining forces with Lou Bender, a white player from Manhattan. By the time they finished their storied careers, college teams were selling out Madison Square Garden. And there was that Jack Robinson guy at UCLA in the early 1940s, a star in basketball, baseball, and track.

But then a more comfortable calculus came to mind. All those years of racial prejudice and the continued aversion of some (most?) to coaching and playing against Black players. All his prejudiced friends in the Big Ten. All those white IU boosters who might resent a Black player.

So McCracken took the coward's way out.

"I don't think he could make my team," McCracken told the crowd.

Let's assume for a moment that McCracken honestly believed that was true (which is doubtful). He was at an Anderson banquet with Wilson looking on in the audience. It's the kind of situation where a coach would go out of his way to praise a bench warmer, never mind the number one player in the state of Indiana.

"He [McCracken] didn't have a single kid on that team," Jumpin' Johnny later told Benbow, "that I hadn't played against in high school and beat."

CHAPTER EIGHT

White Robes

"We didn't make much noise because we were pretty much directed not to."

Crispus Attucks's decisive win over Fort Wayne North set a take-no-prisoners template for the 1954–1955 season. The Tigers won their next game over Sheridan 80–36 and prepared for their "home opener" against Terre Haute Gerstmeyer, a traditional power that had handled Attucks in the past (including losses in both 1952 and 1953), and, like Attucks, drew players from a large pool around its city. Gerstmeyer's lure was a solid technical education and the chance to play for Howard Sharpe, a respected Hoosier coach.

As a sign of how big Attucks had become in the Black community, the *Indianapolis Recorder* ran a full-page notice about the game that included ads from several Black businesses. "Let's Make It the Biggest Game in Naptown's History" read one such ad. It was the third game of the season.

The game was played at Butler Fieldhouse, Attucks's de facto home court. The Tigers were on their way to becoming a full-fledged traveling circus, hamstrung, to an extent, by their lack of an adequate home gym but getting increasingly accustomed to the bright lights of the magnetic fieldhouse, the center of postseason play.

One of Attucks's mechanisms for feeling at home even on the road was "The Crazy Song," a ditty written in 1945 by a graduated Attucks cheerleader named Edwena Bell Payne, considered to be, according to the *Recorder*, "the best cheerleader ever to bark through a megaphone" at Attucks. During her freshman year at West Virginia State College in 1945, Payne heard a tune at a basketball game that stuck with her, worked up some lyrics, and brought it to an Attucks game she attended while on break. She gathered around some of her friends—the *best cheerleader ever* still had some pull—and taught them the yell; the rest is history. That history ended, however; Attucks fans do not sing the song these days.

There has likely never been any substantial piece written about Attucks without mention of "The Crazy Song." In Ted Green's documentary, several Attucks alumni sing bits and pieces of it, including one Oscar Robertson, who at no point in his life has ever been inclined to, shall we say, *put himself out there* in a fun way. Though there have been several slightly differing transcriptions, "The Crazy Song" went roughly like this, accompanied by rhythmic clapping:

Howe [insert school name] thinks they're rough,
Howe thinks they're tough.
They can beat everybody,
But they can't beat us!
Hi-de-hi-de, hi-de-hi;[1]
Hi-de-hi-de, hi-de-ho;

---

1. It goes without saying that the "hi-de-hi-de" part owes a debt to "Minnie the Moocher," a popular jazz song recorded in 1931 by Cab Calloway and his orchestra. It was a runaway hit,

That the skip, bob, beat-um;
That's the Crazy Song!

As silly as it was, "The Crazy Song" held deep significance at Attucks and still does for the older alumni. The school's rooting section, and especially its teams, were *supposed* to be reserved. They weren't *supposed* to lord it over other teams. They weren't *supposed* to complain at egregious referee calls. That was Principal Russell Lane's edict, as well as the way of the world in 1950s Indianapolis.

But "The Crazy Song" *belonged* to them. It was transportable. You carried it with you in your heart and your lungs to every gym visited, which in the case of Attucks meant every gym. Everyone knew it, adults and kids alike. It had just enough vinegar in it to chafe the opposition, a lyrical precedent to the victory cigar that Red Auerbach would light up in Boston Garden after a Celtics victory. No matter how much you might have wanted Attucks to fail, no matter what your feelings about African Americans, the song sent this message: *Right now we* own *you.* It had such meaning that even Black residents of the city who didn't go to Attucks felt its siren call. "I know every word, and I went to Tech and Shortridge," says Eunice Trotter, director of the Black Heritage Preservation Program for Indiana Landmarks, the nation's largest private statewide preservation organization. "My sister was an Attucks majorette, and she would practice it all the time and take me to the games. It was important to them. I understand that completely."

———

Such a song would never have been sung in the formative years of Attucks under the long shadow of the Ku Klux Klan. It is on the subject

though Calloway likely didn't reach the cultural stratosphere until he rendered "Minnie" for John Belushi and Dan Aykroyd in the 1980 movie *The Blues Brothers.*

of the Klan that chroniclers of the Attucks story must strive most dili-
gently for precision and nuance. A few of the basics:

No, the Klan did not literally order the building of the school. Neither did David C. Stephenson, the odious head of the Klan in Indiana.
But Klan fingerprints were all over it.

No, the entire Indianapolis School Board did not show up in white
robes at Attucks's first graduation in 1928. But it is widely believed that
all five members of the school board at that time were Klan members or
Klan affiliated, and they were the ones handing out the diplomas.

No, the Klan was not at its height in the Hoosier state when Attucks
opened its doors in 1927. But the organization absolutely *was* at its zenith
during the years 1922 through 1925 when Attucks was first proposed
and construction got underway.

In short, it's impossible not to talk about the Klan in relation to
Attucks and Black culture in Indiana, where, as Troy Paino pointed out
in a piece for the *Journal of Sports History*, the Klan's xenophobic message
took hold largely because of "its almost exclusively white, native-born
and Protestant population." The Hoosier state was not alone, of course,
in throwing out the welcome mat to the cretins in white. But Indiana has
a deeply disturbing history as a place where race hatred (Catholic and
Jewish hatred too) incubated and where strident Klan beliefs were hidden under coats and ties and overalls and sensible housedresses.

James H. Madison, arguably the most respected historian of all
things Indianan, identifies three distinct Klans. The first was formed
after the Civil War to prevent Reconstruction and deny rights to former slaves. The third comprised (mostly) Southerners protesting civil
rights and school integration in the 1960s, mostly in made-for-TV performances. It was the second Klan, writes Madison, that planted a flag
deep in Indiana's heart around 1920, having been reconstituted, according to most accounts, in the Georgia town of Stone Mountain in 1915.
And when it came, it "came like wildfire," as Madison put it in *Hoosiers*.

Writing in *Ku Klux Kulture: America and the Klan in the 1920s*, Felix Harcourt singles out William Joseph Simmons, a "former circuit-riding preacher and professional fraternal organizer" (there's an interesting double major) as the spark for this second Klan. Simmons lifted many ideas, says Harcourt, from *The Birth of a Nation*, D. W. Griffith's silent film sensation that came out in 1915. (Griffith, the son of a Confederate veteran, borrowed some of his material from an influential racist writer named Thomas Dixon, who was also a Baptist minister. Dixon wrote what historian Nicholas Lemann called a "Reconstruction Trilogy" that concentrated on the supposed horrors of giving Blacks equal rights.)

Simmons's message didn't take off until he hired an organization called the Southern Publicity Association (SPA) to spread the word. The polite-sounding folks from SPA (*eat more grits; sing more "Dixie"; hate more Jews, Catholics, and Blacks!*) did their job well, paying recruiters (called Kleagles) to enlist new members and targeting for Klan membership respected citizens such as Protestant ministers and members of fraternal organizations, like the Masons. It was an organized and efficient campaign that adopted a seductive soft sell aimed at home and hearth. *We're not embittered racists; we're all about the family.*

The campaign was a perfect fit for Indiana, where there had always been racial enmity toward the Black community. Early whites who came to Indiana were most often from southern states such as Kentucky, Tennessee, and North Carolina, and African Americans were seen as rivals for jobs and land, even if, in some quarters, they were as welcome as anarchistic Europeans. There are varying estimates as to what percentage of Indiana's white male population paid the $10 fee to become Klan members in the 1920s, but Madison is on the conservative side when he puts it at one-quarter. Phillip Hoose in *Attucks!* writes that by 1924 nearly one-third of the state's white male population had become Klan members and quotes historian Irving Leibowitz, who believed that more than half the citizens of rural counties, "from the gently undulating prairies of northeastern Indiana to the impoverished hill farms of southern Indiana," were members. Hoosier women joined by the hundreds of thousands too, plugging into temperance movements and supporting Prohibition laws that were often part of Klan dogma.

That was the message that Lillian Sedwick used as state leader of the Indiana Women of the Ku Klux Klan. Sedwick, also an elected member of the Indianapolis School Board, was among those presenting diplomas to the first Attucks graduating class in 1928. Those who have done research into the Klan in Indianapolis are unable to conclude whether all the school board members, not just Sedwick, were actual Klan members, though Emma Lou Thornbrough concludes that "it is not improbable."

But the true messiah of the Klan message in Indianapolis, and throughout much of the Hoosier state, was that particularly vile piece of trash named David Stephenson, known as "D.C." "The Klan owned the state," writes Timothy Egan in *A Fever in the Heartland: The Ku Klux Klan's Plot to Take Over America, and the Woman Who Stopped Them,* "and Stephenson owned the Klan." Hoose describes Stephenson's effect in Indiana as electric: "Overnight, common people—responsible parents good neighbors, community leaders—pulled hoods over their heads and fanned out in mobs under the cover of darkness to terrorize the homes and workplaces of blacks, Jews, and Catholics. Crosses soaked in kerosene blazed on hillsides. Billboards reading Ni**ER, DON'T LET THE SUN SET ON YOU HERE cast long shadows at many Indiana town lines."

Surely these things happened, and Indiana did become known for its "sunset towns," where Blacks knew not to set foot in during the nighttime. But as with many things race-related in Indiana, the effect of the Klan was subtler, more insidious.

On primary election day in 1922, for example, the Klan ran a motorcade through Frog Island, the future home of the Robertsons and already a settlement that was almost exclusively African American. The message was clear: *Don't go to the polls.* It was typical Klan intimidation strategy: *We're not violent; we're just riding around.*

The tentacles of the Klan stretched into every part of life, as long as it was white and Protestant. There were Klan touring stage productions—one ditty from *The Awakening*, reports Harcourt, was called "Daddy Swiped Our Last Clean Sheet and Joined the Ku Klux Klan"—as well as cake sales and youth basketball tournaments. It was more than a movement; it was nothing less than an ecosystem.

For the most part, the press either ignored the Klan or cooperated willingly with it, and not just the *Fiery Cross*, Stephenson's own Klan rag. H. L. Mencken, the Baltimore newspaperman and Klan foe, wrote in 1924, "Whenever the Klan wins, the fact is smeared all over the front pages of the great organs of intelligence; when it loses, which is three times as often, the news gets only a few lines." Indiana newspapers ran regular columns about Klan "goings-on," and at least one reporter for the *Indianapolis Star* openly admitted that he was a Klansman. Writes Harcourt,

> In Klan strongholds like Indiana, newspapers would publish regular front-page columns detailing upcoming Klan events and meetings. Klan officers encouraged members to approach their local newspapers about running a regular "Klan Kolumn" that would carry news of the organization and "constructive arguments for patriotic Protestant Americanism." The Indiana Klans, growing particularly inventive, hired their own photographer, W. A. Swift of Muncie, who would then supply chosen newspapers with illustrations for their articles.

Enthusiasm for the Klan was by no means just an Indiana thing. One of our Supreme Court justices, Hugo L. Black, had been a Klan member (specifically the Robert E. Lee Klan No. 1 in Birmingham, Alabama) in the 1920s, though he had rejected the Klan by the time he was nominated to the Court by Franklin Delano Roosevelt in 1937. (Black ultimately leaned more left in his Court rulings. Go figure.) The liberal *New York Evening Post* ran a regular cartoon strip for months entitled "Our Ku Klux Klan" that portrayed Klan members as loveable and helpful ordinary folk. The *North American Review*, a prestigious literary quarterly, printed a thirty-page explanation of Klan principles from Hiram Evans, who held the position of imperial wizard.

We shouldn't be surprised by this. In later years, we watched David Duke wear stylish suits, talk about Christian values, and let his veneer of conformity put a happy face on his neo-Nazi convictions. The newspapers and publications of the day focused on the Klan's surface niceties and its *activities* while ignoring its *ideas*, which were the foundation of its existence. The Klan didn't cease being a hate organization because it held cake sales; the haters handed out their message on a civic platter.

Stephenson was the perfect Klan gospel spreader, a soulless grifter who didn't wear a robe. He was always impeccably presented in public, every hair in place, ready smile on his face. He was an unctuous, glad-handing, smooth-talking salesman for a coal company, though his real calling was to spread the word of the Klan, which he did with unremitting efficacy. He was an unapologetic capitalist, getting a portion of the money for both Klan memberships and Klan robes and peaked hats. The Klan dressed like it was Halloween, but for Stephenson every day was Christmas. Later, in assessing the danger of Nazism, philosopher Hannah Arendt would write about "the banality of evil." She could have been describing Stephenson.

Stephenson first established a Klan chapter in Evansville, but eventually his voice was heard all over the state, most dramatically at a 1923 speech at a park in Kokomo that drew an estimated two hundred thousand people in lockstep loyalty to the message, widely believed to be the largest Klan gathering ever. Stephenson's true genius was worming his way into the good graces of the people in power—the mayors, the chambers of commerce, the school boards. In the Indiana November elections of 1924, Klan-supported candidates became governor (Edward L. Jackson) and occupied the majority of the state congressional seats. The Indianapolis mayor who had been elected in 1922, Samuel L. Shank, was anti-Klan but, reading the writing on the Hoosier wall, eventually capitulated and allowed the Klan to hold a 1924 march that, according to the *Encyclopedia of Indianapolis*, began at the Indiana State Fairgrounds on the north side, continued through the Black neighborhoods along Indiana Avenue, and wended its way into the heart of the city, "a muscle-flexing parade," as Green put it in his documentary.

According to Kenneth Jackson, author of *The Ku Klux Klan in the City*, Indianapolis from 1922 to 1925 "was the unrivaled bastion of the Invisible Empire in Mid-America." Keep in mind that this period was the exact time that Attucks was being built, a discussion for the next chapter.

What makes sorting out the role of the Klan in the history of Crispus Attucks so confusing is that, by the time the high school opened in September 1927, the Klan's power in Indianapolis had diminished, due in large part to the much-publicized April 1925 arrest of Stephenson for the rape and murder of a twenty-eight-year-old woman named Madge Oberholtzer. (Oberholtzer had been introduced to Stephenson by Klan friend Governor Edward L. Jackson.) "It's hard to overstate what a blow Stephenson's arrest was to the Klan and people who believed in them," says Bill Munn, a historian from Marion, Indiana, a town that will become significant in Chapter 11. "One of the Klan's claims was that it was protecting white womanhood, and here is Stephenson convicted of *biting* this woman."

In 1928, a year after Attucks opened, the *Indianapolis Times* won the Pulitzer Prize for a series that explored the Klan and its oversized influence in Indianapolis politics. But just a half dozen years before its anti-Klan stories, the *Times* took the following "enlightened" positions on race:

- It deplored "the tendency of Negroes to seek homes in white residential neighborhoods."
- It praised a group of "determined white women" who were warning African Americans about moving into white neighborhoods.
- It castigated as "one of the indefensible anomalies of our educational system" the practice of the "co-mingling of blacks and whites in the classroom" and, while encouraging the black race to progress, warned that this path "should never lead to social mingling."

Even when the Klan disappeared—at least from public view—other organizations that believed in the same principles were around, flexing their muscles in mufti instead of white robes. The White Supremacy League and the White Citizens Protective League (WCPL)—beware of organizations touting *protection*; generally, you will need protection *from* them—both exercised undue influence in local elections, particularly school board elections. The WCPL was behind the zoning ordinance that barred mixing of the races. The Indianapolis mayor at the time, John L. Duvall, a favorite of the Klan who was later convicted of corruption, called the measure "a step toward the solution of a problem that has long caused deep thought and serious study by members of both races," a triumph of political nonspeak.

Even benign-sounding organizations like the Citizens School Committee, which presented itself as anti-Klan, put forth a slate of school board candidates who were pro-segregation, particularly in education. All these organizations were bent on protecting the status quo, which in Indiana meant power for the entrenched white elite, some of them with actual Klan membership cards but almost all of them with Klan sympathies. Dr. Martin Luther King Jr. could have been talking about Indianapolis when he said, "The Negro's greatest stumbling block in the stride toward freedom is not the White Citizen's Councilor or the Ku Klux Klanner, but the white moderate who is more devoted to order than to justice." For an African American in Indianapolis, Klan policy or WCPL policy was essentially a Hobson's choice.

———

A few decades later, Oscar Robertson and his teammates did not have to sidestep men in white robes during their years at Attucks. There were no Klan bake sales or Klan-sponsored junior basketball tournaments or white-robed parades through the center of Indianapolis. If there were shouts of the N-word during their games—Robertson later said he heard the word sometimes but not often—they were not persistent or overt.

But the ethos of Indiana, then and certainly through the first decades of Crispus Attucks High School, was a quiet kind of racism, filtered through politeness and a benign disingenuousness.

At the same time, Blacks were prevented from moving into certain areas, ordered into segregated schools, and kept out of certain restaurants, even in their hometown. Attucks players became the princes of the city who ate on the bus. "The coach used to get off a bus, go inside, get us something to eat, come back out," remembers Bill Hampton, an Oscar backcourt teammate. "We all knew it was because they wouldn't let us in there, but we just ate and continued on down the road. We didn't make much noise because we were pretty much directed not to. It just wasn't something we did. It wasn't until later we really realized, 'They're scared of us.'"

That 1954–1955 Attucks team, the one that first achieved true greatness, was a test case for Indianapolis. At the outset of the season, the Tigers were too good not to like but too different to truly embrace. Then the victories kept coming. In the much anticipated third game of the 1954–1955 season, they all but toyed with powerful Terre Haute Gerstmeyer in the second half and won going away by 57–44. South Bend Riley and city rival Broad Ripple went down by double-digit margins—Oscar had twenty-eight points in the former game and hit ten field goals in a row in the latter—and as the Tigers climbed in the polls, now being routinely mentioned as among the best teams in the state, their fan base grew. Over eleven thousand packed Butler Fieldhouse on a Wednesday evening in December to watch them beat hated Arsenal Tech 57–47, the rivalry that had spawned the dueling threats the previous season.

Attucks could play any style. "It was freelance basketball up until we got in a pickle," Hampton said, "and then it was control basketball. A lot of teams could only play a style that put you to sleep." Yet this idea that African American players succeed because of natural ability and Caucasian players succeed using their smarts continues until the present day. Certainly Oscar noticed it and seethed about it throughout his entire pro career. And he's still seething about his basketball IQ being overlooked during his high school days. In his book *"But They Can't Beat Us": Oscar Robertson and the Crispus Attucks Tigers*, author Randy Roberts quotes Robertson thusly: "Reporters always wrote that Attucks players were big and strong, but we were no bigger or stronger than many of the other good teams. In fact, many times we had a smaller team. And never once, not once, did a white reporter write that I was a smart player. A strong player, yes. A talented player, sure. But not an intelligent player. And intelligence, getting the ball to the right player at the right time, setting up a play, making sure the floor was balanced, was what I did best." That's not entirely true; by the time he was a junior, Oscar's smarts as a basketball player were being mentioned in press reports. But his overall point is certainly valid.[2]

---

2. That issue was the backdrop of the much-remembered 1987 NBA controversy involving Celtic Larry Bird (actual Hoosier) and Isiah Thomas (adopted Hoosier from college days at Indiana University) of the Detroit Pistons. After an excruciating playoff loss in Boston Garden, Detroit's Dennis Rodman opined that if Bird were Black, he'd be just another player. Teammate Thomas, frustrated after an agonizing defeat, agreed, and when his assent became public, the basketball world pounced on him. Thomas was wrong to single out Bird, but his larger point was that Black players, generally, were considered great athletes, and white players, particularly someone like Bird, were praised for being "heady."

While there is little doubt that Oscar and his teammates had it easier than those who went before them in terms of the racial climate, it is also true that they endured the slow burn of racism. They lived under a cloud that to be Black was to be second best, not quite the norm, something *other* than the folks who ran the world. Basketball was their salvation, Crispus Attucks their refuge. Always. As teenagers, they probably didn't know the particulars of their school's remarkable creation story. But they did understand that strength and steadfastness were built into the foundation of the place that so many African Americans hadn't wanted to be built in the first place.

CHAPTER NINE

1927: A School Built by Hate but Also with Hope

"This is not a colored high school; it's a *high* school."

Crispus Attucks's basketball success during the 1954–1955 season—at least for the first half of the campaign—was presented in the press as the result of a powerful triumvirate: Sheddrick Mitchell, William Merriweather, and Oscar Robertson. "They were about as hot as three kids can get and still retain their amateur standing," wrote Bob Collins in the *Indianapolis Star* after one Attucks win. It was almost as if no one, even the astute Collins, could see the ascendant brilliance of Oscar without including him in a hoops triptych. Now, to be sure, Merriweather was a certified star. He would go on to be an all–Big Ten player at Purdue who averaged twenty points a game. And Mitchell had a serviceable three years as a rotation player at Butler.

But the fulcrum of all that happened was Oscar, and this wasn't always noticed. His talents snuck up on you because his brilliance came from fundamentals, versatility, and, above all, consistency. He didn't score gaudily (except on one singular night of the following season that would attract some criticism). He was compared most often to Hallie Bryant because both were scorers, but he didn't have Bryant's flash. Plus, Bryant was often a solo act back in the early 1950s when Attucks was just coming to prominence; Oscar was part of a dynamic, thrumming machine.

"People started calling them 'The Attucks,'" Collins would later recount. Pack up the babies and grab the old ladies—the Attucks is in town! "Two minutes into warmups," said Collins, "and the other team would be watching them."

Oscar hit a jumper with 2:13 remaining in sudden death—yes, they sometimes played overtime in a first-basket-wins system back then—to give Attucks a 60–58 win over Shortridge and the city tournament trophy just before the new year. John Gipson, a backup center interviewed at his home in Indianapolis in 2022, remembers that moment well. "Oscar just waved everybody out of the way and said, 'Let me win this.'" Oscar said the team learned a lesson in that game, or at least he did. "Coach Crowe permitted us to load up on food before the game," he writes in *The Big O*. "Naturally we went out there and were sluggish." (Pregame gluttony isn't the province of high school players in the 1950s by the way. It's extraordinary how badly many young NBA players eat before games.)

The year 1955 was ushered in with a 63–44 rout of Sacred Heart (which would play patsy to Oscar in a big way the following year) in a "workout for subs," as the *Star* put it, and then Attucks took the measure of Fort Wayne Central 70–60 for its eleventh straight win. In that game, Oscar fouled out, a theme that would come to light with a vengeance the following year. In a column for the *Indianapolis News*, W. F. Fox Jr., the Bill Fox who had done so much to proselytize for the state tournament, referred to Oscar as "the 1955 Bobby Plump." There is no evidence that Oscar saw that—but he wouldn't have liked it. Down went Michigan City 88–69, Shortridge 93–62 (before a crowd of 11,561 at Butler), and Mishawaka 84–59. For religious believers, the victory over the Shortridge Blue Devils was particularly meaningful. "Tigers Crush Satans" read a headline in the *Indianapolis Star.* Say hallelujah![1]

Attucks had now worked its way to a secure place near the top of the state's scholastic rankings. Herb Banet, a respected coach at Fort Wayne Central, went so far as to place Attucks at the top, ahead of Muncie Central, one of the gilded powers of Indiana basketball. Oh, how different were the creation stories of these two schools, which would meet in a riveting showdown late in the 1954–1955 season.

———

In 1869, Indiana's General Assembly decided that "colored children" should be educated. But it also allowed for "separate schools" that had "all the rights and privileges of other schools of the township." Twenty-seven years later, the US Supreme Court, in *Plessy v. Ferguson,* would rule that racial segregation was not unconstitutional as long as facilities for the races were equal in quality. The decision unleashed the dreaded *separate but equal* phrase upon American society. Long regarded as one of the worst decisions in Supreme Court history, *Plessy v. Ferguson* was tailor-made for Indiana. They should have put it on the state flag.

Granting education to "colored children" but allowing for "separate schools" served as the Indiana template well into the next century. Still, though there were small all-Black schools here and there, education was largely mixed. Remember that proportionately small numbers of Blacks

---

1. And say hallelujah twice more! As Attucks was getting off to its great start in 1955, a Black woman named Marian Anderson, already close to fifty-eight years old, sang the role of Ulrica from Verdi's *Un ballo in maschera* at New York's Metropolitan Opera. That was sixteen years after she was denied permission to sing in Washington by the Daughters of the American Revolution because of a whites-only policy. And it was just three weeks later, according to a piece called "Deceptive Cadence" that ran on NPR, that the first Black male took the Met stage. That was baritone Robert McFerrin, as Amonasro in Verdi's *Aida.* McFerrin was the father of Bobby "Don't Worry, Be Happy" McFerrin. I defy you to catch the video of McFerrin, the late Robin Williams, and the brilliant Bill Irwin and come away with a dry eye.

followed an education path all the way through high school. In Indianapolis, African Americans who went to high school usually went to Shortridge,[2] which had opened in 1864 as the state's first free public high school. "In Indianapolis, the highest thing in the way of education that a Black could aspire to was to be among the graduates of Shortridge High School," John Morton-Finney, a Black educator who would figure prominently in the history of Attucks, once said. "You didn't need anything else in the world. Shortridge was tops."

But by 1920, a decade into the Great Migration that brought some six million Blacks northward from the southern states, about eight hundred African American students were enrolled at Tech, Manual, and Shortridge, and that was increasingly worrisome to a considerable segment of the white population. Several years earlier Indiana's school superintendent had issued a statement that warned, "Sooner or later it will be necessary to remove the colored children from the present high schools." He signed it, "Respectfully, A. K. Kendall." That's how it was done in Indiana: whatever odious opinion you had, express it *respectfully.*

So, at Shortridge in the 1920s, it was okay to go to school with *some* Blacks, just not *too many.* In an academic article titled "The Making of Crispus Attucks High School," Stanley Warren, well versed in the history of this time, wrote, "Reports that black and white students were crowded together in classrooms and the lunchroom exacerbated the situation. Shortridge parents and other supporters, particularly the Women's Department Club, seized upon the idea to build a new Shortridge and use the old Shortridge as a school for black students."

All of those beneficently named organizations "popped up" (in the wry phrasing of David Leander Williams in *African Americans in*

<hr>

2. Shortridge alumnus Kurt Vonnegut once said, "I thought we should be the envy of the world with our public schools. And I went to such a public school. Shortridge High School produced not only me, but the head writer on *I Love Lucy* [Madelyn Pugh]. And, my God, we had a daily paper, we had a debating team, had a fencing team. We had a chorus, a jazz band, a serious orchestra. I wanted everybody to have such a school."

Indianapolis)—the White People's Protective Association, the Capitol Avenue Protective Association, the North Central Civic Association, the Mapleton Civic Association—to promulgate the idea that there were *too many blacks*. The latter organization sounds like something out of *Leave It to Beaver*, but its own declaration of purpose couldn't have been clearer: "To prevent members of the colored race from moving into our midst, thereby depreciating the value of property values by fifty percent or more." It's important to remember that this was not the white-robed Ku Klux Klan marching through the streets. As Emma Lou Thornbrough writes, "Although Klan rhetoric was anti-black, anti-Catholic, and anti-Jewish, in fact the Klan took little action against these minorities." Action came from these benignly named "civic" organizations. "It's in the DNA of Indiana," says Williams. "We don't want to kill Blacks. We don't want them to go back to Africa. We just don't want to *live* with them."

There was also the transparently denominated White Supremacy League, which sometimes carried the name of its founder, Mrs. Otto Jay Deeds, who—you don't really need to know this—wrote dreadful poetry under the name of Daisydean Deeds. Over the next thirty years Deeds was an inveterate letter writer and recipe submitter to newspapers, as well as living proof that crackpots can slither away from their worst moments simply by enduring. "At her death in 1960," writes anthropology professor Paul Mullins, "the *Indianapolis Star* called Deeds a 'civic leader' and did not include the White Supremacy League in her lifework."

The message of these groups was always the same, just as it would be for George Wallace, who said four decades later, in his infamous 1964 stump speech, "In the name of the greatest people that have ever trod this earth, I draw the line in the dust, and toss the gauntlet before the seat of tyranny, and I say, segregation now, segregation tomorrow, and segregation forever."

One sees contemporary America reflected in those times a century ago. In the early 1920s there was a growing sense, in Indiana and other places, that the Black population was *replacing* whites, that a traditional way of life was being overrun by invading hordes, that the minority was becoming the majority. On June 1, 1921, a year before Indianapolis officially set in motion its plan for an all-Black high school, white rioters stormed, looted, and burned Greenwood, a prosperous Black section of Tulsa, Oklahoma, in what is now called the Tulsa Race Massacre. Not long after that, in a speech made before a mixed-race crowd of more than one hundred thousand, President Warren G. Harding steered his listeners toward *The Rising Tide of Color*, a book by a racist nutjob named Lothrop Stoddard. Think about it: the president of these United States promoting a book written by a Klansman who advocated eugenics.[3]

It wasn't just about numbers; there were fears that marauding bands of newcomers (on today's Fox News they're known as *migrants*) bore disease and pestilence that would endanger *our children*. That was always the mother's-milk message in this regressive cant. *Our children must be protected!* The Indianapolis Federation of Civic Clubs, backed by the Marion County Tuberculosis Society, directly used fear of TB as the rationale to build segregated schools. Thornbrough writes of a resolution presented by the federation that reads, "Whereas the public schools have a larger number of colored children in the incipient stages of tuberculosis . . . be it resolved that the honorable members of the board of school commissioners make plans for separate schools for colored children as soon as it is practical and that they secure colored teachers for these schools in all branches."

That was a well-received message in much of white Indianapolis, which led cheers for these "protective" organizations. And so it was on December 12, 1922, that four "aye" votes followed this Indianapolis School Board of Commissioners resolution language: "and the vote upon the motion to approve the foregoing Report of the Committee

---

3. In a 2019 *New Yorker* piece, Ian Frazier writes about a legendary debate in 1929 between Stoddard and W. E. B. Du Bois, the nation's leading Black intellectual. Du Bois scored a TKO.

on Instruction with regard to the erection of a separate high school for negro students."

The clamor to build a new Shortridge school had gone nowhere. The turning against the Klan because of David C. Stephenson's sadism (in November 1925 he was convicted of second-degree murder and sentenced to life in prison) had done nothing to dispel Klan thought. Shortridge would remain as it was, and there would be a new all-Black school, the location of which was never in question: it was to be built on the west side of town, where the majority of African Americans lived, a few blocks north of Indiana Avenue and a few blocks east of the Central Canal, not far from both a dump and a glue factory. The lot facing 12th Street near West Street purchased by the school board cost $3,400, according to author Phillip Hoose.

To summarize with breathtaking understatement: this was not an area that a white realtor would show to a prospective white home buyer. And it cannot be *overstated* how vehemently the argument against building the school arose in segments of the Black community. Morton-Finney described it as "downright hostile." Even before the official board vote, the Better Indianapolis League (BIL), a self-described "civic organization of progressive colored citizens," had expressed its opposition to a segregated school, arguing, among other points, "It is un-Christian, antisocial, divisive in spirit, and pernicious in that it would be the means of stirring up discontent, unrest, and friction among a large element of the community." Two of the BIL leaders were a formidable though seemingly mismatched set. They were Archie Greathouse, the Indiana Avenue saloon operator with deep pockets, and Robert Brokenburr, the estimable local lawyer and leader of the NAACP, who two decades later would be the catalyst to get Arthur Trester and the Indiana High School Athletic Association (IHSAA) to drop its prohibition of Black and parochial schools from the state basketball championship.

The group presented its protest to the school board in person. One imagines the board members listening with plastic smiles, all the while counting the moments until they could reject the proposal in secret. Which they did.

Protests continued but went nowhere. In fact, a ruthlessly effective segregation of elementary and junior high schools followed hard upon the Attucks business. Richard Pierce writes in *Polite Protest* that by 1929 thirteen of the ninety-one elementary schools in Indianapolis were all-Black. Greathouse, with financial help from the NAACP, sued the school board. Predictably, he lost. "Negro School Barrier Gone" read a March 31, 1926, *Indianapolis Times* headline. A new slate of school commissioners had been elected in 1925, and they became widely known as "the Ku Klux Klan board," so closely tied were they to that organization. As Pierce writes, "Klan influence may have reached its zenith in the 1926 election just as Klan strength was being undermined following the murder indictment of [David] C. Stephenson." The Klan as an organization was descending in status while its messages were ascending in importance. *Separation of the races! Protect our children!*

According to Morton-Finney, even some members of the Black community were against the establishment of Attucks for reasons that would have to be classified as racist, had they emerged from the throat of a white person. Morton-Finney theorized that many Black parents believed that, while Black teachers were capable of guiding their kids in elementary and middle school, they couldn't be trusted to do the same in high school. That was a consequence of there never having *been* a Black teacher allowed to instruct a class in a white high school.

But most African American parents centered their concerns on trying to ensure that adequate facilities were available for their kids. That was more important than the philosophical questions of integration propounded by Brokenburr and other Black leaders. Parents were on the front lines. Life was about trying to make the best of a bad situation.

Accommodation—that's a better word than *complicity*—best determined African American behavior in a society segregated by both custom and law. Writes Thornbrough, "In general blacks appeared willing to accommodate and careful not to abuse the 'privileges' accorded them. Middle class blacks were fearful that increase in the black population might endanger their relations with the white community. In repeated editorials the *Indianapolis Freeman*, noting the trend toward increased segregation, warned that Negroes 'should not trifle with our privileges, treating them as license, rather than privileges.'"

Two selling points among segregation advocates were (1) Black kids would be more comfortable among "their own," and (2) Attucks would provide substantial employment opportunities for minorities since all positions would, by mandate, be filled by African Americans. The former contention is spurious, and the latter, while no doubt factually accurate, was described in an *Indianapolis Recorder* editorial as a "small and selfish contribution that means little or nothing to the vast Negro population of this community."

That didn't matter. Never forget that this was Indianapolis. A few months before Attucks opened, Butler University announced that it was limiting its African American enrollment to ten beginning with the fall semester of 1927, which coincided with the opening of Attucks. (It would not rescind that restriction until 1949, a few years before the Attucks Tigers turned Butler Fieldhouse into their personal show palace.) The move was made, most theorized, because the Butler administration reasoned that a good Attucks school would turn out more Black students who wanted to attend college, and many of them would turn their eyes toward Butler instead of the typical choices of Central State, Wilberforce, Kentucky State, and Tennessee State. It was a version of the *they'll-overrun-us* story writ in home-city script. Presumably looking down on this decision with horror was Ovid Butler, the abolitionist who founded the college in 1855.

In 1925, almost quietly, the Indianapolis School Board selected the name of Thomas Jefferson for the new school, even though there was already a Jefferson Elementary School in Indianapolis. The name was challenged in the African American community almost immediately for obvious reasons: Jefferson, despite writing "All men are created equal," had been a slaveholder; in his 1785 book *Notes on the State of Virginia*, he had opined that his Monticello slaves were "lacking beauty, emitting a very strong and disagreeable odor; were in reason, inferior; in imagination were dull, tasteless and anomalous," observed that their "griefs are transient," and stated that "a black, after hard labor through the day, will be induced by the slightest amusements to sit up till midnight, or later, though knowing he must be out with the first dawn of the morning." His personal opinions softened somewhat after his presidency, but he remained an advocate of sending "free Blacks" back to Africa because, as he wrote in an 1811 letter for the American Colonization Society, it was "the most desirable method which could be adopted for gradually drawing off" the Black population. None of these thoughts, as we now know, prevented him from bedding Sally Hemmings, his slave.

Other names for the school were considered, including Roosevelt, after Teddy, and Dunbar, after Paul Laurence Dunbar, a Black novelist, poet, and short story writer. But sometime late in 1925, the name of Crispus Attucks, a runaway slave who was the first person to die in the 1770 Boston Massacre, began to gain favor in the Black community. And by February 1926, a year and a half before the school was to open, the *Indianapolis News* was reporting that "Crispus Attucks was most favored by the colored people of the city."

It remains unclear exactly who first suggested the name. Perhaps he or she was a music fan who knew of the Attucks Music Publishing Company, a small but influential Black-owned firm founded in 1904 in New York City. After a merger it was known as the Gotham-Attucks Music Publishing Company and soon went out of business but not before publishing what one musicologist labeled as "a remarkable number of important pieces," including "Nobody" by Bert Williams, who is credited with being the first Black man (he was Bahamian) to have a leading role in a film (*Darktown Jubilee* in 1914).

Or maybe somebody was just a Revolutionary War history buff.

The school board, to the surprise of some, unanimously agreed to change the name. There had been so many pitched battles by then, and such an expectation that the school would either fail or simply exist unnoticed, that the board no doubt gave into some version of *Ah, hell, let 'em have the damn name.*

The school's namesake lives on in mystery and martyrdom. As a PBS story put it, the real Crispus Attucks was either "a hero and patriot, or a rabble-rousing villain," and it is beyond the scope of this researcher to get to a bottom-line verification of the man's life. But his connections to Attucks High School, metaphorical though they may be, are impossible to ignore.

He was born a slave of mixed descent. Just as Robertson was a slave name, so was Attucks, or in his case Attuck, since he was descended from John Attuck, who, according to a July 4, 2016, story about the Boston Massacre in the *Revolutionary War Journal*, was hanged during King Philip's War, a bloody conflict between the indigenous inhabitants and colonists of New England. Crispus's father was Prince Yonger, who is believed to have been brought to America directly from Africa, and his mother, Nancy Attucks, daughter of John Attuck, was a Native American Natick, an indigenous tribe that practiced Christianity. (How *Attuck* became *Attucks* is unknown, but such alterations, most of them obviously mistakes in translation or transcription, were commonplace.)

So, Attucks, like his father, began life as a slave, and like Marshall Collier, Oscar's great-grandfather in Tennessee, didn't care for shackles. He was a "runner." His "master" was William Brown of Framingham,

Massachusetts, who in 1850 placed an ad in the *Boston Gazette* in hopes of finding his runaway, a "Molatto Fellow named Crispus, 6 feet 2 inches high." Attucks was "tall and thick" and was "regularly called 'stout,'" according to the story in *Revolutionary War Journal*. Sounds like a power forward. Attucks was evidently never caught and lived a hard and colorful life as a seaman, ropemaker, and laborer until the fateful night of March 5, 1770, when he joined a pack of fellow workers and revelers at a Boston "victualling house." (Kudos to the first historically inclined restaurateur to call his or her eatery a "victualling house.")

There are varying accounts of what generated the conflict, but the situation—British troops mingling with hard-drinking colonists already angry about what they saw as England's oppressive tax policies—was fraught to begin with. One account has Attucks being the one who kicked off the row by aggressively going after the Redcoats' company commander, Capt. Thomas Preston, and trying to wrestle away his musket. In the bedlam that followed, eleven men were struck by gunfire with Attucks being the first to fall. Five colonists would die altogether. No British soldiers were injured.

John Adams famously defended the soldiers—successfully as it turned out—and his defense is telling. He argued that Attucks's "very looks was enough to terrify any person" and that his "mad behavior" was the main cause of that "dreadful carnage." Fear of the Big Black Man is still a reliable self-defense strategy today.

Choosing an obscure Black historical figure predictably brought much community derision in Indianapolis. (But what Black historical figure *wasn't* obscure at that time with little or no African American history taught?) One letter writer told the *Indianapolis News* that Attucks was a "barber who simply ran into the street and fell under fire of British muskets" and was not worthy of martyrdom. Can not a barber be martyred? Anyway, there seems to be no evidence that hair cutting was among Attucks's varied vocations. On May 7, 1926, an unsigned article

Oscar with Ray Crowe, the man who helped mold him into a legend at Attucks High School.

(Courtesy of the Indiana Basketball Hall of Fame)

The ultra-aggressive John Wooden was an early Hoosier hero at Martinsville High.

(Courtesy of the Indiana Basketball Hall of Fame)

(right) Dave DeJernett was an early African American Hoosier hero but struggled later in life.

(Courtesy of the Indiana Basketball Hall of Fame)

(below) James Dean was a Rebel WITH a Game as a Fairmount (Ind.) High School basketball standout. (Courtesy of the Indiana Basketball Hall of Fame)

(above) Homer Stonebraker fit the mold of the mythic Indiana high schooler hoopster. (Courtesy of the Indiana Basketball Hall of Fame)

After a storied career at Shelbyville High, Bill Garrett broke the Big Ten's unspoken racial code but still faced his share of trials at Indiana University.

(Courtesy of the Indiana Basketball Hall of Fame)

Stretch Murphy was a legend in the Indiana town that won a state championship and that four years later endured a violent lynching.

(Courtesy of the Indiana Basketball Hall of Fame)

Bobby Plump always said they were lucky to get Attucks when Oscar was a sophomore, but Milan won their 1954 showdown fair and square.

Oscar's primacy as the Hoosier state's No. 1 player earned him that jersey number on the all-star team that routed Kentucky in 1956.

Soon after Riverside Park was finally opened to Blacks, these Indy young people wanted to make sure no one forgot. (Indianapolis Recorder Collection, Indiana Historical Society)

A stern Nebraska policeman named Al Maxey, Oscar's most dependable teammate at Attucks, leads Martin Luther King Jr. around Lincoln. (Courtesy of Al Maxey)

Bailey "Flap" Robertson made Attucks history before his more famous little brother Oscar. And he had a small role in *Hoosiers*.
(Courtesy of Indiana Basketball Hall of Fame)

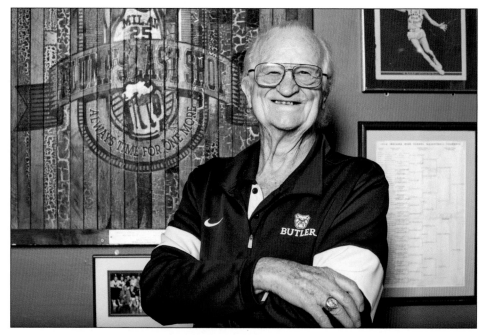

From his roost at Plump's Last Shot, Bobby Plump, whose game-winning shot in 1954 will never be forgotten in Hoosier lore, is the éminence grise of Indiana high school hoops. (Courtesy of Jeremiah Nickerson)

Oscar's teammate William "Bill" Hampton is one of the legends remembered on the wall at Attucks.

(Courtesy of Jeremiah Nickerson)

The tough and talented Willie Merriweather tried unsuccessfully to convince Oscar to join him at Purdue.

(Courtesy of Willie Merriweather)

A mini–Attucks reunion brought together, among others, Oscar, Hallie Bryant, Al Maxey, and James Enoch. (Courtesy of Al Maxey)

"Oscar was a god to me," said the late George McGinnis, who broke some of Oscar's scoring records in the late 1960s.

(Courtesy of Jeremiah Nickerson)

appeared on the front page of the *News* that could serve as a blueprint for veiled racism:

> The new colored high school is to have the name, so it seems to have been agreed, of Crispus Attucks. Of course, nobody knows who Crispus Attucks is, unless he has asked a school teacher or consulted an encyclopedia. It does not appear that his services were such as to call for commemoration of his somewhat unrememberable name. With the best intentions in the world, of course, the name was chosen, but will the pupils of the school be able to remember it, and pronounce it?

It is reasonable to ask if the Black community could have picked a name more befitting Indianapolis's history. Not this chronicler's place to say. Attucks it was, and Attucks it shall continue to be. There are bold-face names from the Harlem Renaissance that could have illustrated what Attucks became, such as Langston Hughes and Zora Neale Hurston. But that movement was only getting started when Attucks was being built. A relevant-to-Indianapolis choice would have been Madam C. J. Walker High School. Walker died in 1919 at age fifty-one, by which point she had established herself, through her salon, cosmetic line, and beauty training school, as one of the richest African Americans in the country. Her businesses were located on Indiana Avenue, not far from the Attucks site, and Brokenburr, a central figure in Attucks's battle to be recognized by the Indiana High School Athletic Association, was her lawyer and confidante. Walker was also a social activist and entrepreneur, whose motivation to build a theater came when she was asked to pay twenty-five cents to enter the Isis Theater on N. Illinois Street, fifteen cents more than the fee for a white patron. Alas, the Madam Walker Theatre, one of the Indiana Avenue structures still standing, didn't begin operations until eight years after her death. That was in 1927, the same year that Attucks opened. It would have been a perfect name, but it was just too revolutionary in the 1920s, one supposes, to name a school after a woman.

———

The Black man selected to lead this new school was thirty-nine-year-old Matthias Nolcox, who had been principal of middle school No. 26, the city's largest at the time. He had come from a tiny town in southwestern Indiana known as Lyles Station, which had been a gathering place for freed and sometimes fugitive slaves. The May 1927 announcement of Nolcox's hiring appeared in the *Indianapolis News* under the headline—not making this up—"News of Colored Folk." The building of a segregated school had been a page-one story for several years, yet the announcement of the man to lead that school was classified as "News of Colored Folk." It was another way to diminutize Black achievement. In fact, the two minority members of the school board, Fred Bates Johnson and Charles R. Yoke, voted *against* Nolcox, not because they didn't think he was a good choice but because, according to them, they had been given no voice in the decision to choose him.

Right before he got the job (which paid $3,500), Nolcox struck and killed a fourteen-year-old boy with his car. He was initially brought in on a charge of involuntary manslaughter but released, and the court concluded that he was not responsible. At any rate, the accident did not affect his hiring at Attucks.

Nolcox's major challenge was hiring a faculty. He was a serious man with a degree from Indiana University and a PhD in education from Harvard, and he took that challenge seriously. A piece in the *Indiana Magazine of History* says that Nolcox "combed the East Coast and as far west as Kansas" in a search for excellent faculty. Some candidates came to him. Teaching applications flooded into Attucks from Black candidates with advanced degrees who couldn't find jobs elsewhere, certainly not at white-dominated institutions. The pay at Attucks, which was a part of a public school system, albeit one that practiced segregation, was generally better than at historically Black colleges.

So, a national-class faculty was waiting when students entered Attucks. As was a national-class facility. Designed by Merritt Harrison (known as "the dean of Indianapolis architects") and Llewellyn Turnock, Attucks was a three-story red-brick building reflecting elements of both the Collegiate Gothic and Tudor Revival styles. The Society of Architectural Historians went gaga over Attucks, describing it thusly in its *SAH Archipedia*:

> The original three-story red brick building rests upon a polished granite foundation and has limestone sills and lavish terra-cotta trim. The main east facade has fifteen bays in groups of three, the center marked by a projecting one-story entrance pavilion topped with a terra-cotta balustrade. Separated by Corinthian columns, its three round arches boast spandrels ornamented with an open book design, all in terra-cotta. Above the entrance, between the second and third floors, are three rectangular terra-cotta tablets depicting musical instruments. The school's name is inscribed beneath the cornice.

The white press was predictably fulsome in its praise for the beneficence shown by the school board in building such a fine school for its minority population. A story in the *Indianapolis Sunday Star* a few days after Attucks opened was typical. Running under the subheadline "Crispus Attucks High School Specially Designed for Negro Students," it suggested that Attucks represented the first time that Blacks had "a building devoted exclusively to them." It never explained what that meant exactly.

But even the Black community, to an extent, plugged into the excitement of a new school. *Maybe this can work.* The *Indianapolis Recorder*, so critical of a segregated school and some of the actions of the "Klan board," waxed positive, at least about the faculty, in a piece about Attucks two days before the opening: "The school authorities are to be congratulated on the type of faculty selected. Practically all of the large colleges and universities are represented and outstanding results are expected from the teaching force. We feel certain that our boys and girls will be well taken care of from the point of view of instruction."

The article went on to compliment the school board, which had "wonderfully equipped" the school, and predicted that parents would be "delighted" that the variety of musical instruments suggested the school would have a band and an orchestra. Indiana Avenue, remember, was booming. Music was important, and, sure enough, Attucks would turn out scores of wonderful musicians.

Indeed, the opening of Attucks happened at a propitious time for the United States in the booming post–World War I era. Writer Bill Bryson would choose the Attucks opening year for his best-selling *One Summer: America, 1927,* which details several monumental moments, like the advent of the talking-picture era with the release of *The Jazz Singer* and the game-changing transition from the Ford Model T to the new Model A. Attucks opened on September 12, four months after the transatlantic flight of Charles Lindbergh, three weeks after Nicola Sacco and Bartolomeo Vanzetti met their deaths in the electric chair, and the day between Babe Ruth's fiftieth and fifty-first home runs. A civic snow blindness had overtaken Indianapolis. Think about it: A school system had gone *backward* in racial education, turning an integrated system, however imperfect, into a segregated one. But in those heady days of the Attucks unveiling, almost everyone spoke the language of the chamber of commerce.

Then again, two days before Attucks opened, the *Recorder* reported— alongside a positive story about Attucks, almost as if the paper wanted to remind everyone that it was business as usual in America—a variety of offenses against African Americans. "Hoodlums Attack Home" told the story of Charles Lewis, whose house on Indiana Avenue was shot up and stoned by white men. "Aged Negro's Property Pillaged" was about a Black man in Georgia named Thomas Murphy whose house had been burned to the ground and his wife and daughter killed by the Ku Klux Klan, apparently because he had amassed a small fortune of half a million dollars.

There were some reports that the Klan marched on the day that Attucks opened. But there was nothing about that in any of the newspapers, including the *Recorder*. What is undeniable is that hundreds of conflicts—less dramatic but all painful to varying degrees—occurred on that first day, as Black mothers and fathers pondered the reality that their kids were being told (not asked) to switch schools, and in many cases travel longer distances, because of the color of their skin. Dozens of young African Americans reported to their neighborhood schools of Manual, Tech, and Shortridge only to be turned away and sent to Attucks. Eighteen Black kids petitioned the school superintendent to allow them to return to their original schools. To no avail.

Nolcox and his staff were as prepared as they could be, but they were overwhelmed from day one. The school was built for 1,000, but by the time the students were corralled on September 12, the number was 1,350. Historian Stanley Warren says that thirty-six teachers were there on the first day, and an additional fifteen were added in the second semester; the *Recorder* puts the total number at forty-eight. Whatever, there weren't enough.

Still, there was a can-do attitude about the place from the beginning, a determination to prove the doubters wrong. In Ted Green's documentary, Morton-Finney reminds everyone that the educated African American was not in any way part of the American Dream. "We didn't *come* here; we were *brought* here. And we weren't brought here to be put in college. We weren't brought here to become lawyers and doctors and college graduates. We were brought here to labor, and that's what they want us to do to this day. And in order to carry out that kind of system, you have to have the people segregated, separated, classified, categorized."

Nolcox invited school superintendent Charles L. Miller (in an interview, Russell Lane, who followed Nolcox, would call Miller a "Ku-Kluxer") to visit Attucks on its opening day. "This is not a colored high school," Nolcox said. "It's a *high* school." There is no word on whether Miller came.

There were countless concerns about this new school, and one of them was the future of athletics. Hoose writes that a few days after Attucks opened, three Black leaders—F. E. DeFrantz of the Senate Avenue YMCA, Freeman Briley (known as F. B.) Ransom of the Madam C. J. Walker Company, and Rev. H. L. Herod of the Second Christian Church of Indianapolis—journeyed to Anderson, headquarters of the Indiana High School Athletic Association. Supplicants at the altar of the czar, they aimed to meet with Arthur Trester, then in his eleventh year as head of the IHSAA, to convince him to lift the manifestly discriminatory ban against Black and parochial schools' membership in the organization. There is no record of that meeting, and a story never appeared in any Indianapolis newspaper. We do know, however, that that delegation won the battle.

It only took sixteen years.

CHAPTER TEN

The Lone Blemish and Ray Crowe Is Not Amused

"From now on, no one has a guaranteed spot on this team."

A few days after his school opened in 1927, Matthias Nolcox was expecting chairs to complete the beautiful new Crispus Attucks auditorium. Before the delivery came, however, he discovered that the school district had ripped out chairs at Shortridge, given new chairs to that school, and was sending the old Shortridge chairs to Attucks. So Nolcox met the delivery on the sidewalk with crossed arms, and said, "Don't bring those in here."

According to his daughter, Joy, a 1948 Attucks grad who was interviewed by Ted Green for his documentary, Nolcox won that skirmish. But there were many, many losses. From the beginning, Attucks was overcrowded and under-resourced. Nolcox, other administrators, and the faculty fought a constant battle to procure (that's the right verb) up-to-date textbooks and materials. The science equipment and band instruments were all second-hand, and many of the athletic teams were outfitted with castoffs from Butler University.

It was never easy. There were transportation issues from the beginning. "For the first ten years or so there was no busing to Attucks," says current Attucks principal Lauren Franklin, "and the only way you could get here was to walk or pay for public transportation for yourself. That was a great hardship for many families." Stanley Warren said that very few kids rode their bikes to school. There was the risk of theft, and, anyway, "riding a bike wasn't considered cool."

And while motivated students could find a rich academic tapestry at Attucks from a talented faculty, the dropout rate was high, perhaps as high as 50 percent. To a large degree, Attucks was a Darwinian experiment: many did very well; many failed.

There were also subtle reminders of who was *really* in charge. Every call made by Nolcox or one of his administrators or teachers to beg for or borrow something needed for the students was received at the other end by a Caucasian. The superintendent, the board, the principals at other schools, the rival athletic directors—all *blindingly* white, an endlessly repeating power dynamic that slapped them in the face. There was even a subtle reminder in the Attucks building. As Randy Roberts points out in *"But They Can't Beat Us,"* the only Caucasian in the building when Attucks opened, and for decades afterward, was Sgt. Frank Whitlow, the school's first ROTC instructor. Writes Roberts, "Attucks would be an African American school, staffed and run almost exclusively by African Americans, but for a sensitive military position a white face was essential."

Also, there was tension from the beginning between Nolcox and the faculty, as well as between Nolcox and the Black community. "Nolcox was a man who pushed," said John Morton-Finney, and pushing wasn't always the way to go in Indianapolis. Green explored that topic in his documentary, noting that Nolcox received death threats at his home and needed a friend to stand guard from time to time. Another daughter, Verona (Attucks Class of 1942), says that at one point someone threatened the family with a shotgun.

More than ninety years later, it's hard to get at the specifics of Nolcox's firing. Even at the time, the *Indianapolis Recorder*, the place to go for accurate reporting about Black Indianapolis, was vague, stating that his administration had been "beset with trials." A story in the June 12, 1930, *Indianapolis Star* related that Nolcox was said to have "experienced difficulty in handling a factional difference among the faculty." Verona conceded that her father was an unbending man, not given to compromise, no sufferer of fools.

Whatever the cause, after three years of working to build a school from nothing, Nolcox was out, and in what would have been a cruelly ironic turn, a replacement named Thomas Jefferson Anderson was going to be in. But Anderson lacked necessary credentials, and Russell Lane, a respected English teacher who had been at Attucks from the beginning, was named in his stead. Lane stayed for the next twenty-seven years, while Nolcox was assigned to elementary schools, bitter that he had been replaced, the firing having "left a hole in his spirit," said his son Noble (Attucks Class of 1945) in the Green documentary.

Even Lane said that he didn't feel he had the full support of the Black community. "The [Black] community was very much up in arms because they didn't want the school, they didn't want Attucks to start off as a segregated school, and consequently I had to work over that," Lane said in an interview with the Indiana Historical Society. "So, I didn't worry about the support of the Black community at all. There were too many diverse opinions. Most of them didn't want it [the school]. And since you had it, I said, 'Let's do the best we can with it.'"

No one can match Lane's twenty-seven years of service. He has to be on any rendering of an Attucks Mount Rushmore. But there seems to be a connection, too, between Nolcox, first on the scene, and those iron-willed Attucks teams of the 1950s. It's not hard to imagine Oscar Robertson, so mature and strong even at age seventeen, standing shoulder to shoulder with Matthias Nolcox at the Attucks entranceway, holding up his hands and saying, "Don't even *think* about bringing those chairs in here."

———

As a segregated school, Attucks was not allowed to be part of the in-crowd of Indiana athletics for the first fifteen years of its existence. So, the athletic department, headed by a man named John Shelburne, had to get inventive to find opponents. The first Attucks yearbook in 1928 outlines a vast checkerboard of venues for the basketball team: Chicago, Louisville, Cincinnati, and Xenia, Ohio. Stanley Warren writes in an essay for the Indiana Historical Society that the 1930 Attucks basketball schedule included two games in Saint Louis and one each in Cincinnati, Lexington, Louisville, and Dayton. Opponents were usually other Black schools—Douglass High School of Evansville was among the integrated schools that would agree to a game—with a smattering of rural schools (which often wanted the sideshow of seeing actual African Americans) and parochial schools, Arthur Trester's other outcasts.[1] Much the same thing was going on at Roosevelt, a segregated-by-mandate high school that opened in Gary, Indiana, in 1928. (Roosevelt and Attucks would make history in 1955, the subject of Chapter 13.)

Things improved, obviously, after Attucks officially became a member of the Indiana High School Athletic Association in the early 1940s. After some initial reluctance, the other Indy city teams played Attucks

———

1. The most overlooked group in any account about Attucks is invariably the Indiana Catholic High School Athletic Association, though chronicling it is beyond the scope of this book. The best estimate is that there were eight African American schools and fourteen Catholic schools in the early 1940s, their pitched battle for acceptance involving not color but religious intolerance.

without protest—at least none that was reported—and the job of athletic director Alonzo Watford got a lot easier. But, for Attucks, it was never *normal*. So, let's put the Oscar-led teams into perspective.

From November 1954 until March 1956, the Crispus Attucks High School basketball team played sixty-three games. They won sixty-two of them. They were captives of a haphazard schedule that was dependent upon other facilities, the ones at Butler University and Indianapolis's Arsenal Technical High School most specifically. Unlike other high schools that adhered to a Tuesday-or-Friday game schedule, Attucks played on any day of the week except Sunday. The players often ate on the team bus, before and after games. John Gipson, a center on the 1955 and 1956 Attucks teams, estimated that 95 percent of the restaurants in the towns where Attucks played wouldn't serve Blacks. They were officiated almost 100 percent of the time by Caucasian referees, whose whistle blowing, to be fair, had improved since the early 1950s but was still suspect. Even when their talents were respected, the Attucks players were singled out as oddities, anomalies, their successes often described as feats of brawn, not brains. And all the time they were high school kids with studies and girlfriends and sometimes chaotic home lives and all sorts of other teenage problems.

Given all that, it is not surprising that Attucks had a brief stumble along the way in the 1954–1955 season. Nor was it surprising that it was well chronicled. It may have had something to do with race, but, on balance, the mainstream Indianapolis sporting press treated Attucks pretty much without mentioning color by the time Oscar was a junior and Ray Crowe was an established fixture on the bench. Attucks's slippage was news because that's the way journalism works. Reporters get tired of spitting out the same story line: "Attucks Dominates. Big Three Stars. Oscar Leads Tigers."

In early February 1955, there was (at last) another stream to follow: "Attucks Struggles." On February 1, Attucks nipped Hammond Noll

72–71. "Undoubtedly the Flying Tigers played their worst game of the season," wrote Wayne Fuson in the *Indianapolis News*. It came after a ten-day layoff ("I can't think of any other reason for all our fumbling and bungling tonight," opined Crowe); further, it occurred in the Hammond gym on what was supposed to be a "home" game at Butler. Plus, Hammond had a fine team that pressed rusty Attucks and was led by a terrific center named Ron Loneski.[2]

The hero of the Noll game was Bill Brown, who hit a late field goal for the winning margin. Brown was Crowe's prized sixth man, "the best relief pitcher in the state," as Bob Collins put it in the *Star*. "Bill Brown was a powerful, powerful jumper," remembers Carl Short, the Manual star. "They had Oscar and Merriweather and Sheddrick, but you never forgot about Brown."

Three days later Attucks beat Washington at the Tech gym by 75–45, yet drew this headline in the *News*: "Tigers Win by 30 but Lack Polish." You know you're a juggernaut when thirty-point wins are considered disappointments. Crowe may have known his charges were tired, as he let Attucks sit in a zone for most of the game. The coach was beginning to feel the strain—he collected the first technical of his career in the Washington game.

Two days later Attucks traveled to Connersville, a town about sixty miles east of Indianapolis, for what can be labeled a "trap game." A coach can often feel one coming in his bones. You won't necessarily lose a trap game, but the ingredients are there. A tired and irritated team yanked around by an irregular schedule. A funky gym with a hostile crowd. An opponent that is not formidable—Connersville had a mediocre 12–6 record—but is scrappy. And no matter how hard you tell your

2. As a Kansas Jayhawk, Loneski was a teammate of Wilt Chamberlain and started in the memorable 1957 NCAA championship game when North Carolina beat Kansas 54–53. Loneski was drafted in the tenth round of the 1959 NBA draft by the St. Louis Hawks but elected to go into the army. He served two terms in Germany and Vietnam, earning Bronze Stars for Valor and Meritorious Service, as well as a Purple Heart.

guys that an upset is possible, they don't buy it. That was the setup for Attucks-Connersville on February 5, 1955.

Connersville played an aggressive zone on what writer Bob Williams described as a "pitifully small floor." The Spartans shot rarely (only forty-two field goal attempts) but wisely (they made twenty-four of them, the .571 a terrific percentage for those days). Think Villanova against Georgetown in the 1985 NCAA final. The fourth quarter was played in what one reporter described as "atmospheric conditions that left the court slippery." Apparently, the floor was built over a swimming pool, and when authorities opened the doors to cool off the overcrowded gym, condensation settled on the floor. Oscar would later explain it meteorologically: "One of those low pressure fields—the kind that Indiana weathermen still like to talk about—moved in."

At any rate, chaos ensued on a surface that was more like a skating rink. Willie Merriweather was quoted in the following day's papers as saying that a Connersville player dribbled *into the stands* to avoid him and coasted in for a layup with no whistle forthcoming. He swears to this day that it happened. "I put my foot on the baseline and he absolutely went up on people's shoes sitting in the front row," said Merriweather in 2022.

Despite Robertson's game-high twenty-two points, which included a jumper from the corner with five seconds left, Connersville held on to win 58–57 and celebrated like they had won the state championship. The following day's *Indianapolis Star* put this headline in type that suggested World War III had broken out: "Attucks Beaten by Connersville."

Starting guard Bill Hampton subscribed to the overdog/underdog theory. "We really didn't take them seriously enough," he said in an interview. "They got a lead on us, and they started playing controlled basketball. But I guess we learned from it."

One thing they learned was that Crowe did not accept losing with the same equanimity that he once had. He openly tossed blame at his backcourt of Scott and Hampton (*nominal* backcourt because Oscar often controlled the ball) and ordered up what some remember as a five-hour practice on the Monday following the Saturday game. Scott told author Phillip Hoose that Crowe ordered his fastest player, Johnny Mack Brown, to lead the team in fifty laps around the court and said that "Johnny better not pass anybody." When the track meet was finished, Crowe informed the team, "From now on, no one has a guaranteed spot on this team. You will have to earn your position every single game." Remember that Crowe was addressing a team that had just lost its first game of the season. By one point. On the road. "I don't remember every-thing that happened that day," says Merriweather now, "but I do remem-ber that statement: 'No one has a guaranteed spot.'"

Oscar says that for the next six decades, anyone he met from Con-nersville would bring up the game. "They seem to forget we beat them by fifty-something next time we played," he said in his podcast with the Indiana Basketball Hall of Fame. (Actually, it was twenty-six points.)

Attucks won its next game easily, by 82–39 over Cathedral, proving that Oscar could take a game off if he so desired. He scored only eight points and fouled out with two minutes to go in the *third* period, "the only Tiger off form," as Fuson put it. The *Indianapolis Star* posited that Cathedral had held Oscar down. Attucks's 53–33 win over Manual was also treated negatively: "Tigers Held to Season Low" was the headline in the *News*.

At this point, Attucks regained its bearings, if it can be accurately said that its bearings had been loose. They beat Howe 90–61 as Oscar's thirty-seven points enabled him to surpass Hallie Bryant's twenty-game record of 417. Fuson wrote that Howe appeared to be "dazed" by Attucks.

From a February 17 game until the state final on March 19, few if any high school basketball teams, certainly among those in a basketball-dominant state, were more consistently brilliant than Oscar's Attucks Tigers (until the 1955–1956 version of Attucks). But it's not like everybody knew that would happen. With the state tournament about to begin, members of the *Indianapolis News* made their championship predictions, among them Fort Wayne Central, Kokomo, and Muncie Central. Attucks got a couple votes, too, and over at the *Star*, Bob Collins went with Attucks all the way.

The first step in the state tourney was frequently the toughest and the one that drew the most attention: the sectional, which drew teams from the Indianapolis vicinity. But this was the wrong year to expect suspense. After Attucks routed Washington 79–51—Oscar had twenty-three points, but the big surprise was Hampton with sixteen—they faced two stalling teams in a row, Manual and Broad Ripple. The respective scores were 87–36 and 33–19. At one point during the Ripple game, Oscar and opponent Dave Freeman (one of Ripple's top scorers with, ahem, two points) were chatting away like they were sitting at a soda shop. As much as Attucks did to obliterate them, vestiges of the old Indiana basketball still surfaced from time to time. Then the Tigers easily beat Shortridge 73–59, behind twenty-six points by Oscar, twelve in a decisive fourth quarter. After the game, Oscar offered a rare observation: "I think we can take it." Players were not routinely quoted in those days; coaches did most of the talking, so that qualified as absolute bravado from the mouth of Oscar. Crowe tried to get Oscar to open up more to journalists, but Oscar usually demurred. It was Crowe's third straight sectional championship, a monumental achievement for an Indianapolis basketball team.

Around this time another Robertson wormed his way into the news: Flap Robertson, now at Indiana Central University (ICU) and once the only Robertson that anyone knew, scored thirty-one points in a game to crack the record for Hoosier college basketball players with 2,201 points. It speaks to the mania surrounding high school basketball that Flap's team rarely got coverage, even though ICU stood on the south side of town and played an entertaining and wide-open brand of ball. Flap had free rein to fire away; Stanley Warren saw him play from time to time and swears that, after a basket by the opposition, Flap would never take the ball out. "He wanted to be the one *getting* the ball," says Warren, "because once he did he wasn't giving it back." "Best brother act" in years ran a caption under a newspaper photo that showed Oscar and Flap together.

Before the regional, which appeared (and turned out) to be a fait accompli for Attucks, Crowe served up a giant-sized bowl of coaching cliché in an interview with the *Indianapolis News*. He said his starters "concentrate[d] on their basketball harder than other boys" and added that they were "above average in school, too."[3]

But the fact that this was pablum doesn't mean it wasn't true. There was indeed a seriousness of purpose around the Attucks team that emitted from several sources. Crowe was the principal one. He, more than anyone, knew what a title would mean, to his race, to the general racial climate, to the school, to the city, and in no small measure to himself. He may have even thought that winning a state championship was *expected* of him in this, his fifth season.

The Crowemen were unusually businesslike for a high school team, particularly the two stars, Oscar and Merriweather. When your best players set a serious tone, there's a good chance everyone will follow. To name one, Edgar Searcy, a 6'4" sophomore who would be one of the best players in the state by his senior year, fed into that maturity and always played beyond his years.

---

3. After the regional, a story and photo appeared in the *Indianapolis News* about Oscar and Attucks reserve Willie Burnley taking an advanced Algebra 4 course, while Willie Merriweather, Bill Hampton, Bill Scott, and Johnny Mack Brown were taking an advanced composition course. (Burnley died from lung cancer at age twenty-five in 1963, and Oscar, by then an NBA star, was one of those who played in a benefit game in his honor.) One could detect principal Russell Lane directing this press operation. Whenever Oscar was asked about his future, he said he wanted to be an engineer. Don't laugh. There was not much talk about an NBA career at that point because the league had such a low profile, something that would change with the coming of Black players like Bill Russell, Wilt Chamberlain, Elgin Baylor, and, eventually, Oscar.

Double-digit wins against Wilkinson (95–42; Oscar had twenty-six points and sat out the final ten minutes) and Anderson (76–51; Oscar had thirty-one points and ten rebounds) pushed Attucks to the state's Sweet Sixteen and a likely showdown with Muncie Central at Butler in what was called the "Indianapolis Semifinal." "That Attucks-Muncie match is floating around in everyone's mind like a lost bomb looking for a spot to explode," wrote Bob Collins, mixing up some metaphors in the *Star*. For much of the season the teams had toggled between one and two in the state. Muncie didn't have anyone to match Robertson as an individual, but it had a solid all-around team and a tough interior player in John Casterlow, an African American with tragedy in his future. Muncie also had a storied basketball history, especially compared to the recent success of Attucks under Crowe. Even more than in its game against Milan, Attucks would play the role of outsider.

CHAPTER ELEVEN

Basketball and Blood in the Same Town Square

"There was a feeling of lawlessness around Marion at that time."

Another detour into the black heart of Indiana's racial past. On August 7, 1930, as Attucks prepared for its fourth season as a segregated school, Marion, Indiana, a town about a ninety-minute drive northeast of Indianapolis, became the racial flashpoint of the nation. What happened on a summer night in Marion is a lurid tale tethered to the darkest parts of American history, yet one with a distinctly Hoosier flavor too, a midwestern Gothic that begins with a bouncing basketball. Its tie to the Attucks narrative is admittedly loose but demonstrates how close to the surface the capacity for racial violence lay, how tenuously held the idea of equality was, and how a veneer of civility hid a simmering capacity for violence in the Hoosier state.

Go back to March 1926. In Indianapolis they are fighting about the construction and the naming of a Black high school. There is precious little basketball tradition in the capital city. But, ah, not in Marion. On the evening of March 14 of that year, there wasn't a town in the state more shot through with joy than Marion. Several hours earlier, at the Indianapolis Exposition Building before about one thousand fans who had made the drive, the town's beloved high school basketball team won the storied Indiana state championship. The local newspaper reported that following the tournament win, "the public square was filled with people," the celebration lasting through the night.

Yes, the public square. It was the center of civic life in the Grant County seat, as it was in so many Hoosier communities. Proudly patriotic, the town elders had just erected a monument to those brave Marioners who had died in World War I. Two of the dead were Black, which you knew because a parenthetical "Col." appeared next to their names. (It took a long while, but Bill Munn, the official Grant County historian, finally got that designation removed from the names of Rollins Wade and William Cromwell.)

Marion's victim in that 1926 championship game—the final score was 30–23 in those low-scoring times—was Martinsville High School, whose starting five included a sophomore guard named John Wooden. Wooden was held scoreless in this game, though greater glory awaited him the next season when Martinsville returned to the state final and won. This Marion team was something special; two of its players are still vividly remembered almost a century after that championship, the first of eight won by Marion, which ties them for most in the state with Muncie Central, another team linked tightly to this narrative (see Chapter 12). Those players were Bob Chapman, a 6'3" scholar athlete who would go on to star in basketball at Michigan—he was also senior class president and was voted "Best Looking Male" in *The Cactus*, the Marion High yearbook—and 6'7" Charles Murphy, who would shortly become a teammate of Wooden's at Purdue, where he would acquire the nickname Stretch. "He is my choice for best center ever from Indiana,"

Wooden would say later of Stretch. A caricature of an elongated Murphy appeared in *The Cactus* with birds resting on his shoulders.

As was the custom, a huge bonfire was built for the celebration in the square—when did fire first follow triumph?—and it burned so hot that the scorched courthouse steps had to be rebuilt. The celebration lasted until daylight and, in a sense, went on for a long time after that. In the weeks that followed, the Giants were guests of honor at countless banquets and civic gatherings. We have seen this before in Indiana, this harmonic convergence of town and team, right? Homer Stonebraker and tiny Wingate. Fuzzy Vandivier and the Wonder Five of Franklin. Were the name of Stretch Murphy to appear on the ballot for mayor of Marion tomorrow, he'd probably get a few votes. A year after the championship, Marion, so proud of its champions, built itself a new arena. Small wonder that, as the city celebrated the victory, Mayor Bob Diglett proclaimed, "Tonight we are the toast of Indiana."

Four years later, in that same town square, a celebration of a quite different character unfolded. At about 6:30 p.m. on August 7, 1930, a crowd began to gather at the square, having heard rumors that a perverted brand of twentieth-century justice was about to be administered. The crowd steadily grew and, according to some estimates, peaked at about five thousand, one-quarter of Marion's population, though surely some outsiders had joined the throng.

They were waiting—many of them *hoping*—to witness their first lynching.

Early that morning, four Black teenagers—Thomas Shipp, nineteen; Abram Smith, eighteen; James Cameron, sixteen; and Robert Sullivan, age unknown—had been arrested for allegedly shooting a twenty-four-year-old local man named Claude Deeter, the friend or fiancé or sometime lover of a nineteen-year-old woman named Mary Ball, who claimed that she had been raped by Smith.

For reasons that remain unclear, Sullivan was subsequently released, but the other three were being held in separate cells in the county jail, a medieval-looking fortress hard by the town square. The mob grew steadily larger and, as is usual with mobs, steadily angrier. Several were armed with sledgehammers from the Marion Machine Foundry, where they were employed. Marion was a union town and accustomed to labor-inspired violence.

In his book *A Lynching in the Heartland*, historian James Madison wrote that Ball's father, Hoot Ball, shouted to sheriff Jake Campbell, "Give us the keys, and let us get the ni—ers. If this was your daughter, you would do just the same as I am doing. . . . [T]he court will give them about two years." That was what the mob used for justification: an alleged lenient justice system.

The police made no move to disperse the crowd, and eventually the men decided to storm the jail. The crowd was estimated at between thirty-five and seventy-five people. It's widely believed that the police hung Deeter's bloody shirt out of a window—"The department absolutely participated in this," says historian Munn—as a kind of signal to unleash the violence. At this point a woman named Flossie Bailey, state president of the NAACP and a Marion resident, called Campbell and warned him that there was a plan to lynch prisoners. According to an *Indiana State History Blog* post, Campbell checked the garage and found that municipal cars had been drained of gasoline and their tires flattened, removing the possibility that prisoners could be transferred in the event of violence. But the sheriff did nothing.

Bailey also called the governor, Harry G. Leslie, and reached his secretary, L. O. Chasey, who was acting in Leslie's stead. The secretary hung up on her. Chasey was a Marion resident and a good friend of the sheriff. So there was no stopping the mob, propelled by its own violent energy.

———

Back in the 1920s, as Indianapolis was building a segregated high school and beginning to separate the middle and elementary schools by race, Marion thought of itself as progressive. The Roaring Twenties were on, and Marion's Blumenthal's Department Store proudly advertised the "new French lingerie."

Certainly Marion was a place open to many and varied viewpoints. The town square itself told that story. In the year 1900 alone, Theodore Roosevelt, William Jennings Bryan, and union firebrand Eugene Debs all came to Marion to speak. That year was one of five times that Debs ran for president as a member of the Socialist Party, and of the three speakers, Debs—the Bernie Sanders of his time—drew by far the largest crowd.

Five years before that, another union favorite, Mary Harris Jones, aka Mother Jones, known then as "the most dangerous woman in America," had spoken in front of the Grant County Courthouse. The sixty-five-year-old Mother Jones was on a crusade for the striking United Mine Workers, and her speech was well received: "Pray for the dead and fight like hell for the living." The Socialist Party had finished second in the 1919 city elections, behind the Republicans but well ahead of the Democrats.

If Marion had one collective community allegiance, it was to the concept of quality public education. The newspapers were full of students competing in spelling and "ciphering" bees, Latin and declamatory contests, and tournaments to determine the best artist, as well as the best typist and shorthand taker. One essay contest that took place right before the violence in the town square was about Abraham Lincoln, who, though not born a Hoosier, was raised one, in southern Indiana; the state still likes to claim him.

A small but vibrant African American community flourished in Marion, which had been part of the Underground Railroad in Civil War times. When Booker T. Washington died in 1915, a Black Marion architect named Samuel Plato arranged for an honorary service and convinced the white mayor to deliver a eulogy. The local Marion newspaper reported on "Black Happenings" from time to time, albeit almost always in a patronizing tone.

And as far as building a segregated school? Not in Marion, where schools were integrated. In 1925, as Attucks was being built in the capital city, an African American student named Leonard Weaver received 190 votes to win Marion High's "School Nuisance" award; he repeated that victory by a larger margin the next year. Surely that *had* to be an honor. Ovid Casey, a terrific football player who in 1928 also became the first Black basketball player for Marion, was another prominent Black student; he went on to star on the Yale football team. Other African American students mentioned in *The Cactus* were Mamie C. Hal, who had come from Chicago, and Lola Fouce, described as "reliable, energetic, artistic" and the winner of a Penmanship Certificate.

But look closer. The Black community had no illusions about equality. They couldn't swim in the public pool in Marion and were restricted to the balcony in the downtown Indianapolis Theater. And African Americans were still the exception in school; those who lasted all the way through Marion High were invariably the strongest and most talented and likely came from parents with the most money, who would not demand that they quit school and go to work.

They also had to endure the slights typical of the day. In his *A Lynching in the Heartland*, Madison writes about a 1921 project at the high school in which the students talked about ancestry and admirably included five African American biographies. Admirable except that the parenthetical "Col." followed each of their names, just as it did on the town square memorial. "It was this peculiar idea that you always had to *mark* Black people," said Madison in an interview.

There was always a sense of separation, a singling out[1] of the African American, a tone-deafness and lack of empathy. Here's an example of "humor" from the 1925 *Cactus*:

White Boy—What have you got such a short nose for?
Colored Boy—I 'spect so it won't poke itself into other people's business.

Marion, like many other places in Indiana, had its dalliances with the Klan. Madison reports on a "massive parade and Klan initiation ceremony" that took place in Marion on November 26, 1922. Seven trumpeters on horseback were followed by an electrically lighted cross mounted on an automobile and hundreds of Klansmen on foot from places like Indianapolis and Muncie. And while the murder trial of D. C. Stephenson had weakened the organization there, just as it had in other places, there was strong pro-Klan sentiment, particularly when things got tough at the foundry, the primary source of employment in Marion. A series of wage cuts helped the Klan message—*Blacks are stealing your jobs!*—resonate with much of Marion.

But remember this: the Ku Klux Klan, as an organization, did not induce what happened in Marion on an August night in 1930. Klan-like beliefs maybe, but not the Klan itself.

"There was a feeling of lawlessness around Marion at that time," says Munn. "There were letters sent to the attorney general of Indiana complaining of exactly that. I know that sounds like the classic economic rationale for what happened. But there were no social services. You ran out of money, you didn't eat. It was a terrible time in the city."

---

1. That didn't happen just to Blacks. Troy Paino writes in his piece for the *Journal of Sports History* that the 1919 Anderson High School yearbook nicknamed the team's center Henry "Jew" and wrote that "in spite of his looks he is some jumper at center."

On October 24, 1929, about ten months before the violence, the big story in Marion was not the fall of the stock market on Black Thursday. It was a bomb set off under the car of a union official, the second such incident in two weeks. Between October 1929 and February 1930, five men died in bombings, all members of Mould Makers Union Local No. 36; no one was ever indicted for the crimes.

So, the Marion lynch mob, already enflamed by economic tensions, the belief that Blacks were *taking over*, and a distrust of what they considered a too-liberal justice system, had learned of the arrests of the Black teens. They knew Deeter, and they knew that Mary Ball was white. The local newspaper, backed by several accounts, said the mob was "encouraged by women, many holding small babies, and young girls." (Racial violence almost always crossed genders.) The mob used heavy traffic signs to batter its way into the prison. Officers later said that the mob leaders were armed and threatened the deputies with death unless keys were produced.

There are conflicting accounts, but Madison writes in *A Lynching in the Heartland* that the mob first reached Shipp and lynched him from the jail window bars as he was being beaten, then later dragged outside. It's not clear—nor does it matter much—whether he died from the beating or the hanging. Smith was beaten inside the jail and then lynched from a maple tree in the town square. There was evidence that Mary Ball had been sexually involved with Smith and that the liaison was widely known around town.

Preserving the virtue of white womanhood against acts of miscegenation was often a factor in lynchings throughout the South. "The third rail in American society for black men is still white women," says Lanier Holt, an associate professor at Ohio State. (Indiana was the second-to-last state, just ahead of Maryland, to have an antimiscegenation law on the books. It was not repealed until 1965.)

Cameron was in another part of the prison, and it took the men a while to find him. They dragged him to the center square, not far from where the celebratory basketball bonfire had burned so brightly four years earlier, and started to put a noose around his neck. But shouts came from the crowd that he was innocent, and he was spared. As the lifeless bodies of Shipp and Smith hung beside him, Cameron was taken back to prison. He later became an activist for Black causes and always claimed that he had been spared by divine intervention. Madison presents two possible candidates who spoke up to spare Cameron's life: Sol Ball, Mary Ball's uncle, and Rex George, head of the Marion branch of the American Legion.

Others point to the pleas of a young man who had been in the Marion High Class of 1926 and who would die a war hero in 1937. Munn identified him as Walter Grant.[2]

As the lifeless bodies of Smith and Shipp swung in the soupy summer air, the rioters continued to stab them, and an attempt was made to burn them. The Marion fire department showed up and unrolled hoses to disperse the crowd, but, according to Munn, "They got a call from downtown, and the chief said, 'Roll 'em up, boys, we're not going to turn the hoses on these people.'"

Inquiring journalists could have secured any number of comments from the murder site, but the *New York Times* selected two telling ones. A barber told the *Times* reporter that the lynching had "served its purpose if it prevented a recurrence of such crimes." And a Sunday school teacher said the lynching was a good thing because "such animals were removed from society." She apparently had her lesson for that week.

The double murder remains extraordinary for two reasons: it was the northernmost lynching ever recorded, and it came so late in time. It laid bare the fact that lynchings were shared civic rituals, almost like

2. Munn believes that Grant stood up amid this raging, out-for-blood crowd and pleaded for Cameron's life. Grant became obsessed by the killing, indignant that no one had stepped forward to stop it or later decried it. "Where were the pastors, the Christian men?" said Grant, who seven years later died by artillery fire in a dusty valley near Zaragoza, Spain.

community picnics. Marion's residents drifted by on foot or in their cars, many of them stopping to chat, as casually and neighborly as if they were viewing a band concert on a warm summer night. Some swear that every white person in town—man, woman, child—came by to bear witness, though that cannot be reliably verified, and Munn believes it an exaggeration. Needless to say, Black Marion residents stayed away.

With the proud lynchers crowding around the bodies, spectators cut clothing from the dead teens and stripped bark from the lynching tree for souvenirs. Many drove through Marion, dragging cans from their bumpers and shooting guns in the air, a sign of triumph known as *belling*. Others, the *Indianapolis Recorder* reported, later drove past the victims' houses, shouting, "We have lynched your sons, now cry your eyes out."

The bodies hung until 5:45 the following morning, when the sheriff finally cut them down. All through the night cars cruised by for passengers to have a look. It was a spectacle, a show, a demonstration of strength and power, the very point of lynching being the postdeath display, the ritualistic warning that *this could happen to you.*

A local photographer named Lawrence Beitler, working in a nearby office, heard the hubbub, ran over to the square, and snapped a photo of the madness, capturing both the limp bodies dangling in the background and the celebratory crowd in the foreground. The photograph defies description. Most of the spectators are looking directly into Beitler's lens, aware and utterly unashamed that they have been snapshotted into a gruesome chapter of American history. A few are smiling. One man, who bears an eerie and uncanny resemblance to Adolf Hitler, points to the bodies, as if Beitler might miss the point of the evening's festivities.

Except for the funeral photo of Emmett Till—his casket open so that his beaten body could be displayed, a decision made by his mother—that single photo taken by Beitler is the most iconic of lynching images, capturing not just the abject cruelty of the act but also the casual complicity of the crowd, the idea of murder as civic amusement.

After taking the snap, Beitler rushed home, developed the photo, and over the next few days sold thousands of copies at fifty cents apiece, working twenty hours a day to get it done.[3] The photo was circulated far and wide and, even to a nation accustomed to violence against Blacks, the image was searing. Of the 4,743 confirmed lynchings (surely there were more) in the United States between 1882 and 1968, the murders of Shipp and Smith, and their subsequent showcasing, remain among the most remembered.

Several years later a New Yorker named Abel Meeropol, a teacher and social activist, saw the photo and became so distressed that he wrote a poem titled "Bitter Fruit."

Black body swinging in the Southern breeze,
strange fruit hanging from the poplar trees.

Eventually Meeropol put his verse to music and gave it to a nightclub owner, who eventually gave it to jazz immortal Billie Holiday, who changed the title to "Strange Fruit" and turned it into her most haunting work, one that she was barred from performing on several occasions because it hit too close to the truth of America.

The closer someone was to Marion, the less likely he or she was to see Beitler's photo. To this day the photo has never appeared in a Marion newspaper. The *Indianapolis Times* said at the time that it would not run the photo because it served "no purpose of journalism catering only to morbid tastes." The *Indianapolis Star* said it would not publish the photo

---

3. That conjures up the first line of "Desolation Row": "They're selling postcards of the hanging." According to several sources, a man named Abe Zimmerman witnessed the 1920 lynching of three African American circus workers in Duluth, Minnesota, and told his son, Robert Zimmerman, about it. The son, by then known as Bob Dylan, turned it into one of his songs on the 1961 album *Highway 61 Revisited*, one of his greatest.

because it showed "grewsome [*sic*] details that might better be left to the imagination of the reader."

But that doesn't mean the press acted responsibly. The *Star* ran a story with a lede that read, "The lynching of two Marion Negroes was not without its humorous vein," followed by the not-at-all-humorous story of two prisoners, James Ailey and William Harrigan, returning themselves to confinement after they were freed in the chaos.

In subsequent days a theme reverberated in newspapers—that the murder and lynching were justified because the crowd could reasonably expect that the guilty parties were going to get off. "Laxity of Courts Is Given as Spur to Lynching Mob" was a headline in the August 12 edition of the *Indianapolis Times*, and an editorial in the hometown *Marion Chronicle* echoed that theme. The reaction to the violence by another local newspaper, the *Grant County Democrat*, is nothing less than flabbergasting, even given the tenor of the times. The same paper that celebrated Latin contests and flapper lingerie wrote this in an editorial the day after the lynching: "Were the punishment of criminals swift and sure, there would be little or no incentive to mob violence. While mob violence is not to be condoned, it is well that we look the situation squarely in the face and recognize the condition out of which it springs."

The editorial went on to decry the spirit of lawlessness that is "going on all over the country," which is what spurred "otherwise good citizens to commit an unlawful act." In other words, it wasn't the mob's fault; it was the country's fault. That's not far from some of the rationale given for the January 6, 2021, attack on the US Capitol.

The county prosecutor, Harley Hardin, in a quite extraordinary piece of legal philosophy, all but echoed that viewpoint in an interview with the *New York Times* shortly after the lynching. Here's part of that story: "Asked concerning possible action against members of the mob, he [Hardin] shrugged his shoulders. 'I might get indictments, but I doubt very much that I could get a conviction,' he said. 'The self satisfaction of the people over the lynching is a psychological matter resting on dissatisfaction of verdicts returned by juries and the sentences imposed. The people feel that the only way to get justice is to take the law into their own hands.'"

It is difficult not to reflect on the 1926 basketball celebration in that same space and a town so happy, so proud, so united. And four years later? Who exactly among the town's leaders was among the spectators? Who gave tacit endorsement to the display? Basketball was still the king in town, drawing crowds of up to seventeen thousand at the Marion Coliseum built after the state tournament win in 1926. Was the basketball coach at the lynching? Any players from the state championship team? The athletic director? Stretch Murphy was preparing for his lone season with the Chicago Bruins, a team owned by George Halas. Did he hear about it? Rush back to town? Say anything about it? Only a few townspeople have ever admitted to being there, the rest apparently subscribing to a kind of omertà of shame, but community outrage was at a minimum. No one from the white Marion establishment athletic community spoke up, at least not in a public forum. The only concerted pushback came from the NAACP's Flossie Bailey, who until her death in 1952 fought unflinchingly for Black rights and against the existential evil of lynching. The 1931 *Cactus* said not a word about the lynching. The world went on.

The best estimate of the total lynchings in Indiana is twenty, all of them except Marion in the early part of the twentieth century. By 1930, acts of racial terror against Blacks had pretty much been decriminalized and moved indoors. Now they were called "executions," many of which followed sham trials. "Marion sticks out in racial history because Indiana had supposedly solved its lynching problems by 1903," said Madison in a 2022 interview. "So, we're left to ponder why it happened. The labor problems, the economic unrest, sure, those are significant. But they're happening in Muncie, Kokomo, Anderson, and all across the state and in America. Certainly the white-woman-black-man factor is significant.

This much we know: If Claude Deeter had been black, there would've been no lynching."

By midnight, news of the murders had spread outside Marion. Rev. John E. Johnson, a pastor at Shaffer Chapel and sometime mortician in Muncie, a town about thirty miles from Marion, was concerned that Marion had no Black undertakers. So he drove to Marion, a parlous trip to be sure, given the circumstances, retrieved the bodies, and drove back with them. A crowd of angry whites congregated at Johnson's mortuary in Muncie. They wanted the bodies. That was often the rule at lynchings—victims were not to be given a proper burial. But a group of white policemen and local African Americans protected the mortuary. Muncie sheriff Fred Puckett, who was white, organized a posse to escort Johnson and the bodies back to the county line, and Johnson delivered them to the families.

An all-white, all-male jury (which pretty much went without saying in those days) found Cameron guilty of being an accessory to voluntary manslaughter. His attorneys were Robert Brokenburr and his law partner, Robert L. Bailey. (Bailey's daughter was Harriette Bailey Conn, an Attucks grad who fought tirelessly for civil rights.) Cameron served two years and was pardoned in 1993 by Indiana governor Evan Bayh. As for the individuals who took part in the murder/lynching, no indictments were ever returned by Grant County grand juries. Does that even need to be said? "That was the problem with lynching," says Bryan Stevenson. "You could engage in lynchings with impunity. They were invulnerable to the law. There would never be any accountability."

From time to time, the events of 1930 are remembered, not in a good way. Several years ago, Illinois's Elgin Arts Commission put into storage a mural by a local artist named David Powers that depicted the crowd (the Hitler-looking guy is front and center) at the Marion lynching. The painting did not show Shipp and Smith, and the commission displayed it for twelve years before realizing what it portrayed. It depicts "monsters" was Powers's take on his work, but the arts commission thought it unnecessarily provocative.

At this writing, movements to erect a memorial in the town square have gone nowhere. The opposition may seem surprising, coming as it does from family members of the victims, but they have a strong reason: they're afraid that any memorial will be desecrated. There is much precedent. A sign near the Tallahatchie River in Mississippi, erected near the site where Emmett Till's body was discovered in 1955, has been repeatedly dented by gunfire.

A postscript: In 2022 Congress passed the Emmett Till Antilynching Act, which made lynching a federal hate crime. Efforts to federalize the crime had been ongoing for 120 years, and some two hundred other measures had failed.

A second postscript: In April 2023, the Tennessee legislature was discussing a bill that would add options for state executions. "Could I put an amendment on that that would include hanging on a tree, also?" offered Paul Sherrell, a Republican. Sherrell was removed from the Justice Committee, though at this writing continues to serve.

CHAPTER TWELVE

Attucks-Muncie: A Game for the Ages

"They weren't on the same team, but they were in the same place."

A t Butler Fieldhouse on March 12, 1955, the fans got what they wanted. First, Attucks dispatched Columbus, which had come within an Oscar free throw of beating the Tigers the previous season. The final was 80–62. Then Muncie beat Rushville 65–48 in the second game of the afternoon. So, what most pollsters considered the two best teams in the state would be meeting in the Indianapolis semifinal that night for the right to be one of the final four teams in the state.

The contrasts between Attucks and Muncie were stark. Attucks was known for its failures in the postseason, Muncie for its tournament successes with state championships in 1928, 1931, 1951, and 1952, a résumé as gilded as any in the Hoosier state. Attucks had a gym so small that games could not be played in it. Muncie played in a showstopping venue, Muncie Fieldhouse, the setting not just for basketball but also community events and big-time acts like the Globetrotters, the Supremes, and Abbott and Costello. You could barely fit all three Supremes in the Attucks gym, and you definitely couldn't if you added Costello.

Muncie Central opened in 1868 with six students, the result of an earnest town wishing to educate its younger generation. Attucks opened in 1927, the product of fear and ignorance. Attucks was an outlier in a bewildering and openly racist big-city educational system. Muncie was such an iconic Midwestern town that it had been the subject of two seminal sociocultural studies about, well, an iconic midwestern town. They were *Middletown: A Study in Modern American Culture* (1929) and the follow-up, *Middletown in Transition: A Study in Cultural Conflicts* (1937), both by Robert S. Lynd and Helen Merrell Lynd. Both books are still staples on college syllabi.

In this battle, Attucks, the big-city team, was more the small-town rube, unaccustomed to succeeding in the bright lights, the avatar for all those failed Indianapolis teams of the past, in contrast to Muncie, comfortably cast as the favorite in an arena where small-town teams usually emerged victorious. Just a year earlier, after all, Muncie had been beaten by even-smaller Milan after Milan had dispatched Attucks.

As some saw it, there was a further contrast in coaching. Muncie's Jay McCreary was already a certified legend. He had been an outstanding player on Frankfort's state championship team in 1936, as well as a key contributor for Branch McCracken's 1940 NCAA champions at Indiana, and had already won a state championship as a coach at Muncie. Ray Crowe? Who was he? What did we know about his playing heroics at Whiteland High School and Indiana Central? Where the hell is Whiteland, and who cares about Indiana Central? A letter writer to the *Indianapolis Star* showed nothing less than contempt for Attucks before the game, criticizing writer Jep Cadou Jr. for "stupid articles" about "how wonderful these Attucks teams are until you get them believing it," and made this prediction: "Muncie will beat Attucks, or any other Indianapolis team, by 20 points if they care to pour it on!"

An idle fan's opinion is one thing; there was also this comment about the Attucks-Muncie showdown from Charles Morris, coach of the Wilkinson High team that had gotten beat 95–42 by Attucks in the regionals: "Get a club with the physical equipment Attucks has and you'll find the club to beat them. I think Muncie will do it. Taking nothing away from Ray Crowe, but Jay McCreary will probably whip Attucks from the bench. All it's going to take is some good tall boys and some good coaching."

It's all there, all the veiled, dismissive, racially cast language about Attucks. *They only win because they're physically gifted. They'll get beat by superior brainpower on the bench. We just need some good tall boys, not these* Black *tall boys.*

———

The portrait of Muncie in the *Middletown* books is nuanced and impossible to boil down in this space; the Lynds, after all, spent over one thousand pages deconstructing this town about sixty miles northeast of Indianapolis. In summary, Muncie came across like many Indy towns, like many towns everywhere, a mixture of good and bad folks, most falling somewhere in the middle, interested in raising their families and bettering their lives. But since this was Indiana—either the southernmost northern state or the northernmost southern state—race played a major part in the Middletown narrative. As it did in so many places in the 1920s, the Klan flourished in Muncie. A 1923 photo shows a huge Klan rally in the town, with an estimated thirty thousand participants. At the same time, Muncie also produced one of the most fascinating Klan opponents of that era: George Dale, editor of the local *Post-Democrat*. In the spirit of H. L. Mencken, Dale capitalized on every opportunity to skewer the Klan, in print and in cartoon. He took particular delight in lampooning the fact that the KKK had managed to get a local resolution passed that Jesus Christ was not a Jew but rather a white Protestant born in America. Dale's life was threatened on numerous occasions for printing anti-Klan satire; *Hoosier State Chronicles* called him "Indiana's

Jazz Age version of a Jon Stewart or Stephen Colbert." Indianapolis had no one like George Dale. The principal press weapon against the Klan was the Black-owned *Indianapolis Recorder*, and journalists there found it hard to turn the Klan into a laughing matter.

Another great source of material about Muncie exists—a memoir titled *Outside Shooter* by Philip Raisor, a Muncie player who became an acclaimed poet. Much of *Outside Shooter* is about two basketball games, for fate brought Raisor into a pair of unforgettable Hoosier state classics: Muncie's loss to Milan in the previous season's state final (Bobby Plump's last shot) and the 1955 game against Attucks.

In the book and in a 2022 interview, Raisor, a professor emeritus of English at Old Dominion, describes a complex racial dynamic within the structure of the town and the team, both of which were racially mixed—but only to a point. As there were for African Americans in Indianapolis, there were places in Muncie that Blacks dare not go, such as the Elks Club, which was the center of Muncie boosterism. In the second *Middletown* book, the Lynds write, "The cleft between the white and the Negro people of Middletown is the deepest and most blindly followed line of division in the community."

Yet Muncie's dominant personality was a Black player—a big center named John Casterlow, who was also an all-state end in football. "I always called him Big John," said Raisor in a 2022 interview. "He was from the south side of Muncie, quick-witted, quick-fisted, law-breaker, jaw-breaker." (Interview a poet . . . expect rhymes.) Casterlow's teammates could joke around with him about race, and Raisor says that their "trash talk was wit not war, a relaxing shower ritual." Like this:

"Hey, white boy. You're a clammy lookin' piece a shell."
"Yeah, Big John, well black is the color of my true love's hair and, by the way, what is the color of your momma?"
"Yeah, uh-huh. And I'll blow you up like a bridge."

There were those moments . . . and then there were others. Raisor describes a night during a road trip to South Bend when the Muncie team was out cavorting in the snow (violating curfew, it should be added), and Casterlow overheard someone say, "That's just some ni—ers being ni—ers." Raisor describes Casterlow's sudden change in demeanor, which speaks to his occasional proclivity to lash out (a tendency that may have led to his death, as we shall see), to react to the casual racism that he so often had to swallow: "I felt his hands shake me and then wrench my testicles. His face grew angry and distant; he spit in the snow and rubbed my face in it, pressing harder into my groin. I tried to cry out but could only cry. This was not play; this was rage."

There is no record of any eruption like that happening to Oscar or any of his teammates, and, at root, maybe the anecdote is about nothing more than two natures, Casterlow's leaning toward anger. But if one were to offer some dime-store psychology, consider that Casterlow, raised in a mixed environment (albeit weighted white), had some understanding of racial equity, some idea that Black and white kids were equals, in school and on the team. And when that idea was slapped back at him, the reality laid bare, his reaction was harsh.

The Attucks kids had no apprehension of equality. They were told, *This is your school. You go* there. *You don't have a choice. And on the weekends, you can't go* there. *Or* there. *Or* there. *Stay in your own neighborhood.* They had almost no interaction with Caucasians of any age, in contrast to Casterlow and two other Black Muncie players, who had daily exchanges with white classmates, white teammates, and a white coach.

Raisor said that he and his teammates had been thinking about Attucks for a long time, even before the 1954–1955 season. On the eve of the state championship game against Milan in 1954, Raisor overheard a group of Muncie boosters talking about their own team and a potentially bright future. He writes in *Outside Shooter,*

"They'll all be back next year. Hinds, Flowers, Casterlow, Raisor, Barnes. We win tonight and, great God! We'll win two States in a row."

"Yeah. But there's Crispus Attucks next year. And that's Oscar Robertson. They'll be one tough bunch of coons."

"But, remember, old bones. They're all black. You put five of them together on the same floor, and they'll be wandering around looking for a cotton field."

Yes, just a bunch of true aficionados deconstructing the game. Perhaps they were some of the same folks who demanded in the summer of 1956 that Blacks be barred from the two Muncie municipal swimming pools. The city stood firm that it would only open the pools if they followed the law and were integrated, and ultimately the city won.

Raisor relates that Casterlow had no fondness for Oscar. These weren't the days of AAU bonhomie. They had never played against each other or met on a playground. They were strangers, and Casterlow was tired of hearing the name Oscar Robertson. "John had him pegged as an uppity jikes [there are several meanings of *jikes* and it's hard to say what it meant in the 1950s; it certainly wasn't complimentary] who needed a face smashing somewhere near the foul line," wrote Raisor. A sportswriter sizing up the game took a more classical approach, pegging Attucks as Zeus and Muncie as Cronos. In ancient Greek mythology, Cronos was overthrown by his son Zeus, so the metaphor must have served as a prediction.

As the players lined up for the opening tip, Raisor[1] sized up the Attucks star. "Oscar was thinner than I expected," he later wrote. That

---

1. Raisor was also a nonplaying freshman on the Wilt Chamberlain Kansas team that lost to North Carolina 54–53 in three overtimes in the 1957 NCAA final. You add up Milan, Attucks, and North Carolina, and Raisor emerges as rather the Zelig of losing basketball; such heartbreak loosed a poet's soul.

was an impression many had over the years, even in the pros, because Oscar managed to be dominant inside without being big framed. Raisor noticed that Casterlow stared and stared at Oscar's face, like he was trying to remember it for later. Intimidation perhaps? If so, that wasn't going to work.

Casterlow, who had been weakened several days before the game by lung congestion, began to insinuate himself into the action in a big way late in the second quarter. Attucks had broken out to an 18–9 lead, but Big John's ferocious rebounding and basket protection enabled the Bearcats to rally and take a 23–22 lead midway through the second period. That triggered something in Oscar, who took over the game and forced his defender, Gene Flowers, a future star at Indiana, into committing his fourth foul before halftime, which ended with Muncie ahead 43–40.

As Raisor headed for the locker room, he stopped for a moment to touch fingertips with his girlfriend, and a fan shouted, "Get them ni—ers, Phil." It's a safe bet that *Outside Shooter* was not a hit in some parts of Muncie.

Oscar was steady throughout the second half, but Willie Merriweather got into foul trouble and finally collected his fifth and final with about a minute remaining and Attucks clinging to a 71–65 lead. Two Jim Hinds free throws cut it to four points, and then Flowers tipped in a missed free throw by Casterlow after a make, and the Attucks lead was down to 71–70.

Bill Hampton then lost the ball in the corner by overdribbling—one can only imagine how loudly Oscar must have been screaming that he should be handling it; almost seventy years later Merriweather still gets angry at Hampton when he remembers the play—and with eleven seconds left it was Muncie's game to win. The contest had been everything it was supposed to be, and the Muncie players appreciated it. A year earlier Raisor had shouted in anger and frustration from the bench as Milan froze the ball in the state championship game: "Move the ball,

Plump! Play the damn game!" The ball never stopped moving in this one, and one could argue that Indiana basketball took a step forward in this game. As Raisor put it in *Outside Shooter*, "This was no Milan vs. Muncie game. No slowdown, coach-crafted, mind-numbing affair; there were no posts-in-the-holes, barbed wire fences, nor tedious flat country land. This was a car horn, screaming fires, chicken run through downtown with the cops taking a coffee break."

There are slightly differing accounts of what happened next. (No video footage of the game appears to exist.) Randy Roberts writes in *"But They Can't Beat Us"* that Muncie substitute guard Fred Scott inbounded the ball to Jimmy Barnes, who took a dribble and looked downcourt for Hinds, who was streaking to the corner, his favorite spot. Phil Hoose writes that Flowers took the ball out of bounds and looked for a teammate. Ray Crowe is quoted in his biography as saying that Raisor threw the pass, but he was not in the game at the time. Flowers agrees that Barnes was driving the ball downcourt and spotted him, Flowers, in the open. "All I had to do was catch a pass and lay it in," he told *Indianapolis Monthly* in 2014.

That didn't happen. There is no argument about what happened when the ball was in the air. Oscar knew where it was headed. He describes the play simply in *The Big O*, saying that he set a "trap" by standing behind the intended receiver. "When he threw the pass I intercepted the ball." On other occasions he said he "deliberately hid well behind his man" to invite the pass.

To others, it was more dramatic. John Gipson said, "Oscar was one of a kind—he saw the whole floor." The *Indianapolis Star* wrote a tongue-in-cheek front-page piece a few days after the win, quoting Indianapolis public health director Henry G. Nester as saying that the intensity of the game was "nothing short of a menace to the hearts and nervous systems of 400,000 residents of this city." Wrote the *Indianapolis News* about the end of a game described as one with "almost intolerable" pressure, "Barnes hurriedly threw [the ball] downcourt—Robertson raced, leaped and cut the pass off. The kid who is quite possibly the best high school player in the state had the ball now and Muncie had about 8 seconds to take it away from him. Oscar kept it."

Oscar hurled the ball toward the ceiling just as time expired. By the time it came down, Attucks had triumphed in one of the great Indiana schoolboy basketball games of all time.

In the mind's eye, the play is reminiscent of one made by another Hoosier three decades later. The Detroit Pistons needed only to get the ball inbounds to preserve a playoff win over the Celtics at Boston Garden in 1987. But Larry Bird, seemingly slow-footed and not near the play, zipped in to steal a pass from Isiah Thomas, turned, and found a cutting Dennis Johnson for a layup that won the game and led to another controversy (described in a note in Chapter 8).

Players, coaches, and fans were left breathless by the game, which had lived up to the hype. Casterlow had twenty-one points and was magnificent. Oscar had twenty-five and was better. It is the gods who send the final message. There remained no doubt about who was the king of Indiana basketball.

After the game Raisor reached for Oscar's hand, but Oscar ignored him and reached for Casterlow. In Raisor's telling, Oscar said, "A war," and Casterlow answered, "I know, man. You did great." And Oscar replied, "You, too. You, too." Perhaps it's a poet's truth, but Raisor remembers apprehending the scene this way: "I watched them looking at each other, then I watched them understand. I don't know what they understood, but they were looking past the eyes into something deeper. Only a year ago I had done that with John and seen a friend, someone who would understand. But Oscar and John had gone somewhere else, I thought. They weren't on the same team, but they were in the same place."

Despite all those returnees the Muncie boosters were counting on, Muncie failed to get back to the state tournament the following season, and their coach, McCreary, left to take a job at Louisiana State University (LSU). Raisor went to Kansas and then to LSU, following McCreary. Casterlow had a short stint at Southern University in Baton Rouge, but it didn't take. He got married and ended up in Detroit, where he worked at a Chevrolet plant. "Coach McCreary wouldn't recruit John," says Raisor. "I don't know why."

On September 7, 1960, three years after his high school days were over, John Casterlow, law-breaker, jaw-breaker, was stabbed and beaten to death on a Detroit street, as his eighteen-year-old wife, Angie, and a nephew watched in horror. According to police reports, Casterlow took exception to insults his killers had hurled at his wife—"That would be just like John," says Raisor—and he confronted them. He was attacked and outmanned. One assailant apparently emerged unseen from behind him. Casterlow was stabbed in the left side of his chest, and the blade penetrated the heart. He was dead on the sidewalk.

"Former Muncie Sports Hero Slain in Detroit" read the headline in the *Indianapolis News.* Raisor got the news when he was passing out pamphlets on the LSU campus. He imagined Casterlow hearing the insults and fearlessly going after the men. Raisor felt the rage build inside of him, wondered what different fate could have unfolded for Casterlow, wondered if he could have had a life something like his own or like Oscar's.

"This is for John Casterlow," he said as he handed out the pamphlets. "Please sign it." Then he grew angrier. "This is for John Casterlow. Sign the son of a bitch!" That's how Big John would have said it.

CHAPTER THIRTEEN

A Triumph of Firsts

"We had Oscar, and they didn't."

O n the Monday before Super Saturday at Butler Fieldhouse on March 19, 1955, the day when the four remaining teams would play for the state championship, a session was convened at the office of Indianapolis mayor Alex M. Clark. Attucks principal Dr. Russell Lane was there along with at least one representative from the police department, the fire chief, a couple of downtown businessmen (all white), and the mayor, who at that time was the youngest in Indianapolis history. It appears that the school superintendent, Dr. Herman L. Shibler, attended, but if not, he was certainly monitoring the proceedings.

The stated purpose of the meeting was to discuss celebration plans if Attucks won the state championship, which now seemed, in the minds of most prognosticators, a fait accompli. The tenor of that meeting, as well as some of the specifics, remains unclear—which is a shame because that meeting serves as a fascinating backdrop to what happened soon afterward on the most glorious weekend in the three-decade life of Crispus Attucks High School.

Consider the multitude of factors that were in play during that land-mark week in March 1955:

- Attucks was set to be not only the first Black state championship team but also the first team from Indianapolis to win it all.

- Its opponent could potentially be—was *expected* to be—another all-Black team. That meant ten African Americans on the court for thirty-two minutes in an arena where Black players were still few and far between. The NBA barely had ten African Americans in its nine-team league.

- Wafting around all of this was the memory of the previous year's state championship celebration—dare we call it *orgiastic?*—after beloved Milan won it all. The police department (more accurately, one policeman, a distinction without a difference) had all but adopted the Milan team, giving it an escort around Monument Circle and stopping local traffic to honor a team from eighty miles outside Indianapolis.

- Amid the anticipation of victory, there floated a sense of unease in some segments of the white community, which had never engaged in wholesale racially integrated celebration. Indianapolis was still a deeply segregated town, and the city was not far from the days when Attucks victories produced stories about how the natives were *whooping it up* down on crazed Indiana Avenue. *My God, what would the Ave-noo be like after a state championship win? And what if a Black boy asks a white girl to dance? Would the world remain on its axis?*

It's impossible to determine if any journalists sat in on the meet-ing in the mayor's office, but all the Indy newspapers reported on it. A story in the *Indianapolis Star* took a downcast tone, bearing the headline "Attucks Victory Plans Leave Out Fire Truck," and said that the championship might "lack one of the traditional thrills" that was a "time-honored salute to [Indiana High School Athletic Association (IHSAA)] kings since basketballs had laces."

But reporting on the same meeting, the *Indianapolis News* related that fire chief Joseph Hancock promised Attucks "a gleaming fire truck" for the celebration. The *Indianapolis Recorder* said that Attucks could have "the shiniest fire truck in town" if it won, and the *Star*, contradicting its earlier story, even laid out specifics: Lane, Shibler, and Clark would ride in the mayor's Cadillac, followed by the coaches and players on a city fire truck, in turn followed by buses for Attucks students.

In other words, it was to be a citywide party, likely the first time a group of African Americans would be recognized by the masses.

But years later, Russell Lane had a different take on what transpired. Ted Green found an audiotape of Lane talking about the meeting and included it in his documentary. Here's what Lane said:

> When we were about to win that championship, the week before they called me down to the school office. The superintendent did—Dr. Shibler. He had the fire chief down there and the police chief, and representatives of businessmen downtown. Sitting around the table. Called me and said, "Mr. Lane, it looks like your team's going to win the championship next Saturday night. The merchants downtown are frightened that after you win that championship, colored people will come downtown and tear up the downtown. Break out the windows and knock out the streetlights, and all that." I said I don't believe they would do one thing.

Narrator Green then paraphrases what Lane said he was told: the parade could include one lap around Monument Circle but would then have to move to the west side of town, to Northwest Park deep in the Black neighborhood. The message was clear: arguably the grandest moment in Indianapolis sports history would be diminished because it was achieved by African Americans.

The stories that appeared after the meeting all say that it was Lane who wanted a bonfire and celebration on the west side. The story in the *News* said that the mayor "offered to close Monument Circle to traffic but Dr. Lane said he felt it was best that the main celebration after the game be held at the park where there is plenty of open space." Having a bonfire was by then already in the celebration rotation. The year before, after Attucks won the sectional but before it lost to Milan, the *Indianapolis Star* ran the headline "Bonfire Rages Despite Rain as Tiger Fans Celebrate Victory," followed by a story about a bonfire behind the high school.

But a celebration after a state championship had to be bigger. Lane then went out of his way, according to newspaper reports, to say that Northwestern Park could hold twenty-five thousand. It seems to make a lot of sense to hold a massive party in a massive park. But . . .

Was Lane misquoted? Did the reporters miss the larger story of the meeting in Clark's office? Was the press misled if no reporters attended in person? Was there another meeting in which Lane was told what everyone *really* felt? Or was Lane's memory of the meeting affected by years and years of being treated like a second-class citizen? Ted Green reacts strongly to that last question. "Russell Lane was, by all accounts, an honest and forthright man," says Green. "To suggest he made it up, or forgot what was actually said, seems out of the question. His audio on the event is, to me, the strongest evidence that the meeting went the way he said it went."

Whatever the answer, Lane spent much of the week reminding the team and the students that they needed to behave themselves, even if the lecture was unnecessary. He always felt like he had to have one finger free to plug a dyke.

But how much reminding did Attucks need? In the years that preceded Attucks's run, going back before Ray Crowe, no team had comported itself as well as Attucks. Earlier in the season, Forest Witsman, the coach of bitter intracity rival Howe, had made this comment: "My kids would rather play Attucks than any team I know. They're gentlemen."

———

Whatever happened in the mayor's office was of little concern to Oscar and his teammates. No doubt they understood the larger significance of being the first all-Black team on such a big stage, but it's doubtful they dug into the granular part of it—all the parade details and celebration specifics. They were kids. They wanted to win, collect the trophy, and kiss the girls.

The *Indianapolis Recorder* had teased this moment a year earlier when the 1954 Attucks and Roosevelt teams were doing so well in the postseason. "It looks like the folks better hurry up and abolish segregated schools for sure," the paper wrote, "if they don't want to be looking at an all-tan final game of these go-rounds." Attucks and Roosevelt then lost, but, as was predicted, the go-round of 1955 was here, and the *Recorder* recognized the moment. In the days preceding the state championship foursome at Butler, the weekly ran a story about a man named Fred K. Dale of Pendleton, Indiana, a small town about thirty miles northeast of Indianapolis. Dale told the *Recorder* that an Attucks victory "should do much to remove the last traces" of Jim Crow laws. "The old tale of Negro inferiority will be dealt a severe blow by an Attucks victory this week. The double-barreled attack, with Gary Roosevelt in the North, should convince even the hardest headed that the days of segregation and second rate living are gone forever. In case you have forgotten, I am a white man. Not all of us are KKK supporters."

On March 19, the date that would decide the championship, the *Recorder* ran a story with this headline: "13 Negroes, 7 Whites Are Big Four Starters."[1]

Obviously, ten of those starters would be from Attucks and Roosevelt. (If you're wondering which Roosevelt the Black school was recognizing, it was Teddy.) New Albany had one Black starter in Harold "Ace" Johnson, and Fort Wayne North had two in Henry Chapman and the exceptional Charley Lyons. As the *Recorder* put it, "Favored to meet in the championship game are Attucks of Indianapolis and Roosevelt of Gary—and there isn't a paleface among them." (Remember that the term African American wasn't even officially enshrined in the *Oxford English Dictionary* until 2001, so the story includes references to "colored lads," "tan hoopsters," and "sepia players.")

The newspaper also felt it necessary to defend its coverage of the race issue throughout the season, writing, "Since the start of the season this newspaper has been writing about the possibility of several Negro teams, making it to the last go round. For our pains we have been accused of 'race baiting' and 'trying to start a riot.' Nothing of the kind. To encourage Negro teams and players does not mean to belittle the whites."

In retrospect, it's difficult to understand why Roosevelt, which would first play Fort Wayne North in the second game after Attucks–New Albany, didn't get more attention as a potential state champion. They had lost only two games (to Lafayette and Hammond, both highly regarded teams) and featured the likely Mr. Basketball, Wilson "Jake" Eison, a 6'5" interior player (only seniors could be Mr. Basketball, or Oscar might have won it), as well as Dick

---

1. On the same day that this piece appeared, the *Recorder* ran an editorial about the notorious Citizens Councils, which it referred to as "a murderous Nazi-type movement [that] has arisen in Mississippi and spread to other states." Much of the reporting about the councils was done by Hodding Carter, the white editor of the *Delta Democrat-Times* of Greenville, Mississippi, which the *Recorder* noted. Carter was the assistant secretary of state for public affairs and a State Department spokesman in the Jimmy Carter administration.

Barnett, an unorthodox southpaw who would have a fifteen-year pro career that included two championship rings with the New York Knicks.

The biographies of the Roosevelt players closely matched those of their opponents. They too were children of the Great Migration, their childhood expectations not much beyond landing a job in the Gary steel mills. Basketball was their salvation. Barnett's family came north from Alabama, and his parents separated in Gary. "My learning and inspiration came from sports, which really changed my life," said Barnett.

Most of the prognosticators were picking Attucks ("Our Gallop Poll: It's Attucks" punned the *Recorder*) with New Albany, the Tigers' opponent in the afternoon, the second pick. (The success of Attucks and Roosevelt overshadowed the strong season enjoyed by the third African American school, Lincoln of Evansville, which went through the regular season unbeaten. The three Black schools posted a record of 78–5 in the 1954–1955 season.)

W. F. Fox Jr., the undisputed dean of doggerel, put it this way:

But we're saluting Attucks
In Attucks we rejoice.
And you will understand, of course,
That Attucks is our choice.
With Robertson and Hampton,
With Merriweather, Scott
With Mitchell, Brown and others,
A triumph we would plot.
Rough the road, supreme the test
For those who win the crown
May Attucks wear the golden rings
Here in the old hometown.

No Pulitzer was forthcoming for Fox, but consider: an old-school Caucasian sportswriter was lauding an all-Black team, rooting them on, connecting them to "the old hometown." This was a new path.

Though Oscar would say fifty years after the game that Attucks didn't play well in the afternoon opener—"If New Albany had possessed half of our talent," he wrote in *The Big O*, "we would've been in serious trouble"—a perusal of the game indicates that Attucks was never in real danger of losing. A fourth-period explosion from Oscar (two straight baskets and two free throws) propelled Attucks, which opened up a 78–63 lead with two minutes left. The final was 79–67.

A film of the great Attucks team of 1951 (Hallie Bryant, Willie Gardner, Flap Robertson) on one side of a screen, juxtaposed with the 1955 team (Oscar Robertson, Willie Merriweather, Sheddrick Mitchell) on the other, would reveal how important Attucks was to basketball's evolution in that pivotal time between the early and mid-1950s. To a large extent, those early-1950s teams were a palimpsest for the Oscar teams that followed. Sure, there were still vestiges of the old game in 1955. Merriweather, a smooth, athletic player, who made an incredible 70 percent of his field goal attempts in his senior year, shot an overhead two-handed set that looked like it came out of the 1930s. Sheddrick Mitchell put up the kind of sweeping hook that pivotmen at all levels of the game were using back in the 1950s. On free throws, Mitchell held the ball high above his head and flicked it toward the basket in what looked like one of Wilt Chamberlain's desperate attempts to achieve proficiency from the foul line.

Even Oscar never really did shoot a classic jumper. He held the ball high with one hand, like a waiter carrying a trayful of food, and shot it with deliberation. Then again, so what? He got it off, and it went in.

But other parts of the game obviously signal the beginning of a new era. Against New Albany, Crowe had Attucks amp up the defensive pressure, forcing the opponent to play a tempo with which it wasn't comfortable. That went against the seeming gentlemen's agreement not to apply intense pressure that was in vogue even with Crowe's early Attucks teams. Similarly, Oscar was one of the few players to "dig" at a center when the center got the ball with his back to the basket, making it difficult for the offensive player to move even if it didn't result in a turnover. He continued to do that in the NBA. (Like many great players—Magic Johnson, Larry Bird, and Julius Erving among them—Oscar wasn't nearly as interested in lockdown defending as he was in getting steals off the ball.)

On the offensive end, Attucks changed the way the game *looked* by taking away its stationary aspect. Perhaps because of the unaggressive defense, passes were highly predictable, lacking creativity. Guard throws it to the wing. Wing enters it to the pivot, who stands with his back to the basket. Maybe somebody cuts, splits the pivot, maybe not. There was a lot of standing around. (Though, to be fair, there's a lot of standing around during contemporary NBA isolation plays too.)

But by Oscar's junior year, Attucks moved the ball quicker. It happened in part because, though Oscar dribbled a lot, he didn't *overdribble*. "He always *went* someplace with his dribble," says Carl Short, an all-city player at Indianapolis Emmerich Manual in the 1955–1956 season. "He could go either way, and he had a way of keeping you from getting it, sort of an arm bar. He didn't do anything in a fancy way, just an efficient way."

The whole Attucks team, particularly Robertson, grew more adept at hitting Mitchell and Merriweather when they were on the move. Was that Crowe getting more innovative or Crowe having Oscar? Probably some of both. Robertson penetrated, and, if stopped, looked inside to Mitchell or Merriweather. He made decisions *in the air*, which had not been part of the early-1950s game.

The starkest distinction between the two "eras" (even though they're only four years apart) is in ballhandling. Even skillful players such as

Hallie Bryant—he was later, after all, a Harlem Globetrotter—didn't look completely comfortable with the bounce. Most players still dribbled with their right hand when they went left, and there was a lot of "defensive dribbling" (i.e., handling the ball carefully with the main objective being not to lose it instead of to initiate offense). By and large the 1954–1955 Tigers moved smoothly in either direction, and it's beyond obvious to state that Oscar was the big reason.

Oscar remembers an unusual atmosphere at Butler before the final, one perhaps resulting from the unprecedented sight of two Black teams playing for a championship. Years later he waxed bitterly about it in *The Big O*: "While the teams were warming up, I remember the crowd being silent. Could it have been because there were no white players on either team? Because Indiana's legendary cultured and diehard basketball fans were not all that excited about sitting there and watching black players, black coaches and black student managers? Because maybe they were worried about us racial interlopers kidnapping their beloved game."

But elsewhere in Indianapolis there was much excitement. The police department ordered up six extra television sets so every officer on duty could watch, and on the other side of the law, prisoners in the Marion County Jail watched on three sets.

Bill Hampton remembers Principal Lane coming in and giving his boilerplate speech about representing Attucks. "You woulda thought he was preaching a sermon," said Hampton. One wonders if Lane's continued presence had grown aggravating by that time. "I can't speak for everybody, but not really for me," said Hampton, relaxing at the home of John Gipson, still a close friend. "You have to remember it was the 1950s. We *lived* by those things that he said. We were just completely focused."

As for Crowe's reminder of the necessity of jumping out from the opening whistle to discount the possibility of bad calls at the end? A different message came out this time. *Both teams are black, so the officiating doesn't matter.* "The fact that we knew we were going to get a fair shake from the officials was a big deal," said Hampton. "It was relaxing to play that way."

The game began with an Oscar jump shot that was so predictable Robertson should have grabbed the PA mic before tip-off and announced, *Ladies and gentlemen. Here's what's going to happen. I control the opening tip, get the ball back, dribble deliberately to the right elbow, where I will shoot a jumper over my defender, whoever he may be, and there's not a damn thing anyone can do about it.*

Every Attucks game did not begin with that scenario, but, as time went on, the Tigers did it more and more, through to the 1955–1956 season. More accurately, Oscar did it. Crowe didn't call the play. It was a scene setter, a sign of things to come, a statement with a capital O. That's how the 1955 Indiana state championship game began. Oscar converted the shot for a score of 2–0. It was 51–32 at halftime, and sensing blood, Attucks applied full-court pressure in the third period. And then it was over. The final score was 97–74. Good thing Attucks stopped scoring when it did because the old-school scoreboard could not register three digits.

The game may have matched two Black teams, but they seemed to have little in common, at least no more than any two teams involved in a rout. Attucks played with confidence, Roosevelt with reticence. When Attucks did slow down on offense, it seemed to have a plan, while Roosevelt flailed. Merriweather says he used to laugh when he heard about Phil Jackson's triangle offense with the Chicago Bulls and Los Angeles Lakers "because we were playing it back then, throwing it into the post and cutting off it."[2]

Roosevelt was a more traditional team than Attucks. In the afternoon game against Fort Wayne North, the Panthers had built a sixteen-point lead when coach John D. Smith reverted to Indianapolis

---

2. Phil Jackson's assistant coach with Chicago and LA, the late Tex Winter, is often credited with inventing the triangle (also called the triple-post), but it really originated with Sam Barry, Winter's college coach at the University of Southern California. But Tex was unquestionably the triangle's messiah.

1950s Basketball 101: he ordered his team to sit on the ball. Sure enough, Fort Wayne stormed back, and Roosevelt barely won 68–66. It was an accepted stratagem back then, but Crowe, even in his early years, wouldn't have done it. Anyway, the Fort Wayne game couldn't have done much for Roosevelt's confidence going against Oscar and Attucks.

Eison, who did indeed win Mr. Basketball, was a solid interior player with a soft touch, but he was a product of the 1950s, a little mechanical and deliberate. (Merriweather, who played with Eison at Purdue, said that Eison was limited, but he liked his game and him personally.)

Barnett, who had three fouls by early in the second period, played more of a one-on-one game, though he did convert a couple of those unortho-dox, legs-flared-at-all-angles southpaw jumpers that would define his style in the pros. He finished with eighteen points but wasn't much of a factor. A few years later, two Attucks players, Bill Brown and Stanford Patton, were teammates of Barnett's at Tennessee Agricultural & Industrial, the histori-cally Black college coached by John McLendon that later became Tennessee State University. "I knew you were good," Barnett told them, "but there's no way I thought you would put that kind of beatin' on us."

The "point forward" position became a major topic of conversation in the 1980s, with tall players like Paul Pressey and Lamar Odom coming to the backcourt to initiate the offense. But one could argue that Robert-son debuted the position in the mid-1950s. Look, great players are always going to get the ball. No doubt the gangly mountain kid named Jerry West, playing for East Lake High School in West Virginia, the cynosure of his state as Oscar was of his, went and got the ball from his forward position when he wanted to score or when his coach told him it was time. But Oscar *really* played the position. He was listed as a forward because that's the way it was back then: tallest is the center, next tallest are forwards, small-est two are guards. But Oscar jumped center, took the first shot, spent the early minutes of the game underneath, then, inevitably, came back to take control of the ball. Crowe didn't have to tell him, and the guards, usually

Hampton and Bill Scott, weren't going to argue. By the third period, Oscar simply headed for the backcourt, got the ball, and directed the offense. Nineteen-fifties, meet the early incarnation of LeBron James.

One play in the second period is illustrative of how far Attucks basketball, and Robertson in particular, had come. Oscar gives a long lead pass to Merriweather that no one is even aware he is throwing. Before anyone can react, Oscar cuts to the basket, gets a return pass, and lays it in. He is perhaps a little too one way (i.e., he favors his right hand by a good bit). But so was Jerry West, and no one stopped him either.

The big difference between the teams was obvious. "We had Oscar, and they didn't," says Merriweather today. "I know it sounds simple, but it's the truth. You could not guard him—they couldn't guard him in the pros either—and he was tough and smart. No one was close to him back then."

With 6:28 remaining, Oscar scored his ninety-third point of the four-game state tournament. Fittingly, the record had been held by Bill Garrett, the future Attucks coach and the great Shelbyville player who had enjoyed a terrific career at Indianapolis, tempered by the racial enmity he experienced from time to time in Bloomington (Chapter 17). In the final two minutes, though, that record transferred to Eison, who finished the game with thirty-one points, one more than Oscar. Eison's final points came on free throws after a personal foul committed by . . . Oscar.

But let us not cry for Robertson, who the following year would break almost every Indiana scoring record and, to be fair, never had trouble getting up shots, heady team player though he might have been. Had the game been more competitive, Oscar would have surely gotten more shots and more points, and as W. F. Fox Jr. noted in a column about the game, Robertson also relinquished a clear shot to slip a pass to little-used reserve William Burnley,[3] adding a minor grace note to the win.

---

3. Oscar wrote in *The Big O*, "Willie Burnley was a senior who hadn't played much all year—he was in the game, getting some mop-up time. He was wide open under the basket and took the pass and got himself a championship bucket, which mattered more to me than the record."

Fox's column praised the sportsmanship shown by Crowe and his team, and it was deserved. Consider this unforgettable moment from the game: Merriweather knocks down Barnett on a breakaway, and a foul is called. Merriweather first walks away, thinks about it, then runs back to offer Barnett a hand. "Don't touch me, motherfucker," is what Merriweather says Barnett said to him. Barnett then goes to the sideline, and Merriweather follows him, still concerned. Finally, Barnett comes back onto the court, and this time Barnett accepts Merriweather's handshake. And remember that Merriweather was Attucks's *enforcer*.

Competitively, Attucks had adopted a completely different mind-set from the days of Crowe's predecessor, Fitzhugh Lyons, who was reluctant to let an Attucks defender get too close to his man lest the physicality get too excessive. But the Tigers under Crowe, who himself had been overly timid at first, had by now figured out how to be both gentlemanly and ruthless.

And so, into the record books went the first Indiana state champion from the capital city and the first all-Black title team, quite likely the first all-Black team in the United States to win a state championship. Eleven years later a team of all-Black starters from Texas Western College drubbed an all-white team from the University of Kentucky in the 1966 NCAA championship game. Hollywood made a movie out of it.

The title gave Crowe a five-year record of 123–14 to go with four sectional championships and four regional championships at a time when it was a safe bet that most basketball fans believed that a Black man didn't have what it took to be a coach. It was like a metaphorical baton had been exchanged, the past giving way to the future, the moment set in stone by the handshake that the previous year's winning coach, Milan's Marvin Wood, gave to Crowe as he headed into the locker room. You wouldn't have understood the cultural magnitude of the game had you listened to the broadcast (available on YouTube), because the announcer assiduously avoided mentioning skin tone. He could have edged into it by talking about the joint cheerleading squad that was put together, combining Attucks students with white kids, something that got a lot of play in the Indianapolis press. But we only see them for a fleeting moment.

But Attucks Nation understood the importance. Said Oscar, "It was the best, most pure feeling I've had in my life."

And then, he says, it turned into one of the worst.

CHAPTER FOURTEEN

Legit Celebration or Veiled Insult?

"Oscar is right about the prejudice, but in this case his reasons
are wrong."

I n 1950, five years before Crispus Attucks made history in the Indiana
state basketball tournament, Japanese filmmaker Akira Kurosowa
released a classic movie called *Rashomon*. The plot involves the murder
of a samurai in a forest, but the film is really about perception versus
reality, how different people view the same event in different ways.

Over the years, few things in the life of Oscar Robertson have gotten him angrier than the memory of the celebration that followed Crispus
Attucks's state championship win. He wrote extensively about it in *The
Big O* and has talked about it repeatedly in interviews over the years. The
post-championship snub has become a major part of Attucks lore. But not
everyone agrees with Oscar's version of events, and of those who do, some
seem to be demonstrating loyalty more to Oscar than to their memory.

Principal Russell Lane's telling of the meeting in the mayor's
office—when he was allegedly warned that town fathers were afraid that
Attucks's African American fan base would tear up the town—serves as

the backdrop to Oscar's version of events. It's highly doubtful that Oscar, as an Attucks junior, would have gotten any kind of read on the meeting at the time (though Lane's admonitions to demonstrate sportsmanship would have come through loud and clear), but he did hear about it later. "In the years to come," he wrote in *The Big O*, "I would also learn about a meeting that took place the week before the state finals."

Another, even stronger factor was in play: Oscar's apprehension, even when he was at Attucks, that he and his teammates were held to a higher standard. That is beyond dispute. And even when they surpassed that standard, they still were cast as the bad kids, the unruly mob, the ones who couldn't be trusted. "You go downtown, they take your money, right?" he says in the Ted Green documentary, almost shaking with anger. "It's unforgiveable."

But, first, let's straighten out the scene and establish several events on which everyone seems to agree.

Deliriously happy, Oscar and Willie Merriweather received the championship trophy from Otton Albright, president of the Indiana High School Athletic Association (IHSAA). It had been only a little over a decade since Black schools had finally been allowed to play by King Arthur Trester's organization, and here they were winning it all. The Tigers spent about a half hour in the fieldhouse getting ready for the celebration. When they emerged, the chilly night air was filled with cheering and loud music from a mobile jukebox (ever see one of those?) owned by Matthew Dickerson, a longtime local promoter well known in the African American community.[1] The *Indianapolis Star* reported that students from both Attucks and Roosevelt were "jitter bugging" on the gravel courts outside the fieldhouse as the Attucks coaches and players

---

1. Among the selections played was "Tweedle Dee" by LaVern Baker, a song that was later turned into a smash hit by a white singer, Georgia Gibbs. Baker complained bitterly about it, but copyright laws did not forbid such appropriation, which was common practice for white singers back then. Just ask Elvis. Baker was married for ten years to the great comedian Slappy White, which has nothing to do with this but is an irresistible fact.

climbed aboard a waiting fire truck from Engine House No. 17. Man, the crowd must have gone crazy when Ray Crowe's wife, Betty, jumped down from the truck and joined Merriweather in the dancing.

The parade—which consisted of eight police motorcycles, the lead Cadillac carrying Lane, Superintendent Herman L. Shibler, and Mayor Alex M. Clark, the fire truck bearing the players, and six buses with Attucks fans—proceeded east on 49th Street, turned south on Meridian, and passed apartment houses "whose dwellers crowded at windows and waved and shouted as the Attucks motorcade shot by," reported the *Star*. Phillip Hoose uncovers a fascinating nugget in *Attucks!*: from the path of the motorcade, some of the players could see the homes in which their mothers and other relatives worked as domestics. Mayor Clark himself employed Bill Scott's grandmother as a maid and nanny. But such grim ironies went unnoticed that night. Sirens filled the air as the six-mile journey stopped at Monument Circle. One newspaper estimated that fifteen thousand people were jammed into the area as the parade made a rotation around the Circle. One rotation? Two rotations? Three? That seems lost to history.

Speeches followed because no one loves a victory parade like politicians. Mayor Clark welcomed the Attucks team and introduced Shibler, who said the predictable things: "Great night for Indianapolis." "We've waited a long time for this." "Attucks is a great team." Lane spoke briefly and said that he was "happy with the spirit of cooperation" shown by everyone. Clark then gave an honorary key to the city to Ray Crowe, who introduced the players one by one. Clark added (and no doubt Lane approved) that Attucks not only won the state championship but "displayed extra sportsmanship."

Then the motorcade took off in a westbound direction, toward Indiana Avenue, where the response was, predictably, delirious. How many nights had the *Ave-noo* celebrated Black sporting achievements? But this was better than a Joe Louis heavyweight victory or a Jackie Robinson win over the Yankees. These were *their* boys. This was *their* team. "Motor traffic came to a standstill, but the horns kept blowing and voices shouting," reported the *Star*, "until the Avenue was a canyon of sound."

From the Avenue the motorcade moved to West Street, Northwestern Avenue, and Fall Creek Boulevard and then into Northwestern Park, where a crowd of between twenty-five and thirty thousand awaited the conquering heroes. The party went on all night long.

Numerous photos of the celebration appeared in Indy newspapers over the next few days. The team and cheerleaders arriving at the bonfire on a fire truck. Oscar and Bill Brown smiling and waving from a fire truck. Sheddrick Mitchell looking joyous on the truck. Clark handing the key to the city to Crowe. Even the *Indianapolis Recorder*, the African American newspaper, ran a photo showing the "whole town" jammed into Monument Circle (it estimated that a crowd of twenty thousand "covered the circle like a blanket"), and many of the faces in that photo were Caucasian.

A mural painted of the whole scene—victory at Butler Fieldhouse, procession to Monument Circle, celebratory bonfire—might have been titled *Absolute Joy*. Plus, the hullabaloo continued into the next week. At a school pep rally on Monday, two days after the title win, Lane declared a free school day and ordered everyone to the gymnasium to dance. A basketball game wouldn't fit in there, but kids could sure as hell rip it up if the music was playing.

As the years went by, though, Oscar came to have a contrary take on the celebration night after the game. He described the Monument Circle trip this way: "[Mayor Clark] and the other city fathers had decided it was too much of a threat to allow us to congregate around Monument Circle. They sent us back to our neighborhood and made sure we had a police escort to guide our way." And he wrote in a 2017 bylined story in the *Undefeated*, "To this day, I cannot forget the pain of being rejected in my own hometown. Our Attucks championship teams have since been celebrated many times, but there's no way to bring back the innocent excitement our group of deserving black teenagers—who had earned the traditional celebration—was looking forward to at that point in time."

Oscar writes—and has reiterated in other interviews—that he got depressed at the bonfire and caught a ride to the home of his father and new wife. His father was excited about the win, but Oscar was downcast. He made a sandwich, stretched out on the living room floor, and said to his father, "Dad, they don't want us."

One can sense Oscar's marrow-deep pain, his visceral feelings of rejection. There can be no doubt that some percentage of the Indianapolis populace was turned off by the very idea that African Americans had come out on top, and some percentage of that same populace wouldn't have come within a mile of Northwestern Park to share in the celebration. There was simply no precedent for Caucasians sharing Black joy.

But is Oscar's take on the evening correct? The motorcade was at Monument Circle long enough for speeches and for Crowe to receive a key to the city.[2] And—understatement alert—although the white press couldn't always be counted on to accurately report Black happenings, the idea that it was Attucks principal Lane who wanted the bonfire in the Black section of town seems solid. Indeed, the bonfire seemed to be the centerpiece of the celebration, planned for days. In fact, on the day of the game, a "prankster" (the *Star*'s word) stole some of the stacked wood from the park.

The story goes on. In succeeding days, the Attucks team is all over the place. There they are onstage at the school getting cheered. There they are eating T-bone steaks at Fendrick's Famous Foods, an Indianapolis institution, the meal later being credited as "a great step forward in

---

2. There was one terrible incident during the celebration—an eighteen-year-old Attucks student named Fred Hicks was hospitalized in serious condition with knife wounds in the lower part of his body. To their credit, the newspapers did not sensationalize or overplay the story; neither did any media outlet appear to follow up on Hicks's condition.

promoting racial equality in Indianapolis." (That's how bad the racism was in Indy; Black kids eating in a restaurant was a milestone.) There they are being honored at the University Medical Center at a dinner hosted by Shibler, the superintendent.

The *Indianapolis Star* carried a full-page congratulatory ad from the Merchants Association of Downtown Indianapolis, some of those merchants having no doubt barred, or at least discouraged, Blacks from shopping at their stores. A proclamation from Mayor Clark appeared in local papers two days after the victory; he said it had been written before the championship and would have run win or lose. Predictably, it praised Attucks's sportsmanship and "gentlemanly conduct" but also noted Attucks's part in the "constant battle against bigotry and intolerance." For the record, Clark was recognized by most, even by accept-no-bullshit *Recorder* columnist Andrew W. Ramsey, for having reasonably progressive views about race.

As the celebrations began to settle down, the *Indianapolis Recorder* ran a March 26 story headlined "City Hails 1st and Greatest State Champs; Parade Is 'Out.'" The first paragraph read, "Attucks's state champion Tigers will have a scholarship fund established in their name and likely will stow away a drumstick in coming weeks, but there will be no Big Parade as fans had expected." The story went on to suggest that "parade and banquet ideas were floating around" but "got lost somewhere later in the week." It's not clear where they were floated. Whether or not Attucks had *deserved* a parade and, more to the point, whether a *white* state championship team would have been given one are separate questions. The best guess from here is that, yes, a state championship by Tech or Manual would have closed down the city in jubilation. But the idea that an Attucks parade had been on the docket, then cruelly taken away because a Black team would be feted, seems a stretch.

Also, there had never been a state champion from Indianapolis, so this "tradition" of fire trucks and Monument Circle celebrations is hopelessly confused. It's undeniable that fans, particularly students, of some teams went to the Circle to celebrate wins in the sectional or even the regular season. Others did not. The Circle seems to have been recognized as a celebration center, which makes sense, but it's highly unlikely that any of those previous celebrations were planned by the city. It was more *Hey, we won—let's ride around the circle and make some noise.* Milan got its triumphant ride to Monument Circle in 1954 because of one policeman; the city fathers did not plan it, and there were, incidentally, no fire trucks, just police cars. In 1953, state champ South Bend had a triumphant fire truck ride . . . in South Bend. In both 1951 and 1952, state champ Muncie Central had a triumphant fire truck ride . . . in Muncie. (And this is the time to note that the losing Roosevelt team got a fire truck ride and a key-to-the-city presentation back in Gary. Good for them.)

There is another dimension to this. In 1949, after city school Tech beat Southport 49–48 in overtime to win the sectional, its rooters took to the streets and made headlines. "Tech Rooters Jubilate," screamed the *Star*, which said that "frenzied students and rooters descended on Monument Circle" and "cheered themselves hoarse," snake-danced "around the circle," and created "as much din as possible." Twenty motorcycle cops were called, and the police had to "disperse" another "band of rooters" who had "invaded the school grounds." Said one "perspiring" police officer, "I never saw anything like it in my eight years on the force."

One could imagine a different cast to the story had a group of Blacks "jubilated" on Indiana Avenue; it would have been called a riot.

Bob Collins, the revered and plugged-in *Indy Star* columnist, believes that the Tech incident is at the bottom of what happened, or didn't happen, in 1955. He said the Tech fans "just destroyed everything within reach" after their triumphant ride around Monument Circle in 1949. Ergo, at an Attucks-Howe sectional final a year later, one that Attucks won, it was announced that there would be no postgame procession around the Circle. Said Collins,

The Black fans immediately believed [the pronouncement] was directed against Attucks, but it was because of what happened before. Just another example of whites not thinking. Please don't get me wrong, there was enough prejudice to go around. But the officials of the High School Association [which made the decision] were teachers and . . . [they were thinking] we're not going to have this happen again. Oscar is right about the prejudice, but in this case his reasons are wrong.

Stanley Warren has this take, which seems reasonable. "I don't know exactly what happened at Monument Circle," he said in a 2022 interview, "but I do know that you'd get the same reaction today, that people would think Blacks will riot if you give them the chance."

Taking a macro view of that seemingly wondrous time in Black history in Indianapolis gives the event a patina of equality, the illusion that everything was fine. Look deeper and you see something else. That's what Ramsey did in one of his follow-up columns after the championship win. The Attucks teacher told his own story about a trip to the supermarket before the championship game. A young white clerk noticed several patrons with Attucks buttons and yelled to a fellow worker, "The Ink Spots will be out at the Fieldhouse tonight!" He then noticed that Ramsey was Black and, nonplussed, hurried into the back. Ramsey must have informed the manager, who apologized for the clerk and said he was a "good Christian." But the clerk was dismissed for what Ramsey called "this breech of good breeding and lack of respect due the feelings of all respectable peoples." That was Ramsey: disrespect me, and you'll hear about it.

Another Ramsey anecdote from his column: he heard from a white Attucks fan that a cashier at a grocery store that catered mostly to a Black clientele told the fan that she hoped Attucks lost because "there would be no getting along with the local Negroes" if they won.

But Ramsey found glimmers of hope in the Attucks win. He saw many white folks gathered along Meridian Street cheering the motorcade. He believed that many of the "calamity howlers" who predicted that race riots would ensue when Black schools were allowed into the sacred IHSAA society were silenced by two African American teams playing in the state final. And he was particularly pleased that Ray Crowe's acumen at the helm had dispelled the myth of a team "needing the guidance of a white man in order to accomplish anything great."

But for Ramsey and many others, this was the time for action, not contentment. "There was in the victory an odd mix of the new and the old," he wrote. "The very existence of three all-Negro schools in Indiana [Evansville Lincoln was the third] is a denial of the democracy that Attucks and Roosevelt's appearance in the final game affirmed." In other words, why in the hell were there still segregated schools? And despite Attucks's success and the advancement of two Black schools to the hallowed state final, segregation went on. And on. And on.

We return for a moment to Monument Circle, whose official name is the Indiana State Soldiers and Sailors Monument, dedicated in 1902 as a memorial to the Hoosier state's Civil War casualties but subsequently expanded to include fatalities of several wars. The inscriptions on the monument, which was designed by German architect Bruno Schmitz, tell a story. "War for the Union" reads one, making it clear that Hoosiers fought for the North. The casualties in the War of Spain list two "Colored Companies," including 213 Blacks who gave their lives.

Whether or not Oscar Robertson's take on the post-championship celebration is correct, nothing describes the Attucks team of that time—serious, steadfast, segregated—better than the monument's top inscription: "To Indiana's Silent Victors."

CHAPTER FIFTEEN

The Cape-Wearing DuSable Panthers and the Angry Brilliance of Russ

"It is high time the school board throw out and abolish its old Klan policy."

After Attucks's breathtakingly easy victory over Roosevelt in the 1955 final, Corky Lamm wrote in the *Indianapolis News*, "Indianapolis waited 45 years to crown its first state high school basketball champion. And it might have to wait 45 more to get another like the Tigers of Crispus Attucks, who Saturday convinced just about every unprejudiced eye that they're the greatest high school basketball team ever collected, bar nobody." And that statement was made before Oscar and Co. stormed through the following season undefeated and all but untouched, a story still to be told.

The Tigers were more than a collection of talent, more than the team that, in one year, transformed the state championship final from Milan stallball into Attucks speedball. They must be seen—they *deserve* to be seen—within the context of their turbulent times, evaluated as much for what they played *through* as how they played. They weren't completely cognizant of that back then, of course. "When you're in the middle of it, in the middle of playing and trying to win a championship, you don't realize everything," says Al Maxey, a star on the 1956 Attucks state championship team. "It's only later that you realize all you went through. And it's very, very satisfying."

Imagine, if you will, the Attucks team—players and coaches—in a flimsy enclosure, semiprotected but still vulnerable. As Ray Crowe was putting together one of the best back-to-back seasons in scholastic basketball history, all these momentous events swirled around them. Consider the following:

On May 17, 1954, the Supreme Court passed *Brown v. Board of Education of Topeka*, which theoretically ended racial segregation in public schools, *theoretically* being the operative word in Attucks's hometown.

On August 28, 1955, Emmett Till was brutally murdered for whistling at a white woman. Photos of his battered body in the casket appeared in a national magazine, the most searing images of racial cruelty since the photo of the lynching in Marion a quarter-century earlier.

About three months after that, a seamstress for a Montgomery, Alabama, department store named Rosa Parks refused to surrender her bus seat to a white man, an action that launched a yearlong boycott that eventually brought Dr. Martin Luther King Jr. to the forefront of the civil rights movement. That happened at about the time that the 1955–1956 Attucks team was beginning an undefeated season.

Throughout the months of January and February 1956, the news was full of bombings in the South that targeted Black churches and the homes of civil rights leaders, including King[1] and Ralph Abernathy.

---

1. Later, the paths of King and Attucks alum Al Maxey would converge. King came to Lincoln, Nebraska, for a speech in December 1964, and Maxey, a young policeman, was assigned as his bodyguard. "I'm almost sure I got the assignment because I was the only Black cop," says Maxey today. Robertson never met King, but on April 4, 1968, the day after King was assassinated in Memphis, Oscar began to organize a benefit game in his honor. It was played in August at the Singer Bowl, an outdoor venue on the site of the 1964 World's Fair in Queens. Oscar did a lot of the grunt work to get the players, and he convinced a bunch of all-stars to

Racial reality always slapped the Attucks players in the face, beyond the fact that they went to a segregated school at a time when segregation was supposed to be illegal. Remember custom, not law, was the order of the day in the Hoosier state.

While the sportswriters who chronicled Attucks gradually learned about covering players of a different color than they were—the *Indianapolis Star*'s Bob Collins was a major factor in educating the press corps—the Indy newspapers breezily tossed around the N-word, reflecting the casual racism of the time. A startling number of classified ads in the Indy newspapers announced pet owners looking for a cat or dog who answered to the name "Ni—er." A local florist advertised popular hybrids for the season, which were called Golden Rapture, Radiance, Will Rogers, and "Ni—er" Boy.

In March 1953, as Oscar was completing his freshman season at Attucks, a major story broke in Indianapolis about a popular children's show hosted by Jeanette Lee, a well-known local personality known as Indiana's "First Lady of TV." She was fired by WFMB-TV after a child guest on her *Town Topics* program exclaimed, "The last one down's a ni—er baby!" The young girl was explaining how her Brownie troop played "Ring Around the Rosy."

The N-word was never censored in the Indianapolis newspapers, which seemed to derive much enjoyment from running stories from other locales where the word could be comfortably used. The *Star* ran a story about the Klan trying to build a new invisible empire in the South and quoted a Klansman from Florida thusly: "The ni—er in Florida has no better friend in the world than a good Klansman. That is, if he's a real 100% American ni—er who stays in his place."

Conflicts over school integration burst into America's living rooms most vividly in the 1960s with the candidacy of George Wallace, but they

---

play, including Wilt Chamberlain. Oscar's East team beat Wilt's West team 77–61, and the event raised $85,000 in a two-hour telethon. That was a lot of money back then. The event lasted only one year, but the players who participated have fond memories of it.

had started a decade earlier, and Indy newspapers were eager to report the chaos, conveniently ignoring their state's own segregated school system. "The ni—er who crosses this line will die," a man was quoted in an *Indianapolis News* story about a standoff at a Texas junior college. The *Star* ran a story about another conflict in Texas at an all-white high school. The school superintendent—repeat, the *superintendent*—told a reporter, "Ni—ers had better not try to register today. The community is agitated. There would be trouble."

On March 17, 1956, just as Attucks was preparing for its second straight state championship, the *News* ran an opinion piece by UPI reporter Al Kuettner on its front page. One imagines the editors gathering around and concluding, "Okay, this works. Nice, objective piece about a difficult subject." In reality, it could have been Exhibit A demonstrating the clueless view of race relations in the Hoosier state. Kuettner asked for a "middle ground" between the White Citizens Council, a manifestly racist organization, and the NAACP, a group set up expressly to protect African Americans *from* groups like the White Citizens Council. It is tempting to classify the argument as anachronistic, yet can't we imagine it being made today? (Remember there were "very, very fine people on both sides" in Charlottesville.) Here is some of Kuettner's opinion:

> The average white southerner is a law-abiding individual to whom violence is repugnant. . . . He is as sorry as other Americans if the controversy over the Negroes place in society is casting his country in a bad light around the world. But he is accustomed since childhood to separation of Negroes and whites in his community. He has come to believe it hasn't worked too badly. The Negroes themselves have been content for the most part, he thinks. The North is mistaken if it pictures all the South's colored people as straining to intermix.

He has a dread of one of his children marrying a Negro. He thinks almost all Northern parents would feel the same. But he feels that will be the outcome if Negro and white children begin mixing freely in the classrooms, the playgrounds, the swimming pools, the high school dances.

He is trying to make up his mind how to proceed. The opinions of his friends and neighbors influence him mightily. Should he get the tag of "ni—er-lover," it may ostracize him socially and ruin him economically.

The story went on to present a famous person ready and willing to offer a compromise: William Faulkner, who just a year earlier had won the first of his two Pulitzer Prizes. Faulkner saw the need for an organization whose aims lay "somewhere between the NAACP and the Citizens Councils." A native Mississippian, the writer was a brilliant and influential novelist . . . and a man with deep roots in Confederate thought, one who always counseled that integration could not be forced upon the South, a tale, in this case, told by an idiot.

———

Interestingly, two other Black basketball teams were blazing trails during this tempestuous time, and their experiences—in markedly different parts of the country—provide a fascinating counterpoint to the Attucks tale.

DuSable is a fabled Black high school in the Bronzeville section of Chicago's South Side. Today, almost seventy years later, the 1953–1954 Panthers, coached by a man named Jim Brown, the Ray Crowe of Illinois scholastic basketball, are still considered among the greatest teams ever in the Chicago Public League. But after winning thirty-one straight games, some by preposterous margins, DuSable lost to Mount Vernon

76–70 in the state championship game, the loss depriving the Panthers of beating Attucks—by one year—for the honor of being the first all-Black high school to win a state championship.

Just as Attucks was the first Indianapolis team to win a state title, DuSable was the first Chicago Public League team even to make a final. Just as Attucks had Oscar, DuSable had *the* player in the state of Illinois: a flashy guard with the unforgettable name of Paxton Lumpkin, who did a Larry Bird before Larry Bird, transferring from Indiana to Indiana State after his high school days. And just as Oscar had Willie Merriweather and Sheddrick Mitchell, Lumpkin had two talented running mates in "Sweet" Charlie Brown, who played with Elgin Baylor at Seattle University, and Shellie McMillon, who played at Bradley University.

Like Attucks, the Panthers were, predictably, victimized by racist officiating[2] and did everything in their power to build a big lead on teams. Several press reports from that championship game against Mount Vernon mention questionable calls that went against DuSable.

At this point the Attucks and DuSable stories diverge. For one thing, DuSable, unlike Attucks, *did* get a parade, the *Chicago Tribune* reporting that it was sponsored by the 47th Street Business Men's Association. (At the time, 47th Street was the thriving commercial address for Black Chicago; had Indiana Avenue been in its prime, with people like Archie Greathouse running the commercial show, perhaps an Attucks parade would have taken place there.)

There are more substantial differences in the stories. During his basketball years, DuSable's version of Oscar never could put aside his taste for liquor and gambling and had a spotty college career. Lumpkin

---

2. John Fraser, who refereed the state championship game, was later barred from officiating in the Missouri Valley Conference after it was found he consorted with gamblers to fix point spreads. Many DuSable fans believed that the championship game was rigged, and Sweet Charlie Brown says that he tried for years to get a copy of the film but "was told the last three minutes were deleted." There is a partial film of the Mount Vernon–DuSable game on YouTube, but large parts are missing, and it's impossible to make a judgment about the refereeing.

played with the Globetrotters for a while (his specialty was the kind of low dribbling in which Marques Haynes excelled), but he never got it together enough to try out for the NBA. He eventually became a postal worker but died at age fifty-four of cancer in 1991, unremembered almost everywhere except where Chicago playground legends are told.

McMillon too died early, at age forty-four, after four decent years in the NBA, followed by a career in sales and public relations. But Brown, who died in August 2022 from complications after a fall, had a sweeter life that fit his nickname. He was a seminal Chicago hoops figure, first at DuSable, then as a referee, and finally as the creator of the popular Windy City Basketball League for players over fifty.

The difference between Oscar (preternaturally mature and goal oriented even as a teenager) and Lumpkin suggests the stylistic differences between Attucks and DuSable. While Attucks was constrained by the restrictive atmosphere of its hometown—hemmed in by both white hegemony and the cautious, toe-the-line principalship of Dr. Russell Lane—DuSable rocked and rolled in wide-open Chi-town. Attucks had the relatively mild "Crazy Song"; DuSable had high-kicking cheerleaders with choreography that presaged the Laker Girls of the 1980s. They wore high socks like the Globetrotters, whose creation story, remember, begins in Chicago as the Savoy Big Five. The DuSable jerseys were a stylish black and red (reminiscent of the early Michael Jordan "devil shoes"), and the players came out for warmups in black *capes*.

The Attucks teams of the mid-1950s could be accurately classified as a running team, but the Tigers ran under control. DuSable ran with *abandon*, relentlessly fast breaking and using a full-court press to jet-start their offense. "They ain't nothin' but a five-ring circus," scoffed one coach at the 1954 state tournament. Oh, the frustration of getting pounded by the different style of a team that's also a different color.[3]

---

3. Willie Merriweather swears that Attucks did one showy thing. "Our jersey numbers were bigger than anybody else's," he says. "We had big numbers before the pros." We'll take his word.

———

In California, another team, not all Black but dominated by a strong African American personality, was doing what Attucks and DuSable did: changing the way the game was played and altering perceptions about African American players. The University of San Francisco (USF), an outlier little known for basketball until a gangly revolutionary named Bill Russell showed up on campus in 1952, won its opener of the 1954–1955 season, then lost to UCLA, then ran off twenty-seven straight wins, the last a 77–63 rout of LaSalle in the NCAA championship game, which came on the same March night that Attucks beat Roosevelt. (And, like Attucks, it went undefeated the following season.) A writer for the *Chicago Defender*, an African American newspaper, sized up the Attucks and USF victories and declared a *mensis mirabilis*: "I'm firmly convinced that March was the greatest month of achievements in the history of Negro athletics."

In temperament and style, the USC Dons were more Attucks than DuSable. Russell and his main running mate, K. C. Jones,[4] were not the kind to wear capes. Especially Russell. He was Oscar-like, or, more accurately, the sixteen-year-old Oscar was Russell-like. Both were focused and intense. They utilized their natural athleticism—Russell was a long

---

Plus, by the mid-1950s Attucks did have small capes on their warmup jackets, though they were subtler than DuSable's. The cape seems associated with Black culture, perhaps because of James Brown, who built an entire routine around his cape. Brown would fall to the ground in seeming exhaustion while performing "Please, Please, Please," at which point MC Danny Ray would drape a cape around him. Sometimes Brown would leave the stage and dramatically return, and sometimes the cape would revive him. In a biography about the Godfather of Soul, author James Sullivan suggests that Brown picked up the idea from "Sweet Daddy" Grace, a cape-wearing, firebrand preacher he saw in his youth in Georgia. But don't take this as the definitive word on capes and Black culture.

4. Russell and Jones came to Indianapolis in October 1956 for an exhibition game at Butler Fieldhouse, a tune-up for the Olympic Games in Melbourne. "K. C." was Jones's given name, from the fabled railroad man "Casey" Jones, which is how most reporters spelled "K. C." until he got to the NBA. K. C., who died in 2020, was a delightful man who could easily be convinced—if he hadn't already convinced himself—to burst into song in any lounge or barroom where there was a piano. He was good too.

jump champion, and, as we shall see, Oscar spent much of the spring on the track as well as the baseball field—but their games had a touch of intellectualism too, like they were *thinking* their way through the chaos. In *The Big O*, Oscar, reaching far afield, digs up an anecdote about a film project that involved jazz genius Charles Mingus and LSD guru Timothy Leary. (It was *You're Nobody till Somebody Loves You*, an experimental film by D. A. Pennebaker.) As Oscar tells us, Leary decided they were just going to improvise the whole movie, which he thought would fit with Mingus's improvisational touch. But Mingus says, "The key to improv is having something concrete to go away from, and something to come back to." It says a lot. Oscar liked the concrete as much as he did the improv.

Oscar's brilliance showed most on offense, Russell's on defense. It didn't become apparent until he got into the NBA, but Russell was a revolutionary player, engineering a devastating fast break by blocking shots under control and/or throwing superb outlet passes. He became such a profoundly gifted defender that his offensive prowess was often overlooked, especially the speed that enabled him to often *finish* a fast break that he had started with a blocked shot or rebound.

Plus, Russell's brilliance came with a dash of . . . let's call it anger. He didn't smile; he didn't play to the crowd; he was a dangerous man. It went over well in San Francisco, which took to those who pushed boundaries.

And so, just as Lumpkin was a creature of wide-open Chicago, Russell was a hero of the Bay Area. That doesn't mean that Lumpkin and Russell didn't face their own battles with racism, and Lord knows Russell was never comfortable in Boston, where intruders once broke into his home, stole some of his trophies, and defecated in his bed. But Oscar faced something else in Indianapolis, a town that, no matter how hard it tried—or appeared to be trying—held on to its racial conventions and its ideas about race mixing. Everyone whom Oscar and his teammates encountered—coaches, principals, the press, public opinion—asked, nay, *demanded*, that they play fair. The city just didn't play fair in return.

The aftermath of a fire that gutted a Black Indianapolis elementary school, No. 63, in 1946 could stand as Exhibit A for the argument that separation of the races was the MO of choice in Indianapolis. School segregation had already been going on for two decades, and the local branch of the NAACP was pressuring the school board to end it. In fact, the NAACP saw the fire (it happened at night, and no one was injured) as a blessing that would force white schools to accept Black students. Meeting at the Senate Avenue YMCA, a coalition of organizations forced the issue into the open and presented three elementary school buildings near No. 63, whose principals all said that they were willing to take in Black students.

Problem seemingly solved. Progress.

But not in Indianapolis. Richard Pierce writes in *Polite Protest* that the Citizens Council–dominated school board "reacted in typical fashion." The decision was made to send some of the 325 displaced students to a previously abandoned building ten miles away and others to School 26, an already-crowded Black elementary school. The board then allotted funds for an expansion to School 26. Charles Preston, the white writer for the *Indianapolis Recorder* who would go on to cover Attucks basketball in the 1950s, wrote, "The spirit of Abraham Lincoln was given the brush-off on the Great Emancipator's Birthday." The Black community was dumbfounded by the decision. The white community barely noticed.

Cries to integrate the schools continued throughout the 1940s and into the 1950s. At one point a group of fourteen Attucks students "commandeered" (Emma Lou Thornbrough's word) a truck and drove to the office of the school superintendent (hard to believe Andrew W. Ramsey wasn't behind that) to protest the fact that they were frequently tardy because so many of them lived far from the school. They got an audience with school authorities but no satisfaction. They appealed to the Indianapolis Chamber of Commerce. Yeah, right. A group of Black parents from No. 87, a junior high school, complained that their kids should have the right to go to Shortridge instead of Attucks because Shortridge was closer. No, said the school board, there is more "convenient transportation" to Attucks—which wasn't true, and never had been true.

In September 1948, a prominent Black attorney named Henry J. Richardson looked the school board in the eye and said, "We have waited, pleaded, and worked on this particular problem for more than ten years. It is high time the school board throw out and abolish its old Klan policy of 1926." Around the same time, a group of Black parents, "indignant at having their children shunted from one school to another outside of their district," in the words of the *Recorder*, gathered in protest in front of a white school and demanded that their children be allowed to enter. In a statement that crystallized white thought at the time, Virgil Stinebaugh, the school superintendent, said that he had no authority to change established segregation policy, "notwithstanding your charges that such policy is undemocratic and unAmerican."

But the winds of protest finally blew strong enough to penetrate the eardrums of Governor Henry F. Schricker, who in 1949 signed a state law that specifically abolished segregation in all public schools. The indispensable Thornbrough explains it this way:

> A growing number of whites, aware of the contradiction between the professed aims of the United States in World War II and the Cold War and second class citizenship for American blacks, supported their efforts. The local branch of the National Association for the Advancement of Colored People and the state conference of that organization took the lead in a campaign to abolish segregation in the schools, strengthen the law against discrimination in public accommodations, and win equal employment opportunities for blacks. Their greatest victory was a state law enacted in 1949 which abolished segregation in all public schools.

The school board said it would comply and promptly set into place all the outer trappings of compliance. By 1950 the directory of Indianapolis Public Schools had stopped putting an asterisk that designated *Negro* beside Crispus Attucks High School. In 1953 the school board announced that integration was complete, and the city was downright hubristic about it. As Pierce writes, "The *Indianapolis Times* was emboldened to counsel southern states to accept desegregation with little worry. Indianapolis had proven that desegregation could be attained peacefully if done correctly. The *Indianapolis News* reported no major upheavals associated with desegregation."

But there are statutes . . . and there is reality. Remember, in Indiana, custom prevailed, not law. In the early 1950s about one-third of Indy's student population was still attending segregated schools, and integration was only marginal at others. But the pronouncement was just sort-of-true-enough to proclaim it true. There was *truthiness*, to borrow from Stephen Colbert, in the statement that integration was policy. Black students went to high schools other than Attucks. Some limited integration had occurred, perhaps because a coach really wanted an African American athlete to play for him or because that Black athlete decided he or she had a better chance of making a team at a school other than Attucks. A smattering of Black players faced Attucks on the court, such as Tech's Adell Turner,[5] who was the *Indianapolis Times* scholastic athlete of the year in 1954. Two other great Black Tech players were Bob Taylor and Freddy McCoy, who emerges in the next chapter. Herschell Turner played at Shortridge and was later a Nebraska Husker teammate and close friend of Attucks's Al Maxey.

Still, most Black kids kept going to Attucks, and white kids—*all* white kids—went somewhere else. Schools were theoretically assigned

---

5. Adell's son was Landon Turner, who helped Indiana win the 1981 NCAA title for Bob Knight. Landon was injured in an auto accident that left him paralyzed, though he eventually regained control of his arms. He and Knight had had a testy relationship, but the coach was a huge supporter of Turner's after the accident. Turner is now a motivational speaker.

by geography, but a waiver system (attached to the 1949 antisegregation law) enabled students to apply for exceptions; predictably, most Black kids applied to stay at Attucks, while white kids opted for Shortridge or Tech. Anyway, even if geographical boundaries were adhered to, long-running de facto housing segregation was powerful: most Blacks continued to live in the more impoverished areas near Attucks.

For the most part, faculty segregation continued. Thornbrough reports that one Black teacher was assigned to a white elementary school in 1951, and two years later only seven Blacks were teaching in schools that were formerly white elementary schools. The first white teachers appeared in Attucks in 1955, but there were only two of them. Attucks had an all-Black student body until the late 1960s, and when one Black principal took a job at a "mixed" school, the *Indianapolis Times* proclaimed that the "last hurdle" to integration in education had been cleared. That's an example of the "complacent, self-congratulatory perception of the process of desegregation," as Thornbrough put it.

It wasn't until these celebrated Attucks teams were long gone and a federal lawsuit was filed in 1968, a battle led by Andrew Ramsey, that school segregation in Indiana could be said to have ended. Even at that, litigation about the suit continued until 1980.

But the disingenuous party line in Indianapolis through the 1970s was always *Color? Why, we don't know from color! Brown v. Board of Education* dropped like a bomb in 1954, but Superintendent Herman L. Shibler said, "My gosh, it doesn't make any difference here. Students are already assigned on a purely geographical basis with no thought to racial composition."

Let's make this clear, though: there is nowhere else that Oscar and his teammates would have rather been in 1955 and 1956. Shortridge? Tech? Washington? No way. Attucks was the place where great things had already happened, and even greater things awaited.

CHAPTER SIXTEEN

Perfection

"I sincerely believe there are college teams they could beat."

A shocking nugget appeared in the *Indianapolis News* in May 1955, a couple of months after Crispus Attucks rewrote Hoosier hoops history. "Oscar Robertson will attend Shortridge High next year." That was it. End of item. It appeared in a column written by W. F. Fox Jr., to which he had given the name—reaching for and achieving maximum cornpone-ness—*The Yarnin' Basket*.

The Yarnin' Basket writer perhaps suspected, as anyone would, that the rumor was fallacious, in which case Fox shouldn't have run it at all. Or, if he thought it was real, he should have amplified it and gotten to the bottom of it. The best player in the state and quite possibly the country switching from his state championship team to a rival team in the city was certainly page-one news in Indianapolis.

The story has underpinnings in confusing Indianapolis school policy. After the Robertson family divorce, mother Mazell's home actually was in the Shortridge district. And Shortridge—who could blame them?—was trying desperately to claim Oscar. But he wasn't going anywhere, and the waiver system enabled him to stay at Attucks.

By the next day there was a slightly longer item in the *Indianapolis Star* reporting that Oscar was scheduled to take one trigonometry course at Shortridge that wouldn't affect his eligibility to play at Attucks. There is no record of Oscar having any reaction to the news (or whether he actually took trig). He was probably too busy to notice. The Indy sports sections that spring were sprinkled with Robertson nonbasketball news. Oscar clears 5'10" in the high jump for third place in the Indianapolis Relays. Oscar sets the Indy mark for the high jump with a leap of 6'1⅞". Oscar runs the high hurdles. Oscar switches to baseball and pitches Attucks to a 7–6 win over Noblesville, going the distance, though not in his customary precise fashion: he allowed only five hits but walked seven. Oscar has some bad luck—he loses a coin flip for a berth in the regional track meet, at which there are only three spots for four jumpers.[1] And some nonsports news: Oscar will play the Dean of Boys in Attucks's annual Student Day. Robertson had clearly become the dominant sports star in the state of Indiana.

Like most coaches, Ray Crowe had long demurred from naming "favorites" or "all-time teams," but he gave in after the 1955 state championship. He took a reporter into his den, glanced at the photos on the wall, and named twelve players. In order from his earliest teams: Hallie Bryant, Willie Gardner, Robert Jewell, Flap Robertson, Bill Mason, Oscar Robertson, Winford O'Neal, Sheddrick Mitchell, Willie Merriweather, Bill Brown, Bill Hampton, and Bill Scott. (The all-time big five from that group would probably be Oscar, Bryant, Gardner, Merriweather, and Brown or Maxey.)

Attucks's run to the state championship was voted the number one story of 1955 by the *Star*, the tale of the Tigers edging out the fatal crash at the Indy 500 that killed Bill Vukovich and Bob Sweikert. As further

---

1. Oscar had also given football a try until his freshman year. He played a predictable position, quarterback, but, according to teammate Willie Merriweather, gave it up after he got "smeared, time after time."

evidence of Attucks's popularity, the Tigers' 71–70 win over Muncie Central was the sixth-biggest story of the year.

So, to state the obvious, Attucks had a target on its back as it headed into the 1955–1956 season. They were *it* in the state of Indiana. The only seeming roadblock was Hammond Noll, a big, strong team with a solid tradition.

Oh, and there was one more thing: public opinion in some quarters had subtly turned against Attucks, and Butler University was listening. Years earlier Attucks was forced to play at Butler because of the inadequacies of a gym that could barely hold a square dance. So it was a novelty: *Let's go watch the Black guys play!* Then the Tigers got good, and it became an attraction: *The Attucks is playing tonight! Let's go!* Then they got *too* good: *Hey, no wonder they win all the time—they have a home-court advantage at Butler.*

So the administrators at Butler, heeding the supplications of some rival schools, were planning to severely cut back the number of games Attucks would play at Butler (which they did). Understand that Attucks administrators had tried to get money for a new gym that would help not only with basketball but also with other school-related activities, such as physical education classes. But they were unsuccessful, and the "Gymless Wonders," as the *Indianapolis Recorder* referred to them, had a "schedule that was more of a mess than ever before."

Years later, in the Ray Crowe biography, Robertson reflected on it: "It wasn't as though we chose to play games at Butler rather than in our own gym. If they'd given us a decent gym in the first place we wouldn't have been in the position of having to play games at Butler. I get a little upset when I'm reminded that we brought the city of Indianapolis its first state championship and that same city didn't even see fit to give us a gymnasium."

You can feel his anger, just as you could when he talked about the celebration following the first state championship. But there was no debate about this. Would Butler have cut back on games for a powerful white attraction if opponents had complained? Perhaps. But the fact that Attucks was *forced* to play at Butler, then told it gave them an advantage, put the situation in a different light.

Attucks enjoyed playing at Butler, for sure, but the venue didn't matter. Oscar said later that they would have beaten anyone "playing in a cow pasture." Trying to beat Attucks that season was as futile as chasing the wind. Just as Attucks was the *it* team, Oscar was the *it* player. Whatever resistance the 1950s press had to anointing one player, he had erased it. Before Attucks's first game the *Star* ran this story:

> Every ivory hunter in college basketball and probably some of the pros have big plans for all-state forward Oscar Robertson once he gets his walking papers next graduation day. Robertson, six-four, 190-pound regular for the third year in a row, already owns just about every record in the book here—499 points for a 21-game regular season, 672 points for a 31-game season, including tourneys 690 for the regular season the last two years and 1,016 the last two years, including the tournaments.

In modern times, someone with Oscar's talent would have been identified back when he was a runt playing junior high ball for Tom Sleet. But not then. To mention colleges was unusual; to conjure up the possibility of the pros for a high school player was revolutionary.

The Attucks starting lineup was projected to be Robertson, Stanford Patton, John Gipson, Bill Brown, and Sam Milton. Patton was clearly a forward and Gipson clearly a center, and because Oscar continued to be listed as a forward, Brown was often listed as a guard beside Milton. But Brown was a tough inside player and the team's second-best rebounder.

Among the reserves was Oscar's brother Henry, whose name crops up from time to time in game accounts. Though he wasn't without some game, it is possible that Henry's surname had something to do with his being on the roster. "Oscar was great and Flap was a real player, but I'd say Henry was more a spectator," said Maxey, who became increasingly important as the season went on. "He could've been a real player maybe, but Henry didn't put as much into it as the rest of us."

Henry did outshine his more famous brother in one respect: as a singer. He and teammates Brown and Gipson and two other Attucks students, Donald Brown and Robert Grider, were members of a doo-wop singing group called the Tigerleers. "We weren't as good as The Counts,"[2] says Gipson today, "but we weren't bad. Sung on the street corner and such. Oscar wasn't a part of it, but Henry was pretty good." The Tigerleers also performed in what was called Attucks's "junior vaudeville show."

Maxey would gain his greatest stardom on the 1956–1957 team, which surprised most experts by getting to the state final, where it lost to South Bend Central 67–55. (In the continuing link to the movie *Hoosiers*, South Bend was the team Hickory High beat for the state title.) But Maxey was of crucial importance to the 1955–1956 team too, if only because Oscar trusted him more than he did any other teammate besides Brown.

A photo of Oscar with Crowe, sportswriter Wayne Fuson, and broadcaster Charlie Brockman, who would call the games for WIRE, appeared in the *News* before the first game. Oscar had been cocaptain of the team (with Merriweather) as a junior, but it was already clear that there was one captain, one leader, one alpha male among the players in 1955–1956. In the Attucks hierarchy there was Ray Crowe and below him—*just* below him—was Oscar Palmer Robertson. There was no one else.

---

2. The Counts, composed of Attucks students and originally called The Five Diamonds, had a national reputation and a couple of R&B hits titled "Hot Tamale" and "Darling Deer." No less a luminary than Wes Montgomery sometimes backed them in the studio. "The Counts are out to make the school as well-known for its singing graduates as for its basketball team," read a 1955 story in the *Indianapolis News*.

Oscar scored thirty-one points in the season-opening win over Fort Wayne Central and followed it up with twenty-nine in a 98–52 rout over Terre Haute Gerstmeyer. The Tigers might have reached three digits except that they were exhausted, having arrived back at 4:30 a.m. from Fort Wayne because of icy roads. Still, the Tigers put on a show. "Before the game my kids weren't warming up," said Gerstmeyer coach Howard Sharpe, who was known as "the evangelist of Indiana basketball." "They were standing around watching Attucks dunk the ball. I told them if they were going to do that they'd have to get off the floor and buy a ticket."

Maxey says today that the pregame show was designed for a purpose. "Coach Crowe didn't like that kind of stuff at first, but, as time went on and we kept winning, he just loosened up," says Maxey. "We know what effect it had on the other team. But we didn't do all that stuff they do today, between the legs and all that. We just went up and stuffed it hard. And it scared people."

As the season progressed, the team was subject to the same trend as the previous season: the Tigers were so relentlessly ruthless that they were held to a different standard, and there was a constant excavation for failures in the routine wins. "Attucks Has Handsful for Three Periods" read one headline after a 55–36 win over Sheridan. Attucks showed "ragged play" wrote another reporter after a 59–46 win over Broad Ripple. Attucks "grounds out" its twenty-first win in a row. But then, the Tigers held themselves to a high standard too. "Disgraceful, disgraceful," Bill Brown said to describe the win over Sheridan, slamming his fist into his hand for emphasis.

What would become a recurring theme emerged early in the season. Oscar scored almost at will—reporters needed to find other words for his prolific output, often settling on *popped*, as in "Oscar popped for 24 points," or *events*, as in "Oscar scored 33 events"—but often got into early and significant foul trouble. In one game he had three fouls in the first period. "They just looked for reasons to blow fouls on me," he said in later years.

What would turn out to be one of Attucks's most harrowing wins of the season occurred in the finals of the city championship when it beat Tech 46–39, a relatively old-fashioned score for Attucks. It was a mixed-blessing kind of game for Oscar, who scored only twelve points, stymied for a large part of the game by a feisty little guard named Freddy McCoy, who had emerged as an "Oscar stopper."[3] McCoy was the sort of player who could give Oscar problems, an undersized (5'7"), speedy track star who was also strong. (McCoy went on to become one of the first great African American athletes at Colorado State, starring in basketball and track.) In modern times, Oscar would have posted him up the entire game and possibly *popped* for forty *events*, but the game wasn't played that way back then. So Oscar battled McCoy most of the way—there was also the matter of the rest of the Tech team sticking to him "like mustard plaster," in the words of another writer—and finally shook loose to "deliver the big one," as the *Star* put it. That was one of his patented one-handed jumpers with 1:08 left that gave Attucks the margin it needed. "It seemed that Oscar suddenly realized that Attucks might lose if he didn't do something about it," wrote Wayne Fuson in the *News*. So he did something about it.

Still, Robertson-McCoy wasn't the battle that caught the eye of the Indy *News* photo editor; that was Oscar and Tech's Eddie Hannon, who, as the caption under their photo read, were "doing their own version of the latest South American dance, the Cha-Cha," one *Cha* short of what the dance eventually became.

---

3. Sports journalists (including this one) have always delighted in singling out "stoppers." Joe Dumars of the Detroit Pistons was considered somewhat of a "Michael Jordan stopper." Seattle's Gary "The Glove" Payton claimed to be as well, though Jordan memorably pooh-poohed the notion in the documentary *The Last Dance*. Other supposed stoppers were Houston's Robert Reid (Larry Bird) and Scottie Pippen (Magic Johnson). Stoppers can be effective for a while, and certainly Pippen was as good as anyone in history in containing an opponent if that was his job. But great players only get "stopped" for a short while.

———

The calendar flipped to 1956, and Attucks flipped a switch. South Bend Adams fell 88–51, but that was merely a warmup. On January 13 Attucks "shellacked" (the *Star*'s word) Michigan City by the score of 123–54 behind forty-five points by Oscar, surpassing Bryant's school record of forty-three. Ray Crowe professed not to know about the record, which sounds suspicious. Assistant coach Al Spurlock,[4] who kept the scorebook at the game, said he was aware of it, which leads one to believe that he must have told Crowe. And why was Oscar still in the game if not to break the record since Crowe was inclined to be generous to victims? But not this one. Apparently Michigan City coach Ralph Hooker had somewhere along the line in the previous season voiced doubt about Attucks's chances of winning a state championship. Or at least Crowe had heard that he had. Anyway, at Attucks, there was no more philosophy of turning the other cheek.

"Man for man, this team is much better," Hooker said when asked to compare the current Attucks team to the reigning state champs.

But was it? This team had no one (other than Oscar) as offensively talented as Merriweather, Oscar's right-hand man, who was beginning a productive career at Purdue. It had no one as tall as Sheddrick Mitchell, who would become a rotation player (though not a star) at Butler. And the backcourt-Bill defensive demons of 1955, Hampton and Scott, were big losses too.

On the other hand, the 1956 team featured, first, a Robertson who simply did whatever he wanted, whenever he wanted. If you look at any

———

4. Spurlock was a highly respected figure at Attucks. Like Crowe, he had been a college track star. Black athletes were often given opportunities in that sport—Spurlock competed at the University of Illinois—because the dearth of personal physical contact, as opposed to what happens in football, basketball, wrestling, etc., made it more palatable to whites. This is not to suggest that Spurlock, who died in 2014 at the age of 101, had it easy. "I didn't become too friendly with white people," he told *Indianapolis Monthly* in 2014, "because if I had gone downtown and wanted to stop for a cup of coffee, there was the potential embarrassment that the place wouldn't serve me."

film of Robertson in his senior year, he is playing a different game than everyone else, as coldly efficient as a Stasi agent. He never appears in a hurry; yet he's quicker than everybody. That might be why he went to the foul line less frequently than might be expected; defenses had a hard time keeping up with him. He never seemed to muscle anyone; yet he got almost every rebound he went after. It is a truism of basketball that if you have the best player on the court, you always have the best chance of winning the game.

Maxey was another wild card. He was one of the greatest athletes in the history of Attucks, a relentless and tough competitor. "I lived to run," says Maxey, who completed numerous marathons and, into his eighties, looks like he could knock one off now. "I never knew anyone who could outlast me," he says. Oscar called Maxey "my cleanup guy." The 1955–1956 team also had a Muggsy Bogues–type weapon in 5'5" LeVern Benson, who was just a sophomore. The newspapers frequently diminished him by calling him a "mascot" and describing him as "loved by the cheerleaders," and just about every photo of him has him peering out from between the arms or legs of a taller teammate. But Benson was a real player, a guard who took care of the ball and locked down his man on defense, and later had a terrific career at Miami of Ohio, where he was twice a Mid-American Conference first team selection. He and Maxey were the main reasons that Attucks made it to the championship final in 1957 sans Oscar.

"The idea that they were just Oscar and four other nobodies is crazy," says Carl Short, the star center for Indianapolis Manual, who had many battles with Attucks in 1955 and 1956. "Oscar was the key, of course, and, no, I'm not sure they win the state championship without him. But they were loaded with great personnel."

Attucks also featured an overload of what can only be called seriousness. Every team will tell you it wants to win, but not every team, quite often at the pro and college levels and certainly in high school, has the collective mental fortitude to do that for every game. Some of Attucks's ability to stay serious came from the notion that they *had* to jump out to a lead to protect against bad calls late in the game. The refereeing got marginally better as the years went on—emphasis on *marginal* since Maxey has in his collection of photos one that shows him getting tackled and still drawing a personal—but the incentive to blast out of the blocks was no less urgent. It was policy.

Hampton, still a strong and forceful man, says it was a business-only team. "We did not get in trouble on or off the court," Hampton said during a 2022 interview. "If I saw somebody getting ready to steal something or get into some other kind of trouble, I'd say, 'Wait a minute, let me get outta here.' We knew the deal. We stayed in our lane."

Occasionally the players would go out on Indiana Avenue to the Walker Casino Ballroom located on the top floor of the Madam C. J. Walker Building. A man named Matthew Dickerson ran the dances, and he would let in the Attucks players—Gipson and Bill Brown were the regulars—for free. "He used to announce us over the microphone when we came in after a game," remembers Gipson. "It was a great feeling." But there seems to be no instance when an Attucks player hit the news for a crime or misdemeanor or any kind of off-court incident.

Crowe had a lot to do with maintaining a serious atmosphere, but much of it came from a certain player. Years later, whenever a conversation with Jerry West turned toward Oscar, "The Logo" would invariably comment on Oscar's maturity. "The big difference between the two of us," said West, the number two pick in the 1960 NBA draft behind Oscar, "was that Oscar was ready to play right away. It takes a while for most players. I know it took a while for me. But not Oscar. The ball went up in his first game and he was a pro. Period."

That maturity and seriousness of purpose was apparent back at Attucks. "Oscar would get on you," remembers Maxey. "'Keep your head up! Watch for the ball!' Stuff like that. And he'd throw the ball at you, too." Indeed, he got on his teammates, sometimes viciously, and his pro-clivity for doing that brought him into conflict with Crowe from time to time. "Ray threw him out of practice a couple times," Maxey says. "The coach would say, 'You go on back to the locker room.' He didn't like losing control, even to Oscar." That happened more in Oscar's senior year than in the previous season, when Oscar felt somewhat less like a boss on the floor because of the strong presence of Merriweather. Merriweather says he remembers Crowe tossing Oscar out of practice only once in the 1954–1955 season.

Robertson never threw a ball at a ref—protracted allocutions about behaving the *Attucks way* from Principal Russell Lane and Crowe were beaten into the heads of every Tiger—but Oscar could look at refs like they were gum on his shoe, which might have fed into his referee problem. He affixed those dark, brooding eyes on officials, and they knew he wasn't happy. He paid a price for that.

That referee problem came to the fore in a narrow 67–62 win over Washington High on January 19. Oscar had collected four fouls, one short of disqualification, by late in the third period, and Crowe had no alternative but to take him out. A 50–36 lead quickly evaporated to 52–51. Oscar returned in the fourth period and scored the key baskets to finish with twenty-two points.

But exactly what the hell was going on with Oscar and the striped shirts?

Bob Collins thought he knew. "It's open season on Oscar Robertson," he opined in the pages of the *Star*. Collins said the refs tended to not just call fouls *on* Robertson but also ignore fouls *against* him. "It seems to this fellow a foul against Oscar is as much a foul as it is against anyone else. . . . [A]t least he can't find any special exemption in the rulebook."

It wasn't just the Attucks-loving Collins. Jep Cadou Jr. in the *Star* felt that Oscar was "the victim of his own brilliance" because the "officials are calling fouls awfully close on him." But the main point of Cadou's commentary was something else: if the Tigers should lose Oscar in a close tournament game, "the Attucks bubble might burst in a hurry." He followed up by concluding that, without Oscar, "Attucks would be pretty ordinary."

One of his teammates remembers Oscar reaching the boiling point over a foul that was not called, and it carried over into an exchange of words with his coach. "Two guys got Oscar in the corner and one of them knocked him down," says John Gipson. "The refs didn't call it. So, then, Oscar's mad and he gets called for a foul, and Ray says to him, 'You can't do that, you'll foul out of the game.' And Oscar said, 'These guys are trying to hurt me and mess me up, and you're just talking about me.'" It no doubt speaks again to the way Crowe was forced to act in the 1950s; he was so conscious of playing by the rules that his best player sometimes felt he was not sufficiently defending his own guys.

The contemporary tale of this superstar-player-versus-referee leit-motif generally bends in the opposite direction: the superstar is protected by the zebras, who wouldn't dare foul out the main attraction. But it's not hard to imagine that things were different seven decades ago. Refs were still getting used to players like Oscar. *Wait . . . he* can't *be doing things that much better than everyone else, can he?* There was a resistance to individual achievement in basketball, a hesitation about accepting the new way of playing, which seemed to be out of the control of coaches. Was it racist? If not, it was certainly *racial.* Oscar was something new, and something new is never understood right away.

The future still frequently collided with the past in Indiana basketball, as when Howe tried to stall its way to victory on January 27 against Attucks. But the Tigers attacked every time they got their hands on the ball and won 55–24. And even in a slowdown game, Oscar picked up three early fouls—perhaps he was understandably impatient and did some hacking—and never got to the line himself.

Attucks avenged the previous season's only defeat by shrugging off Connersville 75–49 and was now four games from a perfect season. Cathedral fell 65–44, and the first specific hint about Oscar's college plans was dropped in a column by Collins: "The United States Naval Academy has now followed up on an early letter to Oscar Robertson through a personal representative." Oscar had no comment himself. It was also reported that he got a "recruiting letter" from the Chicago Cubs. (The Cubs hadn't had a winning record in a decade at that point, so perhaps they were desperate.)

And then something strange happened. In a February 10 game against Sacred Heart played at Tech, Oscar went full-bore Bryant. Not Hallie Bryant, *Kobe* Bryant. He took sixty of Attucks's seventy-one field goal attempts, albeit without his usual efficiency since he made only twenty-three. Oscar scored sixty-two[5] of Attucks's points in a 76–47 win, needless to say an Indiana single-game record. The box score looked like a misprint: Robertson, sixty-two; next-highest scorer, Stanford Patton, four.

It was an absolute anomaly. Did Robertson have something against parochial schools? Did a girlfriend say something to inspire him or piss him off? As was his custom, Oscar never talked much about the game. Maxey, still sharp, doesn't even remember it. "Really? Oscar scored *that many*?" But Gipson remembers, and he knows the back story. "Jerry Lawlis of Washington High," said Gipson during a 2022 interview. "He had broken Oscar's record. I don't know if we realized it at first, but finally someone said—I think it was Bill Brown—'We gotta get Oscar the ball.' I remember Ray going along with it but saying, 'Yeah, but let's still play basketball.' That was the coach in him." Gipson stops and smiles at a memory. "The only thing that stopped it was somebody taking three long jumpers from the corner. I remember Bill Brown saying, 'Damn, why's he doing that?' And it was Oscar's brother. Henry."

---

5. Oscar never scored that many points in a single game in either college or the NBA. He scored fifty-six points in his first college game, which was against Seton Hall in Madison Square Garden. That's officially making a splash. He had fifty in a Missouri Valley Conference win over Wichita State, including thirty-three of the Bearcats' forty-three points in the second half. He scored fifty or more points on two occasions in the pros and, strangely, had no fewer than six forty-eight-point games. For a list of his most prolific NBA scoring games, visit statmuse.com.

Lawlis had indeed set the all-time single-game Indianapolis scoring record with forty-eight points against Speedway High, which broke Oscar's record of forty-five. Lawlis was considered the state's best outside shooter in a state that loved outside shooting. Lawlis went on to have a good collegiate career at Purdue and, during that 1955–1956 season, was considered among the best players in Indianapolis. Oscar likely wanted to emphasize *among*.

Scoring explosions—Wilt with one hundred points against the Knicks in 1962, Kobe with eighty-one against Toronto in 2006 and the sixty-point, fifty-shot orgy in Kobe's final game against Utah in 2016—never come without repercussions. Of Oscar's explosion, W. F. Fox Jr. waxed predictably poetic in a column he titled "Ray Crowe's Theme Song." A sampling:

> Pass the ball to Oscar, boys.
> Pass it to him, please.
> I beg you Brown and Patton
> on my bending knees.
> And Henry, you and Maxey,
> don't try to hog that ball.
> Pass it off to Oscar
> and let him score them all.

In that same column a letter appeared from a 1936 Tech graduate that postulated a dire end for Attucks because of Crowe's strategy that "promotes individual play to such a ridiculous extent." He went on to wag a finger: "It is good for neither the player nor the team, and I would venture to predict that last Saturday's performance against Sacred Heart will cost Attucks the state championship." File that under Freezing Cold Takes. Jep Cadou Jr. wrote this in the *Star*:

Coach Crowe received one of the first really pronounced blasts of public criticism in his highly successful tenure at Attucks. Many persons thought it unsportsmanlike for the Tigers to "feed" Oscar constantly so he could get back the scoring record lifted from him only days earlier by Washington's Jerry Lawlis. There's nothing in the rules against letting one player do most of your shooting, and Oscar's feat was perhaps even more remarkable since he had three or four Spartans guarding him much of the time.

These one-man-team episodes are often cast in allegorical terms: the haughty high scorer contemptuously ignoring his hardworking teammates for personal glory. That was nonsense in this case, as in many cases. It's a good bet that the Tech letter writer found nothing wrong with Bobby Plump holding the ball for four minutes while his teammates stood around like traffic cones, a different form of ball hogging.

But doubtless the response from the press and public would have been angrier five or six years earlier, if, say, Hallie Bryant had taken sixty shots. By the mid-1950s Indianans knew and respected Crowe and had gotten a hoops education from Robertson and his teammates. Fox wrote that no player on the Attucks team was "more considerate of his playmates" than Oscar, and Cadou commented that in six years Crowe "has brought Attucks from basketball obscurity to prominence and fame so notable that it would be hard to find a person in Indiana who doesn't know who he and Oscar are."

Though Oscar said that his arm "wasn't a bit tired," his lone recorded response to his scoring outburst, he scored only eight points in a 52–42 win over Frankfort that followed Sacred Heart, the final game before the sectionals. Beech Grove and Howe both went down easily, and an insipid performance against Cathedral (57–49) nevertheless produced a thirty-ninth straight win, an Indianapolis record. "Go all the way, Oscar," Bob Nipper, the Shortridge athletic director, said to Robertson, and that comment came *before* the sectional final. Shortridge, which broke out to a 10–2 lead, was tough, but Attucks hung on to win 53–48 as Robertson scored twenty-four points.

As usual, joyous news about Attucks basketball was intertwined, in the pages of the *Recorder*, with the harsh realities of Black life. Right above "Attucks Roars into Regional" in the March 3 edition was a story about the horrid threats against and eventual expulsion of Autherine Lucy (who would become known in the civil rights movement as Miss Lucy) from the University of Alabama. Another story discussed the policy of some Indianapolis policemen to keep white people from patronizing and even visiting Black-owned businesses on Indiana Avenue. Another story discussed the ongoing Montgomery bus boycott. (Though the boycott was successful, Dr. Martin Luther King Jr., one of several activists indicted, was actually prosecuted. He was fined $1,000 and received a suspended jail sentence of one year of hard labor.) Another story reported that a Black Chicago disc jockey named Al Benson had chartered a plane to drop five thousand copies of the Bill of Rights upon Jackson, the capital city of Mississippi and his birthplace. Benson, who by the time of his death in 1978 was recognized as one of the most important ambassadors of rhythm and blues music, said he wanted to alert the citizens that "they're living under a democracy" and that the Supreme Court had "ruled against school segregation."

No wonder Indianapolis's segregated school was so often a welcome pause from daily life. And so . . .

Another sectional title—a more difficult task than winning the regional and the fourth in a row for Ray Crowe—was cause for a "Rock An Roll Pep Rally" at Attucks, the *Indianapolis News* unsure if this relatively new genre deserved the *d* in *and* in these days only two years after Bill Haley & His Comets recorded "Rock Around the Clock." Most of the

Attucks players attended in uniform, but Oscar must have been going for the Russell Lane seal of approval in "black suit, colored with pink flecks, white shirt, black and lavender tie." Coach and star offered up reliable clichés for the beginning of the state tournament. Crowe: "We can't turn it on and off." Oscar: "All the tournament teams are tough."

Cadou's musing about Attucks's possible burst bubble came into play in its first regional game, a 99–43 rout of Hancock Central. In the second quarter Oscar went high in the air for a layup on a fast break, and a Hancock player "ran under him," according to a story in the *News*. Sure enough, Oscar was called for a foul.[6] But the bigger problem was that Oscar jammed his right thumb, apparently dislocating it temporarily, when he fell.

Oscar's thumb dominated the news over the next week; he got it treated "by ultrasound waves" under the supervision of Butler University's trainer. Whereas a Black principal's hiring was once carried under "News of Colored Folk," photos of Oscar's injury were all over the place. It's one thing that it was on the front page of the African American–owned *Recorder*, but there it was on the front page of the *News* too. And there's Ray Crowe examining the famous thumb in the *Star*. X-rays were always negative, and Attucks's march to the state's final four continued apace, though not without misprint—an Associated Press story identified Attucks's star as one Oscar *Roberts*.

Remember Oscar's MO before the 1955 state final? Control the opening tip, get the ball back, then announce what's what by dribbling deliberately to the right elbow and going up for a one-handed jumper. That's what he did in the afternoon game against Terre Haute Gerstmeyer. It went in, but a foul was called, negating the field goal. Didn't matter. His presence was announced. *I'm here, so don't get any ideas.*

---

6. The ability of the African American player to "elevate" unleashed the block-or-charge dilemma that still exists today. Refereeing a game essentially played at sea level is a lot easier than judging what happens when players are high in the air and then succumb to gravity.

Still, foul troubles followed him. Robertson fouled out of the game with ten minutes remaining, fouls four and five coming within forty-two seconds late in the third period. It almost defies belief that a player of his stature would collect that many personals at that point in the season. But Crowe, almost always the diplomat, rushed to defend the refs after the game, labeling the fifth foul "a good call," agreeing with Corky Lamm's assessment in the *News* that Oscar committed "a somewhat senseless charge." There is little doubt that Oscar was getting screwed but also that his temper was coming into play too. *You called that foul? Oh yeah, what about this one?*

Attucks led 47–35 when Oscar departed. "Let's show them we're not a one-man team," Bill Brown said to Stan Patton. And the Tigers lost only one point of that margin with Oscar gone. Patton and Maxey, both of whom finished with fourteen points, kept them afloat.

The state final was against Jefferson High from Lafayette, coached by a legend named Marion Crawley. Oscar describes the Bronchos (yes, the Bronchos; later the school would send forth into the world Guns N' Roses cofounders Axl Rose and Izzy Stradlin) thusly in *The Big O*: "Lafayette is a team comprised of white youths wearing dark jerseys. They play an antiquated half-court game that seems to have been dusted out of mothballs." At one point Jefferson passed the ball thirty-four times before shooting. Somebody counted.

Describing his play in the game, Oscar remembers, "I seemed to play every position, bringing the ball up court early, and then posting up like a center at select moments." Well, he's only telling the truth. Once again, he controlled the tip, got it back, made an elbow jumper eight seconds into the game, and Attucks was off. In fact, no other Attucks player took a shot until late in the first quarter.

With about four minutes left in the game and Attucks winning in a rout—"The Crazy Song" had already been rendered by the Attucks fans—Crowe called timeout to make sure the team knew that Oscar needed four points to break the all-time championship game scoring record of thirty-eight points. He got them, the last four coming on two effortless long-distance jumpers that ended the contest with the finality of a guillotine. He finished with thirty-nine points, and Attucks won 79–57. The margin roughly conformed to Attucks's season-long rampage—they won by an average of twenty-eight points in the regular season and twenty-three in the tournament. "The finish," Corky Lamm would write, "was an avalanche of Oscar." An unidentified college coach told Bob Collins, "There is no doubt that was the greatest high school team ever. I sincerely believe there are college teams they could beat. Oscar can do everything and do it better than any high school player I've seen."

Fuzzy Vandivier from the Franklin Wonder Five, then the school's athletic director, echoed that sentiment: "Attucks is the best team I've ever seen."

They were so good that, in the full blush of history, the 1955–1956 Attucks Tigers are almost overlooked. Those who are still alive from that era invariably speak with more emotion about the 1955 team, the *first* Black champion, the *first* Indianapolis champion. The 1955 Attucks yearbook might as well be dedicated to the basketball team; by comparison, the 1956 team is treated almost in *meh* fashion. *Of course*, they won. But anyone who played for them or against them remembers.

In the 16mm video available on YouTube, the 1955–1956 Attucks Tigers, the first undefeated team in the forty-six-year history of the Indiana state tournament, gather for a team photo after the game. Principal Russell Lane is in the front row; Ray Crowe, the orchestrator, is almost unnoticed in the back row. The camera catches the team walking off and settles for a moment on the face of Oscar, a vision of youth. He smiles widely, a smile that will come less and less frequently as the years go by, replaced by a wary countenance. In the following days a dozen photos of Attucks will appear in the newspapers in Indianapolis and points beyond. A caption in one of those photos reads, "Dream Team." That they were.

A postscript: A few weeks after Attucks won the title, Nat King Cole, one of America's first crossover entertainers, was attacked on stage during a performance before an all-white audience at Municipal Auditorium in Birmingham, Alabama. Cole returned to the stage after a while, and the audience gave him a ten-minute standing ovation. "I just came here to entertain you," he said. "That was what I thought you wanted." He mentioned he was born in Alabama. Then he left without resuming the show.

A second postscript: A few years later, after he broke the Madison Square Garden scoring record with fifty-six points for Cincinnati in a game against Seton Hall, Oscar was asked if that was his biggest thrill in basketball. "Nah," he answered. "My biggest thrill was helping Crispus Attucks win two Indiana state championships." A Hoosier has his priorities.

A third postscript: Several weeks after Attucks's dominating win, a fire tore through an apartment on the west side of Indianapolis, killing two-year-old Bettina Ann Bryant and her six-month-old brother Donald Bryant Jr. "The wiring was in deplorable condition," said Michael J. Hyland, director of fire prevention for the fire department. "The neglect of the owner of that house caused the deaths of those children."

David Leander Williams, the Indianapolis-born writer and a former Attucks player, remembers walking by the horrible scene. "It stuck in my mind because the one kid was just a little younger than me," he says. "And they just . . . they just . . . burned up. And they lived in a shack."

It's the kind of story that deserved the headline "Shocking." But it really wasn't. The *Recorder* said that the tragedy brought to thirteen the number of Black children who had burned to death in Indianapolis in less than thirteen months.

CHAPTER SEVENTEEN

Knocking King Kelly off His Throne

"McCracken turned off Oscar really quick."

After another ride around Monument Circle and another Naptown bonfire; after first-year mayor Phil Bayt had promised to "personally drive that fire truck down Meridian Street" if Attucks repeated as state champion in 1957; after Russell Lane told the Attucks students to "cut all the rugs you please" at an in-school celebration; after the Indianapolis Chamber of Commerce, which had ignored the Black school for decades, pledged monies for college scholarships; after another chow-down at Fendrick's Restaurant; after an epic meal at exclusive Broadmoor Country Club hosted by a white Attucks superfan named Harold Stolkin ("a meal that was second to none" as Bill Hampton remembers it), the focus turned to Oscar as an individual.

To the surprise of no one, he was named Indiana's 1956 Mr. Basketball, reprising the honor for Attucks that Hallie Bryant had won in 1953. His exploits in other sports continued to be chronicled in the Indy papers. He struck out ten in one baseball game and continued to be one of the state's best high jumpers and a reliable hurdler in track. And his college plans were occasionally mentioned, though no one seemed to have a concrete idea of what they were, including Oscar. Jep Cadou Jr. of the *Indianapolis News* mused that Ray Crowe should accompany Oscar "to whatever college the Attucks star chooses and take over the coaching reins."

Crowe professed publicly that he would stay out of Oscar's college decision. "That is strictly up to Oscar and his parents," Crowe said, and there's no reason to disbelieve him. At any rate, the guessing game of where Oscar was going to matriculate did not reach the fevered pitch it would these days. Oscar was consistently noncommittal other than to say he was thinking about majoring in math. "And there's always Uncle Sam to consider," wrote one reporter, which, back then, was not as ridiculous as it sounds, though Oscar never considered enlisting instead of enrolling.

But the most newsworthy topic regarding Oscar through much of May was the looming home-and-home All-Star Game that pitted Indiana's top seniors against those from Kentucky. The game was a big deal back then and, to an extent, still is. It began in 1940, took a hiatus for the World War II years of 1943 and 1944, and was played continuously until COVID-19 wiped it away in 2020 and 2021. It always drew much attention from the press of those two states and sometimes even something to write about. There was the 1953 Hallie Bryant game when he starred despite the death threats, and the following year, Indiana won again, 75–74, when—you're not going to believe this—Bobby Plump hit a last-second shot. The newspapers reported that Oscar was chosen for the 1956 Indiana squad "almost unanimously." (There's always an idiot or two; twenty baseball writers, after all, did not vote Ted Williams into the Hall of Fame.)

As the top player in the Hoosier state, Oscar would wear No. 1, as would Kentucky's star, a high-scoring guard named Kelly Coleman, widely known as "King" Kelly Coleman. The King had scored 185 points in four state tournament games (Oscar had scored "only" 106, which was a state record) and an astonishing 4,263 points over his career for

Wayland, a high school deep in Kentucky's mining country, whose jerseys read "WASPS." (To be clear, they referred to the insect.)

And, so, what we had here in the 1956 Indiana-Kentucky All-Star Game was a confrontation with the contours of archetype: the talented Black versus the mythical Caucasian, city versus country, the known quantity versus the great white hope. Corky Lamm reported in the *News* that the magazine *Scholastic Coach* carried biographies of both players and that Oscar's was nine lines while the King's was twenty-two! (emphasis Lamm's).

The King and Oscar (he was not yet known as the Big O) met at a May luncheon in Indianapolis, at which Bob Collins of the *Indianapolis Star* acted as a kind of interlocutor. The two stars talked about the Cincinnati Reds and a little bit about basketball. The King confessed that he liked to dribble behind his back, and Oscar said that his coach didn't like that. One newspaper even ran a tale of the tape: Coleman 6'3½", Oscar 6'5". Both had a thirty-four-inch waist. The big difference was in scoring average: Oscar's was 24.5, while the King's was almost double at 47. Here's another point of comparison: While Kentucky's Adolph Rupp[1] hadn't even considered Oscar because of the color of his skin, he had already called King Kelly "the greatest high school basketball player who ever lived, a combination of Cliff Hagan, Frank Ramsey, and all of the other great stars who have played at Kentucky." Even as an obvious recruiting ploy, that seems excessive.

At some point during the luncheon, the King was asked for a prediction. He said he thought Kentucky would win. One imagines Collins, a shrewd man who had watched Attucks and Oscar change the game,

---

1. Rupp, who began coaching at Kentucky in 1930 and stayed until 1972, had a sketchy rep as a coach of African Americans. His supporters argued that, in ordering that asterisks be put next to the names of Black recruits, he was only doing what his bosses wanted him to do and didn't want to waste either his or the recruit's time. Still, Rupp never recruited a Black player until 1969, three years after he lost the famous NCAA final to an all-Black team from Texas Western. For a detailed analysis of Rupp and race, visit www.bigbluehistory.net/bb/rupp.html.

staring wistfully at the King and thinking, *Son, you know that one about the bug and the windshield?*

Somewhere amid the baseball, the track, the awards (he made *Scholastic Magazine*'s high school All-American team, which also included Jerry West and, of course, King Coleman), and the news that an Attucks student named Jacqueline Gray had nominated him for president during a trip to Washington, DC, Oscar made a recruitment trip to Bloomington and Indiana University.

There were projections that Oscar would go to UCLA, where a certified Hoosier legend named John Wooden had just finished his eighth season, having turned the Bruins into a consistent conference power, albeit one yet to win a national title. (Wooden got the job after Branch McCracken of Indiana University turned it down.) Wooden had even sent Oscar a copy of his "Pyramid of Success." But Oscar thought that Los Angeles was too far from home.

Other rumors had Oscar going to Duquesne, which had a history of treating Black players well, owing in large part to Pittsburgh's being an early haven for African American players. But Oscar recoiled when the school suggested that he spend the summer working at Kutsher's, a resort in the Catskills, and playing hoops at night. Summer bell hopping at a "Dirty Dancing" spot was a popular practice for college players back then. (A short film titled *Wilt Chamberlain: Borscht Belt Bellhop* chronicles Kutsher's biggest summer star. The resort's rich basketball connection is also explored in the 2012 documentary *Welcome to Kutsher's: The Last Catskill's Resort*.) Oscar wanted no part of it. "I told them I wanted to develop into an All-American," he writes in *The Big O*, "but I had to work in the summer, and not as a bellhop."

A dalliance with Michigan went even worse. Oscar took a plane ride (his first) to Ann Arbor, but there was no one to greet him when he got off. "We forgot you were coming," they told him. These days they would have sent the college president, the chairman of the board of trustees, and a dozen cheerleaders for a recruit of Oscar's promise. He took the next plane back to Indianapolis.

But, anyway, Oscar wanted to go to IU. He recalls, "Just about anybody who grew up in Indiana and played nothing more than recreational basketball had a dream, at one time or another, of playing for Indiana University. I was no different." This even though the state's premier university had a much more complicated history with Black players.

In 1951, the same year that the Bryant-Gardner-Flap team made it to the final four, Bill Garrett, the African American star from Shelbyville, was wrapping up his stellar career at Indiana. In a bit of poetic justice, Garrett would later end up at Attucks, where he would coach the 1958–1959 team to a state championship. Garrett, who died from a heart attack in 1974 at age forty-five, is an enormously important figure in Hoosier hoops history, his story told by Tom Graham and Rachel Graham Cody in *Getting Open*. Garrett was the first Black player recruited by McCracken, shortly after he dissed Jumpin' Johnny Wilson at the Anderson banquet. The coach was disinclined to violate the Big Ten's unspoken whites-only rule, and it was only because Indianapolis civil rights activist Faburn DeFrantz successfully lobbied IU president Herman B. Wells that Garrett broke the conference's color barrier. "Dr. Herman Wells is a great hero in my world," says James Madison, the respected Hoosier historian and IU professor.

In Bloomington, Garrett went through the predictable retinue of indignities—racist taunts from opposing fans, discrimination at on-the-road hotels in cities like Saint Louis, being ignored for postseason awards, the ham-handed treatment by McCracken. There was much precedent for mistreatment in this college town. The IU faithful in the late 1940s cheered a talented Black tailback named George Taliaferro; yet he was not allowed entrance to the famed college hangout called the Gables, the place where—wait for it—Taliaferro's *own photo* was displayed on the walls. (The Gables is best known as the place where Bloomington-born IU law student Hoagy Carmichael composed "Stardust" in 1925.) Graham and Cody write that Taliaferro eventually made a deal with the owner that, if he and a date sat in the Gables and no one complained, the place would integrate. It worked, and the Gables "became known as the place to rub elbows with the football star."

Keep in mind that throughout his basketball career, Garrett's was the *only* Black face on the court in any Big Ten game. By all accounts he acted with grace and good humor. In *Getting Open* Graham and Cody write of a practice session when a surly McCracken yelled to his team, "You're gonna stay here and work till you're black in the face!" Responded Garrett, "Does that mean I can go home now?" True, the expression is generally *blue in the face*, but the anecdote, apocryphal or not, is too rich to ignore.

Garrett got a standing ovation after his final game in Indiana's Assembly Hall. "The outpouring, impulsive and cathartic, went on for almost two minutes, momentarily freezing referees and players," wrote Graham and Cody. Two days after that electric feel-good moment, Garrett and teammate Gene Ring were passengers in a car driven by another IU player, Phil Buck. They were heading back to campus after a trip to Indianapolis when they stopped at a diner along State Road 37. It bore, according to *Getting Open*, a marquee that read, "Hurryin' Hoosiers Fans Welcome." Minutes after they sat down, they were approached by a waiter who pointed to Garrett and said, "I can feed the two of you but not him." They left the restaurant, and Garrett sat in the backseat for the remainder of the trip, tears rolling down his cheeks.

A postscript: Garrett played in what is now IU's intramural building, which had been named for Ora Wildermuth, a powerful campus figure from 1938 to 1949, when he headed the university's board of trustees. Wildermuth was a public voice in opposing integration—let's just call him a racist—and a movement began about fifteen years ago to consider renaming the building. In 2009 IU trustees had approved a recommendation that the Wildermuth name remain but Bill Garrett's be added. Many around the IU campus found this a jaw-dropping absurdity, "like naming something the Goldstein-Hitler Center," as IU professor Lanier Holt put it. It is now officially called the William Leon Garrett Fieldhouse.

Oscar's visit with Branch did not go well. "McCracken turned off Oscar really quick," remembers Al Maxey, who went along with Oscar and Crowe on the trip. "He started talking about how he wouldn't give cars and house payments and crazy stuff, and Oscar said, 'I'm not here to get any of that, I just want to play ball.'" When Oscar came out of the meeting, Maxey said his lone comment was, "I'm not coming back here." Oscar wrote that McCracken said to him, "I hope you're not the kind of kid who wants money to go to school," and he has always stuck by it.

In public at least, McCracken never said anything negative about Oscar. "I've never seen anything like him" was one of the IU coach's only on-the-record comments about him. If the exchange with McCracken happened the way Oscar says it did, a backstory involving another high-powered recruit is relevant. A year earlier McCracken and IU were in the hunt to land Wilt Chamberlain, literally and figuratively the biggest potential conquest in college basketball history (as well as the world's tallest bellhop). Wilt visited Bloomington three times, and McCracken thought he had him, but Kansas swooped in and took him away, just as it had done eight years earlier with a Hoosier product named Clyde Lovellette. (Also a center, Lovellette had just lost the 1947 state championship game to Garrett's Shelbyville team.) McCracken claimed that the Jayhawks had paid for Chamberlain, something that Wilt and others all but confirmed years later.

At any rate, Oscar didn't consider IU after his trip. That might also have had something to do with Oscar's believing that McCracken had an unspoken quota of Black players, and he wouldn't have seen as much action as he wanted, something he hinted to Mark Montieth in an interview. It's improbable that McCracken, who knew his basketball, would have been that stupid. At any rate, for Indianapolis fans, at least those who followed Crispus Attucks, Branch McCracken would forever be known as the guy who squandered the talents of Hallie Bryant and sent Oscar Robertson across state lines.

Shortly after he made his decision to go to Cincinnati—a story announced in relatively subdued fashion in the June 11 editions of the *Indianapolis News*—Oscar graduated with his Class of 1956 mates. One of the people most disappointed with Oscar's college decision was Willie Merriweather, who had urged Oscar to join him at Purdue. "I firmly believe to this day that we would've won a national championship," says Merriweather today. "No doubt in my mind." The evidence suggests that Oscar never considered Purdue; if IU wasn't going to be his destination, then no other Hoosier college was going to be either. The Boilermakers had a proud tradition, but it was nowhere near as strong as IU's.

Among Oscar's notable fellow Attucks grads was Jerry Williams, a close friend of Oscar's who would go on to become vice president of a $400-million-per-year auto supplies company and the first Black person to grace the cover of *Fortune*. "What Attucks taught me," said Williams in the Ted Green documentary, "was to dream, to dare and to do." Oscar, like Williams, was a member of the National Honor Society. Oscar had never been involved in any kind of altercation on or off the court. He had led a team of gentlemen for the better part of three years, a team that would go down as the most dominating in Indiana history. His graduation photo in the yearbook is captioned "Oscar Palmer Robertson, Math, English, History, 1956 Mr. Basketball of Indiana."

Yet he did not win the Trester Award for "mental attitude, scholarship, leadership, and athletic ability." That went to Dennis Tepe, a fine player who had helped Elkhart to the final four, where it lost to Lafayette

Jefferson, the team that Attucks scuttled in the championship. There is never a public accounting of what precisely determines the Trester winner. In those days, however, he was almost always white, which is why Robert Jewell of Crispus Attucks High School, the 1951 winner, stands out. He later became the first African American hired as a salaried employee by Eli Lilly, a major Indianapolis employer since the 1950s, and eventually became a product chemist. In the early 1950s, Robert, who died in 1992, was Attucks's jewel, as well as its Jewell.

Before the first Indiana-Kentucky All-Star Game at Butler University, King Kelly started talking like a joker, predicting that he would score fifty points against Indiana and noting, after arriving a day late for practice without proper warmup garb, that he didn't need much work to beat the Hoosiers. The Kentucky coach, Ted Hornback, reported that he could "feed his whole family" on what Coleman ate at the training table, and there were other reports that the King was late because he had gotten married. He was starting to sound like a character out of *Li'l Abner*. Among the Indiana team, there was no shortage of volunteers to guard Coleman, though Oscar settled the argument: "Sorry, boys, he's all mine," then added, "It doesn't make much difference anyway. He's with a losing cause." When the two No. 1's passed each other at midcourt right before tip-off, Oscar said, "Talk is cheap."

There are moments of separation in sports. It boggles the mind, on the one hand, that a player able to average forty-seven points per game would be so outclassed against unfamiliar competition. But it happens when you take a step up and have that come-to-Jesus moment when you realize that part of your sporting life was constructed from myth. Driving lanes that were once freeways are now closed. Shots that were so easy to get off are now spoiled by lightning-quick defensive players.

Getting the ball was usually so easy, but even that becomes difficult with long-armed athletes schooled in the rigors of Indiana state tournament play. Look at it musically. In his league, King Kelly was Jay and the Techniques playing the Allentown Fair, while Oscar was Marvin Gaye at the Apollo. One is reminded of that epic moment in a different sport when Seattle Seahawks talkative linebacker Brian Bosworth, cast in the role of King Kelly Coleman, was run over near the goal line by Oakland Raiders silent running back Bo Jackson, the Oscar figure. It's not fair to judge a player by one game, far less by one play, but Bo bashing Bos in 1987 was an image that stuck.

So it was for Oscar and the King. In the first game, Robertson scored thirty-two points, and Coleman had seventeen, many of them in mop-up time. The final was 92–78. "The King was reduced to a more loyal subject," Collins wrote in the *Star*. The rematch in Louisville, Kentucky, went worse for Coleman. Oscar had forty-one points in a 102–77 rout, and the King had only four. "Oscar's a pro playing against high school boys," commented Kentucky coach Hornback. Attucks's biggest press supporter went further: "If there is anyone in the world who doubts now that Oscar Robertson is the best high school basketball player in the world," wrote Collins, "he is speaking in very faint tones."

Coleman claimed, even at the time, that he never said he would score fifty points and that the boasts he did make were at the suggestion of "a press agent" who wanted to increase ticket sales. He regretted that he looked like a "nitwit." Oscar dismisses him in *The Big O* as a "braggadocious white boy from the Kentucky hills," and there's an element of truth to that. But Coleman had a good college career with Kentucky Wesleyan and even made it to the NBA with the Knicks for a few years. He just came along at the wrong time, when the real king was on the court.

Coleman has not been forgotten, incidentally. A couple years ago Jason Frakes of Louisville's *Courier Journal* wrote a piece about Wayland that included this sentence: "People from around Kentucky and the entire nation still come to Wayland, just to see the gym where Coleman once played." King Kelly Coleman died in 2019, still a certified hero in his neck of the Kentucky woods.

———

A couple of postscripts to the Indiana-Kentucky classic.

First, about a month after the second game in Louisville, another Kentucky town, Sturgis in the northwest corner, was in the news. At the orders of the Kentucky attorney general, National Guardsmen with riot guns and fixed bayonets formed a protective wall around nine Black students as they left a high school among threats from five hundred townsfolk that they would "get you ni—ers if it takes all year." The Guardsmen also brought in four tanks. The school grounds looked like a war zone. The hubbub went on for days as the African American students, buttressed by law, tried to integrate a previously all-white school. Truancy among protesting white students on some days early in the term was as high as 50 percent.

The white guys won one. Two weeks later, the Union County Board of Education, acting under advice from the state attorney general, barred Blacks from entering Sturgis High, as well as schools in the nearby town of Clay. Proclaimed the *Indianapolis Recorder*, "School integration was halted as voices of segregationists were heard in rumbling overtones throughout the tense Southland."

The second postscript is from the following season, when Attucks's Al Maxey was chosen for the Indiana team. He headed out to a cafeteria the night before the first game in Louisville. Maxey remembers,

I was with a bunch of the white players. I handed my tray in to get a helping of something, and the guy behind the counter says, "We can't serve you." It stopped me cold.

I just froze. The white player in front of me turned around and saw what happened and said, "Let's get outta here." We went past the coaches in the back, and they left, too, and we got something to eat back at the hotel.

But Maxey and another Indiana Black player, Herschell Turner, got the last laugh. The whole team went to a movie together—Maxey was angry and didn't want to go, but the coaches insisted—and ended up at an African American theater. "Everybody was talking and yelling through the whole thing," remembers Maxey. "'Watch out! He's got a gun! Don't go in there!' All those white boys got an education that night."

It's not that Indianapolis was necessarily a more open place than Louisville. It's more that kids like Maxey were aware of the boundaries when they were home. "You forgot that sometimes when you were in other places," he said.

That kind of thing didn't happen just to high school kids. Three years later, at an exhibition game before the beginning of the 1961–1962 NBA season held in Lexington to honor Frank Ramsey and Cliff Hagan, two of Adolph Rupp's former stars who were now in the NBA, Sam Jones and Satch Sanders of the Celtics were refused service in the coffee shop of the Phoenix Hotel. Furious, they huddled with Bill Russell and K. C. Jones, and though coach Red Auerbach urged them to stay, they flew home. The Celtics played the exhibition with seven white players that evening, none of whom honored the boycott.

No wonder Rupp was in no hurry to recruit Black players to the Bluegrass State. Except three nights earlier the African American Celtic players had been turned away at another hotel restaurant before another preseason game.

That was in Marion, Indiana.

CHAPTER EIGHTEEN

Did Attucks Unite a City?

"Attucks made his life important."

The golden era of Crispus Attucks basketball began with Ray Crowe at the dawn of the 1950s, reached its apotheosis with Oscar Robertson in the mid-1950s, and didn't really fizzle out until 1960. Under Bill Garrett, the Hoosier schoolboy star who had broken the color barrier in the Big Ten Conference, the Tigers won the 1959 state championship. By that time, Crowe was the Attucks athletic director.

But after all this wonderful basketball played at this segregated school, after death threats and racist officiating and epic games and varying venues and sandwiches on the bus and white fans jumping on a Black bandwagon, these questions should be asked: Did Crispus Attucks accomplish something meaningful? Did those teams change minds? What was their impact? Documentarian Ted Green called his terrific film *Attucks: The School That Opened a City*—but exactly how far did it open? And for how long?

Those answers are, to some extent, unknowable. No reliable metric exists to assess ignorance; no barometer besides the anecdotal to study racial progress from one decade to another. Remember, too, that Attucks was—*is*—more than a basketball team, and Green's film was about more than hoops. The collective power of Attucks came from its roots as a racial outlier in a town whose DNA was white hegemony. From the beginning, Attucks existed simultaneously as afterthought and dream, and the mere fact that it not only endured but also prospered is substantial proof of its worth.

In trying to assess the Attucks legacy, let's take the easy things first.

Robertson, whose three-year record at Attucks was a mind-bending 85–6, with only one of those losses coming after his sophomore season, changed basketball in a state of seminal importance to the game. He was a revolutionary player without appearing revolutionary. His scoring numbers are dazzling, a numbing chronicle of consistency. After Attucks had secured its second straight championship, Oscar held scoring records (without a three-point shot, remember) in the following:

- Single game (62 points)
- Single season (541 points)
- Season including tournaments (764 points)
- Three-year tally excluding tournaments (1,231 points)
- Three-year tally with tournaments (1,780 points)
- Championship game (39 points)
- Four-game state tourney (106 points)

Oscar also shot .505 from the field, an outstanding percentage back then, particularly for a volume shooter. (Traditionalists love to talk about how much better shooters were in yesteryear. They weren't. Shooting is more accurate now; three-point shooting averages are nearly as good as regular averages were back in the day.) Oscar was one of the first great shooters, as were many of those Hoosier farm boys who learned their perfect releases on hoops attached to barns.

Yet Oscar's scoring was not the first thing people mentioned when talking about him as a player. It was his court sense, his ability to control the flow. "He just *ran the game*," Crowe once said, as if he were talking about a casino pit boss. "It was something special when you were on his team," said Carl Short, who played against Oscar in high school and on Indy playgrounds and with him once in an exhibition game when Oscar was a pro. "There was just a level of expectation, an understanding that you had better perform. He just raised everybody up."

Robertson had the qualities that the press had previously reserved for white players—leadership and smarts—combined with the athleticism that African Americans brought to the game. He redefined the common misperception that the Black athlete was 99 percent brawn, 1 percent brain. Oscar was fifty-fifty, his athleticism sometimes even overlooked because of his high-IQ, blue-collar MO.

As a team, Attucks changed the way the game was played. "They swept through the state like a chemical fire," Bob Collins wrote after Attucks's two-year run, "building and exploding and growing into an awesome, almost uncontrollable force." Collins was never one for holding back on metaphor and overstatement ("Pull out your adjectives, garble the syntax, throw it in one big stream and you'll have a word defining the show Attucks gave 15,000 high school addicts last night," he wrote after the first championship in 1955), but his enthusiasm speaks to how Attucks animated fans who resisted change. Angelo Angelopoulos, another reporter who covered Attucks, put it simply but profoundly: *Attucks brought fun back into the game.* Bobby Plump's mind-numbing stall was, to be fair, dramatic when he attached a fifteen-foot jumper to the end of it. But it was not fun. It was a waltz. Attucks played thirty-two minutes of rock 'n' roll.

A group of Black teenagers became an economic engine that drove not only the school but some of Indianapolis at a time when whites rarely shopped at Black businesses—sometimes they were even chased off—and Blacks dared not venture where they were not welcome. Attucks's appearances in Butler Fieldhouse generated substantial income in an era long before super high school teams crisscrossed the country and raked in money on ESPN. When Attucks played, say, intracity rival Tech at Butler, the place was packed, with as many as fifteen thousand fans. The college got parking and concessions, and the schools split the ticket revenue, somewhere between $3,000 and $4,000. That was real money. Phillip Hoose reported in *Attucks!* that by 1953, even before the Oscar glory years, the Attucks Athletic Fund had socked away $25,000, primarily from the revenue gleaned by playing at Butler. That bought the school a new printing press and equipment for tailoring and shop classes. It also brought in money to sponsor golf and tennis teams at a time when a Black person couldn't have picked up a club or a racket at most discriminatory American country clubs. Attucks was one of the first cross-racial attractions in the capital city, perhaps in the country. They were Louis Armstrong without a trumpet.

Then, too, Attucks was indispensable to African American–owned businesses, which attached themselves to the basketball team like aphids to tomato plants. Their ads were all over the *Indianapolis Recorder,* game programs, and yearbooks.

"Wash 'Em, Steam 'Em, Wipe 'Em Dry Attucks Tigers"
—Stancy's Auto Laundry.

"Hey There, You Attucks Tigers Pour on the Cool, Pour on the Oil—Get Real Hot, Make 'Em Boil"
—Indianapolis Ice and Fuel Co.

Once the Tigers had won their first state title, some white businesses even jumped aboard the Attucks train.

Attucks's success helped establish a different life paradigm for the Black Attucks athlete. As Oscar and teammates were winning their second championship, Bill Hampton was playing at Indiana Central,

Willie Merriweather was playing at Purdue, and Bill Scott and Sheddrick Mitchell were playing at Butler. That's Bill Scott, who would later teach at Attucks and coach the basketball team. Bill Scott, who worked within the once-racist Indianapolis Public School System as a counselor for forty years. Bill Scott, who was raised in what amounted to a garage after his mother was murdered. But before the Crowe teams came along, the best of those players dreamed of being Globetrotters, a temporary career that worked for precious few, and most of them didn't dream at all.

Similarly, the success of Attucks gave hope to all young African Americans throughout the city, at least those who were paying attention and for whom the cards fell right. The Tigers were a guiding light (Tyger tyger, burning bright). True, many of them might have also been athletes, and one of the best who followed Oscar was George McGinnis, who led Washington High to the 1969 state championship and is generally considered the second-best player in Indianapolis history.

McGinnis's story followed the pattern. His father brought the family north from Alabama looking for a better life. They were originally targeting Chicago, but a stopover in Indianapolis changed the plan. "My father's sister told him, 'Look, you won't have to live in those high-rises,'" McGinnis said in an interview, "'and you'll have a wide-open-spaces-type job.'" If you call foundry work the *wide-open spaces*, the senior McGinnis got what he wanted. They moved to Naptown. One side of George's street went to Attucks, the other to Washington; he was on the Washington side. But he remembers Attucks:

> I was five, six years old when Oscar was the king of Indiana basketball. I remember it like it was yesterday. We had this old TV we had to adjust with a clothes hanger. The games came in fuzzy, but they came in. And Attucks represented something we had never seen before—a Black kid winning a state championship and getting a gold ring.

Oscar was a god to me. We all wanted to be just like him. And that never changed, you know? When I got to Washington High, it was always Oscar I heard about. "You're coming up on Oscar's record." "You're going to eclipse Oscar." Really? As far as I was concerned, *nobody* ever eclipsed Oscar. The first time I met him—I was a rookie with the Indiana Pacers—I was shaking.

Ray Tolbert, who starred at Indiana and had a six-year pro career in between stops in Italy and the Continental Basketball Association, put it this way: "He [Oscar] was like our Rosa Parks," he told Hoose.

Attucks educated the press and countless others about the game. At one point early in Crowe's tenure, Jep Cadou Jr. of the *Indianapolis Star* was predicting the day when kids with "jumping jack legs" would disturb "basketball's traditional patterns" and ruing the fact that Attucks had six players who could dunk. That subtle kind of racism crept into stories when Black players started, to use Nelson George's elegant phrase, elevating the game.

But by the mid-1950s, Cadou was looking at things differently. In a story he wrote a few weeks after Attucks's second title, he interviewed Globetrotters owner Abe Saperstein during a Globies visit to Indianapolis and came out with this:

> It isn't that Negro boys are becoming any bigger or any faster these days than they ever were, Abe believes. It's simply that great basketball interest has been kindled among them during the last decade. . . .
>
> As evidence of the increased prominence of the Negro in basketball, Saperstein points to the fact that three out of the five collegians on most all American teams of the last season

were Negroes. Bill Russell of San Francisco made everybody's dream team. His teammate K. C. Jones made quite a few.

The relationship between the Attucks players and Collins, the *Star*'s star, could be a Hallmark movie . . . with some language deleted. To be sure, Collins knew everybody. From time to time Collins would send Bobby Plump into a barroom to fetch food and drink, and one night, as the owner handed it over, he had a message: "Tell Collins to pay his goddamn drink tab."

But it was the Attucks teams that gave meaning to Collins's journalism. He championed their cause in the early 1950s when he routinely received hate mail calling him a communist or, predictably, a "ni—er" lover. "You know where to find me," he told them all. He got close to the players when they were in high school and maintained those relationships. Many was the night that Bill Hampton would go to Collins's desk in the *Star* newsroom and, with the writer's blessing, lift a few complimentary tickets to Indiana Pacers games. (Collins had led the charge for Indianapolis to get an American Basketball Association team.)

Collins drank Early Times whiskey, sometimes with a dash of vermouth and sometimes without, but usually too much of it. His drinking killed him. He died of cirrhosis of the liver in 1995 at sixty-eight. This is what Zak Keefer wrote in the *Star* in 2015 in a reminiscence twenty years after Collins died:

> But as he lay on his deathbed during those final months, sipping those beers topped with tomato juice, laughing, reminiscing, one topic would cause his words to slow and his voice to crack. That was Attucks.

"The day he died, there was nothing he was more proud of than what he wrote about Attucks," says Dale Ogden, a curator of history at the Indiana State Museum and a Collins friend. "It made him feel like he did at least one thing right. In his eyes, Attucks made his life important."

The most significant person in the Attucks equation might have been the coach, who provided something new to Indiana basketball: a Black person in charge. By the time Hallie Bryant, Willie Gardner, and Oscar and Flap Robertson had come along, Indiana fans had seen at least a sprinkling of color on the basketball court—Dave DeJernett, Jumpin' Johnny Wilson, Bill Garrett, and Ray's brother George, to name a few—but Crowe was something different. He was a dark face on the sidelines matching wits with all those chalkboard gods celebrated in Hoosier lore.

Crowe cut a dashing figure at Attucks. He dressed well. His wife, Betty, sixteen years his junior, added a dimension of youth and hipness. A daughter from his first marriage, Katherine, was also a popular figure at the school and the subject of a particularly peculiar headline in a November 1956 edition of the *Attucks News* that read, "Attractive Crowe, Junior White, Enjoy Being Teachers' Kids." The story began, "Katherine Crowe, attractive, brown-eyed daughter of basketball coach Ray Crowe, confided: 'I like it, as long as I'm not in my father's classes.'" She confessed in *The Ray Crowe Story* that several players wanted to ask her out but were afraid of her dad, and she told of a night that he "made a surprise visit to a dance at the community center" that neither she nor Attucks players were supposed to be attending. When someone spotted him, "all of those basketball players and I headed for the emergency exit. I hid with them until he left." That qualified as big-time trouble at Attucks during the 1950s.

Crowe struck a balance between being tolerant and being a hard-ass. He threw Oscar out of practice but also gave him the ball and let him run the offense. His record seems like a misprint: 193–20. He coached for seven years and made the final state game three times. Only one of his teams, in the 1952–1953 season, lost two games in a row. He never lost a game in the regional and won six of seven titles in the sectional, perhaps his most striking achievement and the one that stuck in the craw of opponents. Yes, he had a string of very good players and one great one. So does every coach who wins.

But this startling fact remains: Ray Crowe was never voted Indiana's coach of the year by the Indiana Sportswriters and Broadcasters Association, not in his state title years of 1955 and 1956 and not the next year, 1957, when an Oscar-less team went all the way to the championship game, where it lost to a powerful South Bend Central team. Some said that was Crowe's best coaching job.

There seems to be no other logical explanation than this: he was Black. It was too difficult for some at that time to accept that a Black man could outcoach a white man. Acknowledging the athletic brilliance of Oscar and Merriweather was one thing; appreciating the coaching pedagogy of Crowe was something else again. "The people doing the voting were usually white males and a lot of them thought we had no business playing basketball anyway," Oscar was quoted as saying in the Crowe biography. "I guess it's no surprise Ray never won one."[1]

Crowe lived a long and productive life. In 1967, he was elected to the Indiana House of Representatives and became chairman of the House Education Committee. He became director of the Indianapolis Department of Parks and Recreation in 1976 and served on the Indianapolis City-County Council from 1983 to 1987. He was named to the Indiana Basketball Hall of Fame in 1968.

---

1. You never have to look far for other egregious examples of racism in sports in those days. In 1956 Jim Brown of Syracuse, an African American who was so far and away the best college football player in the country it wasn't even funny, finished *fifth* in the Heisman Trophy voting. The winner was Notre Dame golden boy Paul Hornung, who had quarterbacked the Irish to a 2–8 record, throwing thirteen interceptions against three touchdowns. Not that Hornung didn't become a great pro; he just wasn't Jim Brown. Nobody was.

But the athletic side of his life at Attucks could have—should have—turned out better.

To this day it's not clear if he was nudged out of his coaching job. He was only forty-two when he left the bench, though opposing coaches must have thought he was ninety-two for all the beatings they absorbed from the man. Yes, the athletic director is technically the boss; yes, in that position he would make more money, $300 more than the basketball coach, and Crowe told the *Recorder*, "Salary is one of the best ways to measure advancement." That is quite often a mantra among a class of people who grew up with very little (and also quite often among a class of people who grow up with millions).

But a powerful coach usually has more power within an institution than the athletic director. The *Indianapolis Recorder* announced the change with the headline "Promotion of Crowe Floors Attucks Fans" and suggested in the story that he had been "kicked upstairs." Collins wrote in a column after the change was announced that it was a "shock to many," and it's a solid guess that Collins knew the whole story—and the whole story was not merely that Crowe wanted a promotion and the salary bump. Attucks was in a state of flux at the time. Russell Lane, who had been at the helm since 1930, retired in 1957, and a new man, Alexander Moore, took over. Newspapers described what was going on at Attucks as a "general reorganization of the faculty." In all probability, Ray Crowe, for all his success, got reorganized.

His successor, Bill Garrett, was already in the public school system as a teacher, and some thought that he had been groomed for the Attucks job even when Crowe was so successful in it. At any rate, after a few years of calling the shots from an office, Crowe said publicly that he wanted back on the bench. Or maybe he had never wanted to leave in the first place. Or maybe he was furious that Garrett was named the Indiana High School Athletic Association's coach of the year after his state championship when he, Crowe, had been snubbed for all those seasons. The Ohio Touchdown

Club, hardly a civil rights organization, was so appalled that Crowe had been ignored so often that it gave him its 1959 High School Coach of the Year Award—even though he wasn't coaching or from Ohio.

Crowe said in Kerry Marshall's *The Ray Crowe Story* that he had had offers over the years from Prairie View in Texas and "from teams in Florida and Tennessee" but was not specific about what kinds of schools or what kinds of offers. He had been told that he had a chance at getting the Shortridge job when their coach retired. But Crowe never got that call. Muncie Central, the team Crowe had beaten in that memorable 1955 game, was also in need of a coach after Jay McCreary left, but Crowe never applied, believing they had no interest in him. Tom Graham and Rachel Graham Cody report in *Getting Open* that Shelbyville's Frank Barnes, a white man, had nine high schools and two universities contact him about coaching jobs after his Garrett-led team won the 1947 state championship. Barnes stayed and parlayed the win into a new three-year contract with a salary bump. Ray Crowe, he of the 193–20 record, seemed to have no such leverage.

Bob Collins knew that Crowe would have a hard time getting a job at any white school and, to prove it, started a rumor that the school board of Lebanon, a high school about thirty miles northwest of Indianapolis, had made Crowe its first choice for the open head basketball job. Crowe went along with it and might possibly have taken the job. Said Collins in the Crowe biography, "Well, not more than two or three days passed before every racist in Lebanon was up in arms ready to lynch the school board. They had cross burnings, white hoods, the whole business. Even in the late fifties and early sixties, predominantly white schools were not going to turn their basketball programs over to a black coach—even one as successful as Ray Crowe."

Which brings us back to Ted Green's documentary, *Attucks: The School That Opened a City*. Just how widely did it open?

Collins always maintained that Attucks's success helped integrate Indianapolis high schools. "They became so dominant that the other schools had to get black basketball players or forget about it," he said in an interview with writer Phil Hoose. Is that the best road to integration? No. But it's a road.

Even Robertson, anyone's least likely candidate to express a positive opinion, says that the Attucks team "opened up" Indianapolis a little, if only for the Black population. "It gave them [African Americans] something to feel good about," he said to Indy author Mark Montieth. Montieth asked Oscar if he thought that the Attucks run of victories and consecutive state titles were popular. "Probably 50–50," he said before reconsidering and putting it at "seventy loved us and thirty didn't." That's not bad.

Willie Merriweather, Oscar's rock-solid teammate on the 1955 championship run, is more positive. "I think we changed the way people thought about us in Indiana," said Merriweather in a 2022 interview.

> Suddenly, the theaters, the stores, some of the restaurants, felt like places that Blacks could now go. They were a little more welcoming. We had a lot to do with changing the racial atmosphere, at least in Indianapolis.
>
> You take the mixed cheering squad that rooted for us in the state championship games. Attucks cheerleaders combined with white kids from other city schools. It sounds small, but it was a big thing. And it happened because of our basketball team.

Herman Shibler, the school superintendent during Attucks's run, is even more positive that the title of Green's documentary is accurate. "That basketball team accomplished more for race relations in one season than you could accomplish in ten years of forums and discussions," he said after the 1955 title. "The white people here have a completely new impression of the colored race. It's marvelous." (It would have been even more marvelous had he found a word other than *colored*, but those were the times.)

Chances are, the whiter your face in Indianapolis, the more you believed—the more you *wanted* to believe—that things had changed, that the Attucks basketball team had pushed an equality button and suddenly the city was more egalitarian than it had ever been. Now, there can be little doubt about how much pride (for African Americans) and how much pure joy (for all audiences) those magic years of 1955 and 1956—and to an extent the whole Crowe era from 1950 to 1957—brought to the city.

But then some fans began to tire of Attucks's dominance. The team wasn't so novel, so fresh, so beautiful in its precision as it had been during the Oscar years. The idea that Attucks should deliberately lose to restore competitive balance started to seep into the mainstream newspapers. Now, that was *never* the suggestion in the small towns of Hoosier hoopdom, where the citizenry wanted to keep winning forever. Black Attucks was never gathered as deeply into the civic bosom as were other teams in other places for the simple reason that African Americans, even athletes, were not accepted as equals off the court. "Whites saw no hypocrisy in cheering Attucks on as an Indianapolis team while at the same time denying African Americans full participation in civic affairs," wrote Richard Pierce in *Polite Protest*.

In the 1958 sectional, with Oscar two seasons gone and the Tigers coasting to another title win over the nearby teams, unhappy white fans tossed ice cream carton tops onto the floor during the closing moments of Attucks victory over Ben Davis, a city rival. And Andrew Ramsey, the *Indianapolis Recorder* columnist and Attucks teacher, had seen enough. In two consecutive weekly columns, he unpackaged all the anger he had been carrying around for decades. He wrote about the "restrictive covenants" and real estate "collusion" that kept Blacks from these "glorious communities of suburban living" and castigated the Indianapolis Redevelopment Commission for its seeming commitment "to a policy of more and more racial segregation." The expansion of Indiana University–Purdue University Indianapolis and the construction of Interstate 65 continued to push minority residents out of the areas around Attucks and Indiana Avenue, and often they quite literally had nowhere to go.

Most everyone in Butler Fieldhouse saw ten players and two referees take the floor for the sectional final. Ramsey saw this: "As the players started peeling off their street sweat clothes to do battle with each other, America 1958 was again in evidence. Five Negro boys coached by a Negro and cheered by Negro fans formed a team that represented segregation. The failure pattern of America passed, while four white boys and one Negro composed the team representing integration, the pattern of America to come."

He wrote about the opposing crowd cheering when an Attucks player went down. He decried the top-tossing as "an almost unheard of display of poor sportsmanship." He gazed at the cheering sections at the Attucks–Ben Davis game and saw nothing but separation, white fans over here, Black fans over there, the seating reflecting an economic divide that prevailed in the real world because "that's the way America lives." In fact, the headline over his March 8, 1958, column read, "Net Tourney Represents America in Microcosm."

Ramsey noticed, too, that the comments about the athletes only related to the game, one fan ruing that a certain player was a senior, "as if graduation was something to be deplored." (That was the educator in him talking, and, Mr. Ramsey, that battle is still being fought.) And this paragraph lets us remember how much the Indianapolis of the 1940s and 1950s needed an Andrew Ramsey, someone to see through the public relations pablum, someone whose eye bored straight to the truth—this final cri de coeur: "Here in Butler Fieldhouse was a fair sampling of America in 1958. Here was the new beside the old, the strength alongside the weakness, the hopes elbow to elbow with the fears."

On another page of the *Recorder*, but as if in symphony with Ramsey's sentiments, was a story about a fan witnessing "hideous and repulsive remarks" hurled at a college basketball player during a game at Duquesne and seeing another fan walk onto the floor after the game and "berate" the athlete, who took it all in expressionlessly. The player was Cincinnati sophomore Oscar Robertson, who scored twenty-seven points in the Bearcats' 72–61 victory. It was a perfect snapshot of a moment in time, incidentally, and a forecast of things to come: Oscar stood in first place in the national collegiate scoring race with 34.3 points per game, just ahead of Elgin Baylor at Seattle University, with a "third Negro cager," as the story identified Wilt Chamberlain of Kansas, right behind Baylor. In just a few years, those three, along with Bill Russell, already a Boston Celtic, would dominate the NBA, elevating the game.

———

One more story from 1958. Although Attucks remained all Black, school officials trumpeted the fact that more and more African Americans were going to Shortridge and Tech, and more and more teachers were working in mixed schools. One of the teachers who demanded a transfer out of Attucks was Ramsey, who believed that Black teachers would help white students "understand that America was a multi-racial society." (He finished his forty-two-year teaching career with twelve years at Howe and Shortridge after thirty at years Attucks.) The cross-integration numbers were actually quite small, and in a few years' time the federal government would rule that, of 350 school boundary changes since 1954, more than 90 percent promoted—one might say *protected*—segregation. Again, in Indianapolis, custom, not law, prevailed. Who helped generate that investigation? Ramsey, through his position in the local NAACP.

Later in 1958 there was the story of Betty Jean League, a white teacher at School 60, a mixed elementary institution near Shortridge High. In what the *Indianapolis Recorder* was calling the "Indianapolis Little Rock Case," a coalition of white parents demanded League's removal because she was married to a Black man. He happened to be Bailey D. League Jr., who had played basketball at Attucks in the late 1940s and continued at Indiana Central. League had served in the US Army and had a good job at Kingan and Company, an Indianapolis meatpacking plant.

The issue came before the school board, and it was a hot one. The best way out, according to the board and Dr. Shibler, the "progressive" school superintendent, was to transfer Betty Jean to another school despite her having received a review of "excellent" for her teaching performance.

Only one voice on the board, that of Grant Hawkins, who in 1955 had been elected Indy's first Black school board member, spoke against the transfer. "Don't let this happen in this country," he pleaded. Norman B. Gesner, a white parent who said that he and his wife "were looking forward" to their seven-year-old son being taught by League, said, "I think it is outrageous that a teacher should be transferred because of a matter that is of no proper concern to the board."

Outrageous? Not in Indianapolis. Shibler ruled that the transfer should take place not because League was a bad teacher but because "she could no longer do an effective job at School 60." Remember what Shibler had said about the effect of Attucks basketball? That white people *have a completely new impression of the colored race.* That it was *marvelous.* If there had been an over-under bet on leaders doing the right thing back in 1950s Indianapolis, you should have always taken the under. A delegation from another elementary school showed up with a message: *Don't send her here.* "It's against the law for them to be married," said one man from that delegation. Sadly, he was literally correct. As the meeting broke up, a white parent loudly berated Gesner. "There aren't ten thousand people in the world who think like you do!" she shouted. Shibler told reporters that morale was low at School 60 because other teachers "resented her being married to a Black man." League reported that she had received several abusive phone calls.

The story never did get much attention in the three major Indy newspapers, and even the *Recorder* couldn't follow it forever. Alas, there is no denouement to the Leagues' saga from this chronicler. It is a revolting tale, but one that, for sure, was simmered in an all-too-familiar Indiana broth.

CHAPTER NINETEEN

A Tiger in Winter

"Oscar could have all the money he wanted just by having a different kind of personality, but that wasn't him."

On a Tuesday night in January 1964, Oscar Robertson, in his fourth year in the NBA and already one of its established stars, sat in a dreary Boston Garden locker room with nineteen other NBA All-Stars as a blizzard raged outside. There was one inside too. Robertson, the Cincinnati Royals representative to the National Basketball Players Association, was one of the leaders of a coalition that had demanded change in an NBA that played in rundown arenas and compensated its players with average salaries and second-class travel accommodations, while sapping their energy with a killer schedule at a time when trains and buses were frequently used to get from city to city. Robertson was anticipating the birth of his second child around that time, but he wouldn't be there for it. Male maternity leave in the 1960s? What the hell was that?

Tip-off for the nationally televised NBA All-Star Game—TV exposure for the pro game was a rarity back then, and it was a big, big night for the league—was just minutes away, and the players were adamant that they weren't taking the court unless they received concessions from the league. "I was scared to death," Jerry West would say years later. "Our owner [Bob Short] had told Elgin [Baylor] and I that, if we struck, we'd never play for the Lakers again." Boston's Red Auerbach had roughly the same message for his players. Baylor had a message too. "Tell Bob Short to go fuck himself."

There have been countless accounts of that night, but Oscar says that it was less than ten minutes before tip-off when the twenty All-Stars, responding to a vote conducted by union president Tom Heinsohn of the Celtics, St. Louis Hawks star Bob Pettit, and Oscar, finally agreed to play, a desperate NBA commissioner J. Walter Kennedy having promised that union lawyer Larry Fleisher (who would a few years later march arm in arm into sports labor history with Oscar) could file papers that would begin the process of creating a players' pension plan. That was one of several issues on the table.

The game was anticlimactic, but Oscar did what he always did: played seriously and to the hilt. He scored twenty-six points, grabbed fourteen rebounds, and handed out eight assists while playing forty-two of forty-eight minutes in the East's 111–107 win over the West. He was voted the game's MVP at a time when the All-Star Game was not a meaningless exhibition, as the no-defense-allowed scrimmages are these days. It would set the stage for a more important award Oscar received a couple months later: league MVP, the only time he would win the award. Most importantly for Oscar, Tia Robertson arrived in the world sometime during that Boston Garden evening, which unfolded without the Garden spectators or TV audience realizing that the game almost didn't happen.

From that night emerged perhaps the sports world's first trustbusters, men who stood up to the ownership at a time when players' rights were a pure fiction. Yet no band of brothers was formed from that struggle, no united front, at least nothing like the contemporary coalitions of players like LeBron James, Chris Paul, and Carmelo Anthony, the kind of strength-in-numbers bonding that results in power.

A little more than a year later, at an offseason meeting at Kutsher's in the Catskills, Heinsohn, Fleisher, and Oscar's well-respected teammate Jack Twyman asked Robertson to take over the job of union president from the retiring Heinsohn. (Heinsohn's handoff represented one of the few times that Tommy Gun actually passed.) Oscar became the first Black president of any national sports or entertainment organization at a crucial time. "Playing conditions were still dismal," Oscar wrote in *The Big O,* and most of the issues the players had fought for in their Garden standoff had not been addressed. He held the position for the next decade during the most tempestuous time in sports labor history. Fleisher used to say that Oscar had the number one attribute for a labor agitator: complete distrust of the other side. The walls around Oscar that he began to erect at Crispus Attucks High School kept getting higher and stronger. Yet his name is not whispered in the same obeisant tones as those reserved for Muhammad Ali, Bill Russell, Kareem Abdul-Jabbar, and Jim Brown, recognized as masters of defiance.

Oscar alone. It became a theme.

In 1967, when a who's who of athletes[1] met to discuss the intersection of sports and civil rights, Oscar was not there.

In 1969 the NBA needed to up its marketing game, something to distinguish it from the American Basketball Association (ABA), which was playing with a three-point shot, a red-white-and-blue ball, and a balls-out spirit. A graphic artist named Alan Siegal was hired to design a logo. At that point the biggest candidates to represent the league, based on legacy and productivity, were probably Robertson, Russell, Baylor, and Wilt Chamberlain, all African Americans, and Jerry West, the Big O's longtime Caucasian counterpart. Going back in time, Bob Cousy

---

1. The most famous attendees at what came to be known as the Cleveland Summit were the four mentioned above. Also attending were Willie Davis, Curtis McClinton, Bobby Mitchell, Carl Stokes, Sidney Williams, and John Wooten.

and George Mikan, two white pioneers of the game, could have been chosen, but the NBA needed currency.

Siegal came upon a photo of West dribbling to his left, his face locked in a mask of concentration, an image at once static and charged. It was chosen as the logo, and the silhouette of West going left endures (even though he usually went right). Jerry West *is* "The Logo," and no one could reasonably argue that he isn't deserving. But others are too. The subject pains West, who on occasion even denies that it's his silhouette. "It should be Oscar," he told this chronicler several years ago.

As the 1960s rolled into the 1970s, the ABA was providing that reliable capitalist staple known as *competition*, and player salaries started to rise. The league executives and owners began to talk about a merger, and union leadership wanted to challenge it. They needed a big name to step forward, knowing full well that it would be unpopular with the public, which was still under the impression that players raked in millions while owners in tattered clothes scrounged under their seat cushions for loose change. Oscar said, "I'll do it."

So, *Robertson v. National Basketball Association* was filed on April 6, 1970, which was class action litigation that claimed any proposed merger would violate the Sherman Antitrust Act. The Robertson suit got nowhere near the attention given several years later to the labor strife in baseball led by the bravery of player Curt Flood and the strategy of union president Marvin Miller. "Henceforth and forever," wrote William C. Rhoden in 2017, "the NBA should designate July 1 [the annual beginning of NBA free agency] as Big O Day, in honor of Oscar Robertson, namesake of the rule that put NBA players on the road to free agency." But it didn't happen.

Oscar alone.

A year after the suit was filed, thirty-two-year-old Robertson walked into a US Senate hearing room in Washington, DC, to stand before the powerful and largely hostile nine-member Senate Subcommittee on Antitrust and Monopoly. The group seemed likely to vote against the players union and in favor of granting owners the antitrust exemption that would allow for the merger, thus limiting player movement and reducing players' earning power. With the brilliant and acerbic Fleisher at his side, Robertson, for all his life both an assister and a scorer, at least had a wingman.

"Mr. Chairman, my name is Oscar Robertson," he began. "This will be my twelfth year in professional basketball, and I've seen some of the ills that were brought on the ballplayers when I first started playing basketball, and I think it's terribly wrong for anyone to limit anyone's ability to earn more money."

Some of the senators, no doubt avowed capitalists, found this idea shocking.

"You seem to have done pretty well," said Senator Roman Hruska, a conservative Republican from Nebraska who, throughout the hearing, seemed to be one step away from calling Robertson "uppity." "Do you think you are worth more than the one hundred thousand dollars you are getting?"

At this point, Fleisher whispered to Oscar, "There may be those who wonder if you're worth the money you're getting from taxpayers." Fleisher loved him some verbal warfare.

Robertson smiled ever so slightly. It might have been the time for showmanship, the time to go metaphorically behind the back with a dribble. But not for the no-nonsense point guard from Attucks.

"To be honest and frank," Oscar answered, "I think so."

The room erupted in laughter. Oscar stayed sober as a sphinx.

The proposed amendment never made it out of committee, and the legal battles, helmed by the kid from the shotgun shack on Colton Street, led to the dismantling of the odious reserve clause and the advent of free agency. Now, the poet-heavyweight would have handled it differently. Yuk it up with the senators, get them licking out of your hand, then nail them with the killer line. But Oscar was no Ali.

Oscar alone.

It would be ridiculous to posit that Oscar is forgotten. He surfaces casually in NBA conversation weekly, usually when Denver's Nikola Jokic or Dallas's Luka Doncic hangs up a triple-double, and he was a daily subject in the years when Russell Westbrook broke both his season and career marks for triple-doubles. The video game NBA 2K23 uses Oscar's distinctive lay-it-on-the-palm J—thank you, Dust Bowl, circa 1950—for several of its jump shot models, bestowing him with a particular kind of contemporary immortality.

But that's the point really: Oscar is more number than man, more myth than flesh and blood, his off-court accomplishments, his stands against authority, his stubborn unwillingness to back down . . . all but forgotten. Though he had to make his way through both the northern and southern strains of racism, he's not Ali, not Russell, not Abdul-Jabbar, not Jim Brown, not Jackie Robinson. How many people know that the rule that eliminated a team's ability to hold on to a player for life bears the name of an Attucks immortal?

"Oscar is a man of conviction," Pat Riley, the Hall of Fame coach and Miami Heat president, told Sam Smith for *Hard Labor*. "He probably was bulletproof as far as his career, but it wasn't popular to speak out against corporations. . . . He put himself out there, like Muhammad Ali, like Jim Brown. Oscar was the one who would tell us to stay the course, be tough, get your rights and freedom."

In any protracted conversation with West, Oscar, whom he affectionally calls Donut—get it?—will come up. They're a perfect (un)matched set, one Black, one white, the Magic and Bird of their time, cocaptains of the 1960 Olympic team, numbers one and two in the 1960 draft, backcourt rivals, champions, immortals. "I always admired his game, of course, but what was most admirable about Oscar was his willingness to speak out," West said. "It was much harder to do that back in our day, and very few had the courage that Oscar did."

Yet only one of them, West, has remained tethered to the league since their retirement in 1974, the West Virginia star's fame as a general manager—he's also been a scout, consultant, and de facto Yoda—almost eclipsing his rep as a player. The other, Oscar, is, if not quite estranged from the NBA, then distant from it, a lone boat drifting near the dock but rarely mooring, perceived as gloomy, unreachable, hard to please.

Why, we ask? Why, Oscar, can't you play ball with the league? Why, Oscar, can't you be *easier*? Why, Oscar, can't you be *happy*?

As the years passed, Crispus Attucks's place in Indianapolis history began to diminish. It didn't have anything to do with what Attucks did or didn't do, and it doesn't change all that the team accomplished in uniting the city in the 1950s. It resulted from the realities of life for urban Blacks. Highways and roadways—*white men's roads over Black men's homes* became a saying on the west side—and the expansion of the Indiana University–Purdue University Indianapolis campus and hospital rolled on, and properties continued to be bulldozed. There was no more Frog Island, no Naptown, not even a legit Lockefield Gardens, which lost half of its apartment buildings to demolition, according to writer Phil Hoose. One day in the winter of 2022, IUPUI professor Paul Mullins and a visitor searched the Lockefield area in vain for a sign that indicated where the Dust Bowl court once stood. "It was here last time I looked," said Mullins, clearly frustrated and disturbed that it couldn't be found.

As the Attucks feeder population decreased, so did the Attucks enrollment. Some of the brightest Black students were taken to the suburbs under a busing plan, and members of the Black middle class started to leave the west side. There was a brain drain of teachers too, some of the best African Americans opting to teach in more modern suburban schools, while few of the best white teachers chose Attucks.

The alumni watched in agony, praying that the school could stay open.

Most sports teams, including the Tigers, kept a full schedule albeit without postseason glory. But in 1986 once-proud Attucks High became a junior high, and for the next two decades, Tigers hoops fans who remembered the glory days had only memories. That was the same year that Tuskegee Airman Charles DeBow, Class of 1936, died. By then Lieutenant DeBow had gone on record as saying that the school should have been razed a long time ago, representing as it did the worst instincts of man to separate and define by color. He was joined in that wish by someone named Ray Crowe, who had done as much as anyone to bring attention to the school. "A sick social experiment," Crowe called Attucks.

Still, one gets the feeling that many more alumni—people whose destinies had been changed by attending Attucks—felt as bad about what happened as people who wished that the school had never been built. Those people most assuredly felt the sting of Andrew Ramsey's words when he wrote, before his death in 1973, that opposing the elimination of Attucks because of "nostalgia" was like "freed slaves longing for the security of chattel slavery."

Attucks was just part of the story of change on Indy's west side. Some cities take care to preserve their historic ethnic neighborhoods. Not Indianapolis. There is a revamped Walker Theatre on Indiana Avenue that is part of the Madam Walker Legacy Center, the result of a $15 million infusion of cash from the Lilly Endowment in a partnership with IUPUI. But there is nothing else—at least not right now—to remind anyone of the bright Black life that happened there, no stars on the sidewalk, no plaques on the buildings, no retro jazz emanating from speakers. *Satchmo played here? Really?* Bethel African Methodist Episcopal Church at 414 W. Vermont Street, the city's oldest African American church right around the corner from Indiana Avenue, is now a Hampton Inn.

"That whole area," says Attucks grad and writer David Leander Williams, "has been culturally destroyed." Adds Mullins, "It's not inevitable that things disappear. There's still Beale Street in Memphis, right? There are cities that save those sections and turn them into cultural tourism or whatever euphemism you want to use. We didn't do that. We tore everything down." Mullins called the razing of the west side no less than "the decimation of one hundred years of Black neighborhoods and culture."

So it goes, as a Hoosier writer named Kurt Vonnegut might have put it.

There are people who are working to change that. In her position as director of the Black Heritage Preservation Program, Eunice Trotter hopes to undo the "awful, awful job" of (non)preservation done by city authorities. Trotter knows it won't be easy, but this is no rookie taking on the job. She's a lifelong Indy resident, familiar with what she calls the city's "economic racism," policies of simply pricing minority populations out of housing, and its "paternalistic" treatment of those groups. Trotter also wrote a book called *Black in Indiana*, detailing the history of her great-great-great-grandmother Mary Bateman Clark, whose 1821 Indiana Supreme Court case resulted in ending indentured servitude in the state. From 1987 through 1991 Trotter was the owner, editor, and publisher of the *Indianapolis Recorder* and on occasion had to use her own credit cards as collateral to secure new equipment and vehicles for the paper because Indianapolis banks were reluctant to deal with Black-owned businesses. "They ignored the one-hundred-year history we had in this community," said Trotter, shaking her head. Trotter's organization is looking to put interactive and interpretive touches back on Indiana Avenue, such as audio systems on the tops of buildings that would "broadcast the sounds of the Avenue." She describes herself as "hopeful but clear-eyed," aware always that, in Indiana, there is reverence for the past (though not the Black past), an affection for entrenched custom, and a reluctance to engage in dialogue that might be painful. "Indianapolis values civility above all," says IUPUI professor Mullins. "Where I came from [a native Virginian, he was educated at the University of Massachusetts and the University of Maryland] discussions of race involved a fair amount of tension. Here? They would prefer just not to talk about it."

But Crispus Attucks High made a comeback, so perhaps the Avenue can, too. In 2006 Eugene White, the superintendent of Indianapolis Public Schools, announced Attucks's conversion from a middle school to a medical magnet school, grades nine through twelve. Not incidentally to scores of alumni, in 2008 back came its hallowed basketball program after a two-decade hiatus (with that state championship to follow in 2017). Decades earlier, Matthias Nolcox, the first principal, and Dr. Russell Lane, his successor, who stayed for twenty-seven years, had to decide whether they would follow the philosophy of (1) W. E. B. Du Bois, who believed that Blacks should get a liberal arts education and integrate society from all angles, or (2) Booker T. Washington, who advocated a vocational path. Washington was infinitely more palatable to white society than Du Bois, a member of the intellectual class, and the Attucks motto, there on page fifteen of the first yearbook in 1928, was right out of the Booker T. playbook: *Labor Omnia Vincent*. Work Conquers All. To be sure, industrial training, woodworking, auto shop, tailoring (where tattered hand-me-down athletic uniforms could be fixed), welding, home economics, plumbing, engineering, printing, all sorts of things, were long a part of the Attucks curriculum. But both principals wanted to split the difference, and much of the vision of its distinguished faculty aligned with Du Bois, who believed in "social power," the training of "quick eyes and ears and above all the broader, deeper, high culture of gifted minds and pure hearts." So it was that Attucks, from its earliest days, was the model of a well-rounded school.

The magnet designation turned Attucks to the vocational, the curriculum leaning toward training medical school professionals, veterinarians, and even crime-scene forensicists. It carried another significance too: the change was made largely because of Attucks's proximity to the

Indiana University School of Medicine, thus aligning the high school with one of the institutional engines of Black displacement.

———

The surviving basketball players from the 1950s represent an Attucks fraternity within the larger Attucks fraternity. They are special, and they know it. Yes, Attucks has sent out into the world generals and music stars and politicians and police chiefs, but, ah, nothing could beat the 1950s, when the game was theirs, when "The Crazy Song" rang out in so many enemy gyms, when all of Indiana knew that the road to Hoosier hoop heroics cut right through the heart of Naptown.

They talk often—Oscar and his brother Henry, Willie Merriweather, Bill Hampton, Al Maxey, John Gipson, Stan Patton from Florida, and occasionally LeVern Benson. Hallie Bryant from that earlier team that first put Attucks on the map will check in too. But so many are gone: brother Flap, the great Willie Gardner, Sheddrick Mitchell, Sam Milton, Edgar Searcy, and the coaches Ray Crowe and Al Spurlock. When they talk about a departed brother, they use *passed*. As in, "Bill Brown? No, he passed." Almost seventy years ago now, they reached the heights, as far as they could go in high school, and some of them went on to play in college and semi-pro. But only Oscar, first among equals, reached the sky.

Their memories are mostly positive, but there is a tincture—maybe more than that—of collective discontent among them. To varying degrees, they feel that the Attucks story has been hijacked, told and retold, hashed and rehashed, the reflected glory of their achievements shining back on every Attucks grad . . . with them getting nothing in return. Ancient grievances and petty jealousies surface now and then. None of the players has made serious bank except for Oscar . . . and Oscar reached the sky.

The Big O is not a man who puts on airs. The best guess is that none of them feel that Oscar acts superior. Never has. That's not how he operates. There's too much Colton Street in the man. Yet the basketball brotherhood knows that the Attucks Dream Machine runs on O-fuel, that without the youngest Robertson brother, they'd be just another really good team, a nostalgic iteration of *That Championship Season*, the 1972 play about a bunch of guys who never got over their shared seminal moment. It is Oscar who puts them over the top; it's Oscar who makes them special.

And, so, they wonder, Could Oscar have done more to make them more celebrated? Has Oscar's intransigence cost them opportunities? They wonder, as we do, *Why can't Oscar be happier?* Don't misconstrue this. They would never speak against Oscar, particularly in any kind of dialectical battle with a journalist or a TV producer or a documentarian. But Oscar's stubbornness, his impatience, his *fury* sometimes confounds even them.

From his home outside San Antonio, Willie Merriweather, a tough man, considers the question *Why can't Oscar be happy?*

"I just have a different type of feeling about things than Oscar does," Merriweather begins, choosing his words carefully. "Even though I grew up the same way, I wasn't, I guess, affected the same way he was. Even though we didn't have much, I happened to go to an all-white school from fourth grade to ninth grade, and during that time Oscar was exposed to a lot of things that maybe I wasn't. His interactions with people seemed to end more often as a negative thing. He had some kind of feeling that he was threatened by things that were being said and things that were being asked of him."

Merriweather pauses. He wants to make it clear that he's not criticizing Oscar. They just see things differently. This happens even to men who come from what seems like the same world.

"He gets a call in high school that he'll be shot if he plays a game," continued Merriweather. "I never experienced that, and I don't know what feeling that leaves you with. He had some negative experiences at Cincinnati[2] that I never had at Purdue, and he kept that inside of him. Oscar could have all the money he wanted just by having a different kind of personality, but that wasn't him. He's been blackballed by the NBA and for all that he's done. Man, the players ought to give him a hundred thousand dollars a year for what he did."

George McGinnis was a friendly, openhearted man despite a series of orthopedic indignities that have left him almost crippled. He was a strong player, the very definition of a power forward in his playing days, but late in his life he was stooped and dependent upon walker and cane and sometimes a helping hand. But he mostly smiled when he talked about his memories.

"I came along a little later than Oscar, and it was easier for me because he blazed that path," said McGinnis from his home in Indianapolis, where he lived most of his life. McGinnis smiled. "But it still wasn't perfect." After McGinnis signed with the Indiana Pacers in 1971—like a lot of Hoosier schoolboy stars he longed to play at Indiana University, where he averaged thirty points per game for a terrible Hoosier team and turned pro after one year—he and a girlfriend tried to rent an apartment in the city. "I still remember what they told me," said McGinnis. "'We don't rent to coloreds.' Can you imagine that?"

But McGinnis put it behind him. He loved the city where he grew up and became a legend. "I wish Oscar could somehow wash everything away," McGinnis said. "I wish that he could've stayed in Indiana, you

---

2. There are too many racial incidents involving Oscar at the University of Cincinnati, and later in his pro career with the Royals, to detail here. He writes about them in *The Big O*. The takeaway, again, is the idea of fences, that Blacks in Indianapolis learned where they could go and where they were not welcome but found things different in the open world. What makes this chronicler sad is the thought that Oscar didn't fully enjoy his four years in college—yes, even the great ones stayed four back then—that he didn't have the experiences of Lou Alcindor (before he was Kareem Abdul-Jabbar) and Bill Walton at UCLA or Michael Jordan at North Carolina. They threw themselves into the college experience and still made their mark in basketball. For Oscar, it was more of a trudge. For Oscar, it's always a trudge.

know? But he got out of this place and never looked back. And he has every right to do what he wants to do. I'll just . . . I'll just never forget the man."

Neither will Chris Hawkins, the current Attucks coach, the man who every day sees the names of the Attucks heroes from the 1950s on the walls of the Attucks gym, which is still not a showpiece but is adequate for high school games. Hawkins is one of thousands of faces that represent Indianapolis's struggles with a segregated educational system. He lived in the Shortridge area but in the 1990s was bused to Southport High, eight miles south of center city in Perry Township. (Busing in the Indianapolis Public Schools, the result of federal mandate, went on from the early 1970s to the late 1990s.) But his wife, as well as her mother and father and various other relatives, all graduated from Attucks and all know the history. Hawkins also made a Ray Crowe–type mistake—winning the state championship (Attucks was in the second-highest class of the four-class tournament) in his first season in 2017, just as Crowe unexpectedly won the 1951 sectionals in his rookie season. It's been an uphill struggle for Hawkins since then.

"Oscar talking to us before and after the game, then hanging the medals around our necks?" said Hawkins before an Attucks game in 2022. "Man, that is a memory that will never leave. The history of Attucks is just in the air around here. A bunch of the guys, Hallie Bryant, Willie Merriweather, they come around for our golf tournament."

Hawkins, like many others, wishes Oscar were more amenable to showing up, that when asked to do something, he wouldn't list a litany of things that once went wrong and ancient promises that weren't kept. "But he's Oscar, right?" says Hawkins. "Only been one like him. Our kids understand the tradition, best they can. They hear about Oscar and ask, 'How can I have a career like that?' I'll tell them, 'You can graduate, you can play in college, you can have a great life. But following what Oscar did? Well, good luck with that.'"

Only Oscar touched the sky.

Many Attucks graduates, particularly the older ones, will talk about how fortunate they felt to have attended the school. *Fortunate* is the word they often use. They were taught by people like the unwavering civil rights fighter Ramsey, who was no fan of polite protest; like John Morton-Finney and a colleague in the foreign language department named Frances Connecticut Stout, who held several degrees; like Merze Tate, the first Black woman to earn a degree at Oxford and the first Black woman to earn a PhD in government and international relations from Harvard, who taught history and social sciences at Attucks before going on to Oxford and a career as an international traveler that brought her into friendship with Eleanor Roosevelt; like Fred Parker, a Phi Beta Kappa graduate of Amherst who taught math at Attucks and later taught at Yale; like Dr. Joseph Cephas Carroll, a Baptist preacher who taught history at Attucks and wrote a seminal book about slave history; like Dora Ann Hodge, who taught math and Latin at Attucks and died at twenty-seven from a respiratory infection because she was refused medical attention at an Indianapolis hospital; like George Roddy, who taught industrial arts and started the golf program at Attucks while he won a couple Indianapolis city golf titles.

Talk to any Attucks grad and chances are he or she will bring up one of their teachers. *I had Miss Walker for history. Mr. Harris turned me on to zoology. Mr. Brown taught me everything about music.* Two Attucks basketball veterans, Bill Hampton and John Gipson, were chewing the fat a while back about that very subject.

"Stan Patton and I had a project due for Miss Pierce—she taught us English, great teacher—about the Civil War," says Gipson. "And Stan, see, doesn't get his part done, and we have to tell her the next day. 'Miss Pierce, we didn't finish because we had a game last night.' And she looks at me up and down and says, 'What? Did you play *all night*?'" Gipson laughs out loud. "That was Attucks, man. You got no breaks."

But if there were substantial reasons to feel fortunate you had Attucks, there was no rule you had to feel happy about Indianapolis. Happy about your lot as a Black kid in the 1950s, happy that there were places you couldn't go in your own city, happy that people assumed the worst about you because you were Black. "What I have always admired about Robertson, in addition to his honesty," William C. Rhoden wrote in the *New York Times* in 2015, "is his unwillingness to validate past racist misdeeds by participating in ceremonies that he felt were designed—consciously or not—to erase or minimize past slights."

We can complain—with justification—that Robertson seems to take it too far. He sees conspiracy where there is none; mistakes the unstoppable flow of history that favors the modern athlete (more money, more publicity, more, more, *more*) over the old-timer as a plot against him; considers the most innocent queries as invasions of his privacy. The walls are up, and even his closest friends sometimes wish they would come down if only a little.

But there is this about the man: he stands indomitable and constant, guided by his own North Star, principled, wary, hard, the man about whom the New York Knicks' Walt Frazier, upon considering Robertson's relentless nature, once said, "Oscar just *overwhelmed* you." It is entirely fitting that one makes a turn off Dr. Martin Luther King Jr. Street and onto Oscar Robertson Boulevard to enter the parking lot of the place where the kid from Colton first brought the magic seventy years ago. Attucks, too, stands indomitable, weathered by time and urban insult, but looking largely the same as it did when it opened its doors in 1927 and let in hope and doubt in just about equal measure. "So many things are gone over on this side of the city," said David Leander Williams, a man not given to sentiment when asked to consider his alma mater. "The city has taken them and the college has taken them. Indiana Avenue, the clubs, the music, the African American church. So, Attucks, in a way, is the last jewel." He stops and nods his head. "Yes, it is. The last jewel."

ACKNOWLEDGMENTS

This section begins with a *non*-acknowledgment—which I suppose is a kind of acknowledgment. Oscar Robertson declined to be interviewed for this book. I reached out a half dozen times before getting a flat no, after which I tried once more. Still no. It's complicated.

There was never a thought of reducing Robertson's presence in the book. His upbringing in Indianapolis, his exploits at Attucks, and his outsized place in Hoosier basketball—indeed, in basketball in general—mandate that he be at the center of the narrative. Not featuring Oscar would be like doing a history of the Globe Theatre without featuring Shakespeare.

Nevertheless, I have gathered much of what Oscar has said on the record and in his 2010 autobiography, *The Big O: My Life, My Times, My Game*, and you get to know him in these pages. In my opinion he has hurt his legacy by being so suspicious and prone to exaggerate any slight that has come his way. But that's his business. This will probably come across as rationalization, but I came to appreciate Oscar's first-person absence. It added to his mystery, his legend, his essential *Oscar-ness*. Just as Ray Crowe said he had run the game, Oscar kind of ran the book.

Several of Oscar's Attucks teammates were willing to share their memories. I spent a pleasant afternoon with Willie Merriweather in his home in suburban San Antonio and another in the condo/art studio of Al Maxey in Lincoln, Nebraska. They were Oscar's two most trusted teammates on, respectively, the 1955 and 1956 state champions. I interviewed Bill Hampton twice, once at the Crispus Attucks Museum in the high school and on another occasion at the home of his friend John Gipson. John was a gracious host, and I enjoyed hearing him talk about his singing days as a member of the Tigerleers.

Hallie Bryant kick-started the Attucks phenomenon and shared his memories about those early-1950s teams and his later career with the Harlem Globetrotters. Carl Short, an outstanding player at Emmanuel Tech in the 1950s, was generous with his time in providing perspective on what it was like to go against Attucks. There were fewer nicer gentlemen than George McGinnis, who, despite severe orthopedic difficulties, was warm and welcoming and provided his memories of coming up behind the Attucks teams of the 1950s and eclipsing some of Oscar's records at Washington High (not to mention a nice digression into his Philadelphia 76ers days).

I began the reporting for this book by talking to Lauren Franklin, the current Attucks principal, who led me on a tour of the building, which made an obvious impression—the prologue to the book came out of that visit. Bill Munn, the official Grant County historian and a longtime public school teacher, was an enormous help in the section about the lynching in Marion.

I was honored that Bryan Stevenson, author of the riveting best seller *Just Mercy* and executive director of the Equal Justice Initiative (EJI) in Montgomery, Alabama, sat down with me for an interview. Travel tip: visit the EJI and Montgomery in general; you will never think about race the same way.

One inviolate rule for book writers: always interview people smarter than you (not a high bar for me). Dr. Stanley Warren provided Attucks perspective both as an alumnus and a scholar. The depth of research done on all aspects of the west side of Indianapolis by Dr. Paul Mullins, an anthropology professor at Indiana University–Purdue University Indianapolis, was enormously helpful in my understanding of the city and the Attucks phenomenon. Ditto for Dr. Richard Pierce, a professor of history at Notre Dame who studied at Indiana University. Dr. Pierce and I spent a pleasant morning together in South Bend and, as a bonus, enjoyed the company of former Notre Dame women's basketball coach Muffett McGraw and her husband, Matt.

Dr. Pierce's mentor at IU was Dr. James Madison, a professor emeritus of history at that institution. I devoured two of Dr. Madison's books about Indiana and assumed he must have been a native Hoosier for his depth of knowledge. No, we discovered a common alma-mater-dom at small Pennsylvania liberal arts colleges.

David Leander Williams and Edna Trotter provided tremendously helpful perspective. Both are authors and lifelong Indianapolis residents who can look upon their city with a loving yet critical eye. Trotter once owned the *Indianapolis Recorder*, the city's African American newspaper, and I spent so many hours in its archives that I felt like a 1950s subscriber. Many years ago, at some now forgotten sporting event, I met the late Bob Collins of the *Indianapolis Star*, a first-class character. But I got to "know" him—as well as reporters from the other Indy dailies back in the day—more from frequent visits to newspapers.com. Similarly, I wish I had been able to meet two forthright chroniclers of this era, both of whom died years ago: historian Emma Lou Thornbrough and *Recorder* columnist and Attucks teacher Andrew Ramsey. Thanks, also, to another Andrew, this one Andrew Jackson Pope III, for research assistance.

Sorry, Attucks fans, but you can't cover this territory without talking about the movie *Hoosiers* and its real-life inspiration, Milan High School. I enjoyed an afternoon with Bobby Plump at his bar near Butler University, and another in Bloomington with Angelo Pizzo, the screenwriter of *Hoosiers* and, not incidentally, *Rudy*. One more Attucks opponent was on my list: Phil Raisor, a poet/professor and former Muncie Central guard.

This book started off in another direction and required a number of three-point turns to get it going the correct way; my agent, Susan Canavan of Waxman Literary Agency, helped with the steering. Brant Rumble, editorial director at Hachette Books, was there to direct the book to a parking spot.

There were two previous books written about Attucks—*Attucks! Oscar Robertson and the Basketball Team That Awakened a City* by Phillip Hoose and *"But They Can't Beat Us": Oscar Robertson and the Crispus Attucks Tigers* by Randy Roberts—and, yes, of course, I read them. If I learned something that I had no way of researching or confirming myself, I gave credit to Phil and Randy in the book. I would describe the process as tilling the same soil but with a different tool.

As usual my wife, Donna, did some reading, some suggesting, and, most importantly, some listening. She's never been a hoops addict, but she's spent much of her life listening to basketball stories, and sounding boards are integral to the writing game.

My loudest shout-out goes to Ted Green, who made the 2016 documentary *Attucks: The School That Opened a City*. Ted's contributions, though, went beyond offering up material. He provided copyediting, fact-checking, and, not unimportantly, phone numbers. Hoosiers by choice not birth, he and Dr. Madison are cut from the same cloth, truth seekers with storytelling souls.

The basketball experiences of a white kid from a small town in New Jersey could not—understatement alert—match those of the Attucks Tigers. I didn't have the talent, the size, or the determination to go far as a player, so the fact that I didn't have a Dust Bowl as a learning ground didn't matter much. I did have a backyard hoop nailed to the garage. The cesspool cover was kind of out of bounds, but a jump shot hit from there was good.

But basketball got into my blood, same as it did for the Attucks Tigers, same as it did for many people involved in the Attucks story. "I spent so much time in the homes of Attucks grads, their children, and their grandchildren," said Ted Green, "that their story became a part of me." I feel similarly. It's hard to let the story go, and I feel fortunate that I had the chance to lose myself in it.

SOURCES CONSULTED

Books

Davis, Seth, *Wooden: A Coach's Life*

Du Bois, W. E. B., *The Souls of Black Folk*

Egan, Timothy, *A Fever in the Heartland: The Ku Klux Klan's Plot to Take Over America, and the Woman Who Stopped Them*

Ellsworth, Scott, *Death in a Promised Land: The Tulsa Race Riot of 1921*

Ellsworth, Scott, *The Secret Game: A Wartime Story of Courage, Change, and Basketball's Lost Triumph*

George, Nelson, *Elevating the Game: Black Men and Basketball*

Graham, Tom, and Rachel Graham Cody, *Getting Open: The Unknown Story of Bill Garrett and the Integration of College Basketball*

Guffey, Greg, *The Milan Miracle: The Greatest Basketball Story Ever Told*

Harcourt, Felix, *Ku Klux Kulture: America and the Klan in the 1920s*

Hodge, Aleta, *Indiana Avenue—Life and Musical Journey from 1915 to 2015*

Hoose, Phillip, *Attucks! Oscar Robertson and the Basketball Team That Awakened a City*

Johnson, Claude, *The Black Fives: The Epic Story of Basketball's Forgotten Era*

MacKean, Nancy K., *Behind the Mask of Chivalry: The Making of the Second Ku Klux Klan*

Madison, James, *Hoosiers: A New History of Indiana*

Madison, James, *A Lynching in the Heartland: Race and Memory in America*

Marshall, Kerry, *The Ray Crowe Story: A Legend in High School Basketball*

Martin, Charles H., *Benching Jim Crow: The Rise and Fall of the Color Line in Southern College Sports, 1890–1980*

Packer, Billy, and Roland Lazenby, *The Golden Game*

Painter, Alex, *Blackball in the Hoosier Heartland: Unearthing the Negro Leagues Baseball History of Richmond, Indiana*

Pierce, Richard B., *Polite Protest: The Political Economy of Race in Indianapolis, 1920–1970*

Price, Nelson, and Joan Hostetler, *Indianapolis Then and Now*

Raisor, Philip, *Outside Shooter, a Memoir*

Roberts, Randy, *"But They Can't Beat Us": Oscar Robertson and the Crispus Attucks Tigers*

Robertson, Oscar, *The Big O: My Life, My Times, My Game*

Shaughnessy, Dan, *Wish It Lasted Forever: Life with the Larry Bird Celtics*

Smith, Sam, *Hard Labor: The Battle That Birthed the Billion-Dollar NBA*

Thornbrough, Emma Lou, *The Indianapolis Story: School Segregation and Desegregation in a Northern City*

Wilkerson, Isabel, *The Warmth of Other Suns: The Epic Story of America's Great Migration*

Williams, David Leander, *African Americans in Indianapolis: The Story of a People Determined to Be Free*

Articles

Freeland, Sharon Butsch, "HI Mailbag: Marshall 'Major' Taylor," HistoricIndianapolis.com, January 29, 2013.

Gottlieb, Robert, "The Rise and Fall of Booth Tarkington," *New Yorker*, November 4, 2019.

Goudsouzian, Adam, "Ba-ad, Ba-a-ad Tigers: Crispus Attucks Basketball and Black Indianapolis in the 1950s," *Indiana Magazine of History*, March 2000.

Lighty, S. Chandler, "Finding the 'First' Indiana Basketball Games," *Indiana History Blog*, March 14, 2016.

Mullins, Paul, "Commemoration and African-American Place: Remembering Basketball and the Dust Bowl," *Archaeology and Material Culture*, April 27, 2015.

Mullins, Paul, "Indiana Avenue: The Story of Indianapolis African American Cultural Hub," *Encyclopedia of Indianapolis*, November 20, 2020.

Paino, Troy, "Hoosiers in a Different Light: Forces of Change v. the Power of Nostalgia," *Journal of Sports History*, spring 2001.

Paschall, Wildstyle, "When Indianapolis Accidentally Did Public Housing Right," *New America Indianapolis*, December 1, 2020.

Rhoden, William C., "A Tribute to Oscar Robertson's High School Team, 60 Years Overdue," *New York Times*, May 22, 2015.

Schenawolf, Harry, "African Americans in the American Revolution: Crispus Attucks Was the First to Fall for Liberty," *Revolutionary War Journal*, July 4, 2016.

West, Evan, "Remember the Tigers: Crispus Attucks, 1955 State Basketball Champs," *Indianapolis Monthly*, March 24, 2014.

Film

Green, Ted, *Attucks: The School That Opened a City*

Other Sources

Indianapolis News and *Indianapolis Star*, various stories enumerated within

Montieth, Mark, various interviews available on markmontieth.com

INDEX